LET THE CHILDREN PLAY

PASI SAHLBERG AND
WILLIAM DOYLE

LET THE
CHILDREN PLAY

How More Play Will Save
Our Schools and Help
Children Thrive

OXFORD
UNIVERSITY PRESS

OXFORD
UNIVERSITY PRESS

Oxford University Press is a department of the University of Oxford. It furthers
the University's objective of excellence in research, scholarship, and education
by publishing worldwide. Oxford is a registered trade mark of Oxford University
Press in the UK and certain other countries.

Published in the United States of America by Oxford University Press
198 Madison Avenue, New York, NY 10016, United States of America.

Library of Congress Cataloging-in-Publication Data
Names: Sahlberg, Pasi, author; Doyle, William, author.
Title: Let the children play : how more play will save our schools and help
children thrive / Pasi Sahlberg, William Doyle.
Description: New York : Oxford University Press, 2019.
Identifiers: LCCN 2018045120 | ISBN 9780190930967 (hardback)
Subjects: LCSH: Play—Psychological aspects. | Play schools. |
Child psychology. | Child development. | BISAC: EDUCATION / General. |
EDUCATION / Educational Psychology. | EDUCATION / Preschool & Kindergarten.
Classification: LCC BF717.S324 2019 | DDC 155.4—dc23
LC record available at https://lccn.loc.gov/2018045120

1 3 5 7 9 8 6 4 2

Printed by Sheridan Books, Inc., United States of America

This book is dedicated to our families:
Otto, Noah, Eero, Brendan, Petra, and Naomi.

The lifelong success of children is based on their ability to be creative and to apply the lessons learned from playing.

It could be argued that active play is so central to child development that it should be included in the very definition of childhood. Play offers more than cherished memories of growing up, it allows children to develop creativity and imagination while developing physical, cognitive, and emotional strengths.[1]

—American Academy of Pediatrics Clinical Report

Children discover the world through play and reveal their creative abilities. Without play, full intellectual development is impossible. Play is a huge open window through which a life-giving stream of concepts and ideas pours into the child's spiritual world. Play is a spark, igniting the fires of inquisitiveness and curiosity.[2]

—Vasily Sukhomlinsky, Founder, School of Joy

The playground at Maple Street Elementary School is quiet these days.

The only movements on the swing sets are a result of a strong west wind edging the swings back and forth. The long lines that once formed for trips down the sliding boards are empty. There are no softball or kickball games nor are there any games of tag or duck-duck-goose being played. There won't be a fifth-grade musical this year.

Children will not be learning to play the recorder nor will they be learning to march to rhythms or learn the traditional songs that have transcended the years of music instruction in elementary schools. There will be no art to display. Daddies' old long sleeved shirts that were handed down to children to cover up school clothes to keep from being stained with tempera paint and water colors are no longer needed.

No, Maple Street Elementary School is not closing. It is squeezing every minute of the school day to meet the mandates of the No Child Left Behind Act (NCLB) and in so doing many parents and educators are questioning whether the nation's elementary school students are being robbed of their childhood.[3]

—Joan Henley, Jackie McBride, Julie Milligan, and Joe Nichols

They ran among the trees, they slipped and fell, they pushed each other, they played hide-and-seek and tag, but most of all they squinted at the sun until the tears ran down their faces; they put their hands up to that yellowness and that amazing blueness and they breathed of the fresh, fresh air and listened and listened to the silence which suspended them in a blessed sea of no sound and no motion. They looked at everything and savored everything. Then, wildly, like animals escaped from their caves, they ran and ran in shouting circles. They ran for an hour and did not stop running.[4]

—Ray Bradbury, "All Summer in a Day"

CONTENTS

FOREWORD

When you were a child, how much time did you spend playing outdoors? By playing, I mean making up games on your own or with friends, running around and falling over, all for the sheer fun of it. I expect it was many hours every week. I'm a baby boomer and when I was growing up in inner city Liverpool, my siblings and I took every opportunity to get out of the house and play. Like cats, we only went home for the food. We played in the streets, in the back alleyways and in the local park, with each other and with other kids from the neighborhood.

We played running and chasing games, hiding games, ball games; and improvised adventure games, often based on stories we'd read in comics or seen at the Saturday cinema matinées. Our parents did much the same when they were children and so did their parents. From time immemorial, children have spent countless hours outdoors immersed in physical, imaginative, social play. Not any more. Children now spend much less time playing like this than ever before, and the consequences are incalculable.

Let the Children Play argues vividly that play is vitally important in young lives. Child's play may be highly enjoyable but it is not trivial. To grow and thrive, children have to play. Active, physical play is a primary way that children learn about themselves and the world around them. It is essential to the healthy development of their minds and bodies and to cultivating the complex personal and social skills they need to make their way in the world. Active play should be a regular part of every child's daily life. As this book also shows, for many children the reality is depressingly different. For a variety of reasons, and in many parts of world, children from the earliest ages are being systematically deprived of their need, and their right, to play.

I know this from my own experiences in education and more broadly. I am currently senior advisor and chair of Dirt is Good (DiG), an international initiative funded by Unilever to promote better provision for children's play. The campaign emerged from a growing concern that children's lives are now increasingly out of balance and that active, physical play is being squeezed out by other demands and constraints. In 2015, the campaign commissioned an international survey of parental attitudes to play. The survey included over 12,000 families in 10 countries: Brazil, China, India, Indonesia, Portugal, South Africa, Turkey, the UK, the United States, and Vietnam. It confirmed that children everywhere spend much less time than previous generations on self-directed outdoor play.

Almost two-thirds of parents say their children have fewer opportunities to play outside than they did themselves as children. Over half of children spend less, often much less, than 1 hour a day on outside play. Play is increasingly an indoor rather than an outdoor experience. Almost 1 in 10 children never play outside at all. By the way, the accepted convention for the treatment of high-security prisoners is that they spend at least 1 hour a day relaxing and exercising outdoors. Evidently, many children around the world are now spending more time indoors than convicted criminals. This does not mean that children are not playing at all, but they are playing differently. As you'll see in the chapters that follow, these days, when children play outside, they are often supervised by adults in organized games and activities. When they play indoors they spend most of their time on screen-based games. What's wrong with that and what sorts of play matter most?

When the DiG campaign asked parents that question, the phrase that kept coming up was "real play." When we asked what they meant, they said things like "play that promotes the shiny-eyed, engaged state of being in 'flow'"; "play that generates exuberant, happy feelings"; "play where children express their natural personalities"; and "play that encourages children to develop their natural curiosity." So what is "real play," and why is it so important?

Real play is not a particular activity: it is a state of mind, in which all sorts of activities are done, such as playing with sand and water, painting, skipping, climbing, chasing, role play, juggling, and hiding games. It involves all the senses and being physically active. These are some of the common characteristics of real play:

- *It is self-initiated and self-motivated:* Real play is freely chosen. If children are forced to play, they may not feel in a state of play at all.

- *It is creative:* Children engage in make-believe that bends reality to accommodate their interests and imagination.
- *It is active:* Real play engages children physically as well as mentally.
- *It has negotiated rules:* The rules of play come from the child, including entry to and from the game and what counts as acceptable behavior within it.

Sahlberg and Doyle cite numerous studies that confirm that real play is essential for a happy childhood and for becoming independent adults. Real play is vital for the *physical development* of healthy bodies. Growing children need the stimulation that comes from vigorous physical activity, good nutrition, and a safe environment in which to explore their abilities. Real play stimulates children's *cognitive development*. Children's brains are immensely plastic. Through play they tap into their natural curiosity and creativity. Real play helps to form new neural connections in the brain while strengthening existing pathways. Real play facilitates children's *emotional development*. Through play they explore their personal feelings and ideas and learn how others feel and think. Real play has essential roles in children's *social development*. Through play they learn about give-and-take, and how to get on with others in reaching common goals; they practice teamwork, communication, and problem-solving.

If real play is so important to children's well-being, then why don't they have as much of it now as previous generations did? There are several reasons. One is the pervasive reach of digital media and the compulsive attractions of screen-based games. In a second survey, the DiG campaign looked at how much time children spend on screen-based activities at home. The survey included 4,000 parents of children from newborns to 7-year-olds, across the UK/Ireland, France, Spain, and Portugal. Three-quarters of parents said that, from a very early age, their children spend significant amounts of time every day in front of screens. By the age of 3, screen time becomes the dominant way for children to play. The survey calculated that by the age of 7 children have spent up to 2 years and 3 months (818 days) in front of screens. Less than half this time is spent with family and friends playing games or watching films together. The rest of the time children are alone with the screen.

By the time they are 7 years old, children have typically spent up to 1 year and 3 months alone with a screen, more than two and half times the amount of time they spend playing outside with others. For example, four out of five parents say their children would rather play virtual sports indoors on screens than active sports outdoors in real life. Screen-based activities are not all bad, and this is not an argument against video games or digital culture. Playing video games can have positive benefits for children, but as *Let the Children Play* convincingly shows, they don't begin to match the social, emotional, cognitive, and physical benefits of real play in children's development.

There is a second barrier to real play. Evidently, many adults think children's play is an enjoyable leisure activity, but unimportant compared with other priorities, especially in education. In the last 20 years or so, public policies in education have put unprecedented pressures on schools, teachers, and students to demonstrate academic achievement through endless batteries of standardized tests. Many parents are deeply worried about the uncertain futures their children are facing. This uncertainty is fueling an intense focus at home as well as in school on structured learning and achieving high grades. Since the benefits are not widely acknowledged, provision for real play is usually low on the agenda in homes, schools, and public policy alike.

In many schools, playtime is being cut back to make way for extra study time. Increasingly, children's time out of school is also being closely managed on the assumption that this is the best way to cultivate the skills and understanding they need to compete in education and in the workplace. Even parents who believe their children should have a better mix of play styles and more creative, outdoor play often don't make any changes to their daily routines to make it possible. Play just slips off the "to do" list.

A third reason for the decline in outdoor play is fear. Children across the globe spend less time playing outside because of parents' worry about their safety. These fears may be largely unfounded but they are exacerbated every day by the relentless, alarmist tendencies of the 24-hour news cycles. Partly for this reason, when children do play outdoors, they are often oversupervised by adults, which limits the benefits of playing or even whether children perceive it as real play at all.

There is another problem. As urban populations grow and rural populations decline, there are too few designated spaces for real play that are free of cars and other obstacles. In many urban areas, city planners make play a low priority and fail to provide enough safe spaces for children to play. The DiG campaign argues that here, as in other areas of social provision, the need to tackle "the play deficit" cannot be allowed to slip off the agenda.

It is simply too important. Reintegrating diverse forms of play into children's daily lives calls for a practical and concerted plan of action to raise awareness and drive change. That is what this book is about.

Let the Children Play is a passionate, eloquent, and substantiated argument for a radical change of priorities in how many parents, educators, and policymakers provide for the education, health, and well-being of children. It includes outstanding examples of alternative practices, which illustrate the changes that are needed and the benefits they bring, and it concludes with an action list to help bring them about. The case that Sahlberg and Doyle make here is clear and concise. It is based on current research and on ancient principles of human flourishing. I trust you will be convinced by the arguments, the data, and the examples they have marshaled with such authority. More than that, if you felt the benefits of play when you were a child, I trust you will know in your heart why all children must feel them now.

Sir Ken Robinson

ACKNOWLEDGMENTS

We thank our interview subjects, and we thank Petra Sahlberg, Brendan Doyle, Naomi Moriyama, Marie Louise Doyle, our editor Abby Gross and her colleagues at Oxford University Press, our agent Mel Berger and David Hinds of WME Entertainment, Sir Ken Robinson, James Meredith, the faculty and students of the University of Eastern Finland, Andy Hargreaves, Jukka Mönkkönen, Risto Turunen, Jukka Pietikäinen, Janne Pietarinen, Sari Havu-Nuutinen, Ritva Kantelinen, Helmi Järviluoma-Mäkelä, Heikki Happonen, Jyrki Korkki, Tuomas Järvenpää, Sam Abrams, Ivana Andrijasevic, Marija Franetovic Cvitic, Marija Majic, Rachel Cowper, Kirsty Gilchrist, Cathy Ramstetter, Kathy Hirsh-Pasek, Charles Adams, Michael Rich, Tim Walker, Gwen Colvin, Jerri Hurlbutt, Jouni Mölsä, Leonie Haimson, Terhi Mölsä and her colleagues at the Finland Fulbright Center, and the staff of the Rockefeller Foundation Bellagio Center for their support of our work. We are grateful to Jesse Coffino for translating our interview with Cheng Xueqin of Anji Play in China.

LET THE CHILDREN PLAY

1

The Coming Golden Age of Childhood

There can be no keener revelation of a society's soul than the way in which it treats its children.[5]

—Nelson Mandela

It is good for young children to play and to learn through play. Please let your children have their childhood![6]

—Lee Hsien Loong, Prime Minister of Singapore

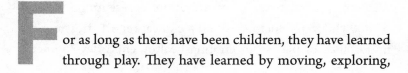or as long as there have been children, they have learned through play. They have learned by moving, exploring,

discovering, practicing, simulating, and experimenting with life, without punishment or penalty, with freedom and encouragement.

Play, both intellectual and physical, is critical for the healthy growth and learning of a child.

This is not a fringe opinion, or a liberal or conservative opinion, or an idea that is relevant only to certain eras, cultures, or countries; it is today a settled, global consensus among leading educators, childhood development experts, researchers, and pediatricians—for children to learn best, they need to play.

In 1930, a White House conference of 3,000 childhood development experts from around the United States issued "The Children's Charter," a declaration of national policy which stated that every child, "wherever he may live under the protection of the American flag," has "the right of comradeship, of play, and of joy," the right to a community that "provides him with safe and wholesome places to play and recreation," and the right to "wholesome physical and mental recreation, with teachers and leaders adequately trained." It was endorsed and co-signed by a Republican president, who insisted on putting the force of the presidential office behind the declaration.[7]

In 1989, the United Nations adopted the Convention on the Rights of the Child, Article 31 of which declares, "Every child has the right to rest and leisure, to engage in play and recreational activities appropriate to the age of the child and to participate freely in cultural life and the arts." In 2007, the American Academy of Pediatrics, the organization representing America's 67,000 children's doctors, issued a clinical report stressing "the importance of play in promoting healthy child development" and that "play is integral to the academic environment."[8] In 2010, the Centers for Disease Control and Prevention reported that there is "substantial evidence" that physical activity, including school recess, "can help improve academic achievement, including grades and standardized test scores," and "can have an impact on cognitive skills and attitudes and academic behavior, all of which are important components of improved academic performance," including "enhanced concentration and attention as well as improved classroom behavior."[9]

In 2011, the European Parliament and Council of the European Union declared that "all children have the right to rest, leisure and play" and recognized "the importance of play, which is also crucial to learning in the early years."[10]

In 2011, the American Academy of Pediatrics issued another clinical report on play, stressing that in order for children in poverty to reach their highest potential "it is essential that parents, educators, and pediatricians recognize the importance of lifelong benefits that children gain from play."[11] In 2013, the American Academy of Pediatrics issued yet another clinical report, declaring that "recess is a crucial and necessary component of a child's development" and that recess is essential for a child's performance in school.[12]

Also in 2013, the highly prestigious Institute of Medicine of the National Academy of Sciences [now called the National Academy of Medicine] recommended that schools provide physical education and daily access "to at least 60 minutes per day of vigorous or moderate-intensity physical activity,"[13] much of which can be accomplished by scheduled breaks for free-play recess. This message was from an organization that the *New York*

Times has called "the most esteemed and authoritative adviser on issues of health and medicine," whose reports "can transform medical thinking around the world."[14]

In 2017, the U.S. Centers for Disease Control and Prevention announced that physical activity and recess are essential parts of students' school experience and can improve academic achievement.[15]

Also in 2017, China's national Ministry of Education announced that promoting play in early childhood education was "a matter of the highest importance," stressed "the important value of play in the lives of children," and declared that play is "a unique way in which the child encounters the world and learns." The ministry urged parents and educators to encourage and support children "to engage in self-determined, joyous play," to "reverse a contemporary emphasis on knowledge and skills learning, the neglect and interruption of play, adult 'direction' of play, the substitution of electronic games for play materials and other factors that rob the child of the right to play, and reverse a trend towards 'primary-school-ification' and 'adult-orientation' in early education that impacts the physical and emotional health of the child."[16]

In 2018, the World Bank's World Development Report declared that "children's brains are most efficient at incorporating new information through exploration, play, and interactions with caring adults or peers."[17]

And also in 2018, the American Academy of Pediatrics yet again issued an urgent call for play in children's lives, stressing, "Play is fundamentally important for learning 21st century skills, such as problem solving, collaboration, and creativity, which require the executive functioning skills that are critical for adult success." The doctors' report stated, "Play helps to build the skills required for our changing world; and play provides a singular opportunity to build the executive functioning that underlies adaptive behaviors at home; improve language and math skills in school; build the safe, stable, and nurturing relationships that buffer against toxic stress; and build social–emotional resilience."[18]

Despite this strong medical and scientific consensus that play is a foundation of children's lives and education, play is an increasingly endangered experience for many of the world's children.

Why is play dying in our schools? There are many social and cultural factors, and one major political reason is "GERM," or the "Global Education Reform Movement," a term that co-author Pasi Sahlberg has coined to describe an intellectual school reform paradigm that places academic performance as measured by standardized tests before children's engagement, well-being, and play in schools.

GERM is the belief among some politicians and policymakers that education can be improved by increasing the academic workload of younger and younger children, by "survival of the fittest" competition between schools, by de-professionalizing the teacher force and standardizing teaching and learning, and by basing school system management on data derived from the compulsory, universal standardized testing of children in a few subjects, as early as the third grade. For schools and children under intense government pressure to generate optimal standardized test data, play—and many other essential things like the arts, music, physical education, life skills, field trips, ethics, civics, and hands-on STEM (science, technology, engineering, and math) projects—is increasingly dismissed as a disposable, unnecessary luxury.

However well intentioned they might be, these misinformed, misguided, and ineffective policies of GERM, which began in the 1990s and are thoroughly infecting the public school systems of the United States, the United Kingdom, and Australia and are spreading elsewhere, have not improved children's education by any meaningful measure but are helping to devalue, squeeze out, and eliminate the critical cornerstone of play in education. Thanks in part to GERM, play is becoming forgotten.

Parents know what is best for their children. But when it comes to education, they aren't always being told the truth or being given complete information. For example, parents may not understand that there is little concrete evidence that forcing a child to master academics at an early age (like 4, 5, or 6) results in any long-term learning advantage. Parents may be unaware that there is little concrete evidence to support most forms of homework before high school other than independent reading and short "refresher" assignments. They may not know that there is little independent, rigorous evidence to support most classroom technology products in childhood education. And many parents may not know that in order to learn best, children, especially younger children, need regular periods of indoor and outdoor play, in school and outside of school.

Co-author Pasi Sahlberg was startled to witness a vivid example of this when he was in Mexico City recently to give a speech to an education conference, a speech in which he mentioned the subject of this book. After the talk, several teachers from a private preschool in the city came up and asked him, "When is your book coming out? We need it now! We need it right away!"

When Pasi asked why, one of the teachers explained, "Our school parents don't understand how important play is. We have parents asking us for a tuition discount—they think they shouldn't have to pay for the times their child is napping in school, and especially for the times they are playing in school, which looks like a waste of time to the parents."

Pasi replied, "But these are 4- and 5-year-olds! The whole point of school for children that young is to learn through play!"

"We know, we know!" the teachers responded, "but parents don't know that."

It's not just in Mexico City, either. On a New York City park bench one day, while watching his son race around a playground, co-author William Doyle struck up a conversation with a kindergarten teacher who was moonlighting as a babysitter for two small frolicking children. She was a highly trained childhood educator with a masters degree who taught at a highly selective, elite, religiously affiliated private school just off Park Avenue.

"I'm thinking of quitting," she abruptly declared.

When asked why, she explained, "We're doing so many things wrong in our school. All we give our children is stress, pressure, and insane amounts of overwork. There is no play. In order to learn, children must play in school. But at our school there is no joy, no discovery, no feeling of ownership or independence for them, no breaks, just stress. This is not right for any child, rich or poor."

"What about the early grades?" asked William, "is there any play in your pre-K and kindergarten?"

The teacher laughed wistfully. "No way," she said. "There used to be lots of play in school, when I started 15 years ago. It was a different world then. But now, the parents wouldn't allow it. We have parents of 3-year-olds drilling their kids in counting and word recognition so they'll have a better shot at winning a place in our school. Our school doesn't tell the parents how wrong this is and how important play is to a child's learning, and the parents don't know. It's a vicious cycle. I hear the same thing is happening in our public schools. Play is fast becoming a thing of the past, and stress is the daily life of children in school—from pre-K through college."

It is time that we, as parents, teachers, and citizens, insist that our government officials and school administrators tell everyone the truth about what our children need to learn best in school—which includes regular doses of physical and intellectual play—and give it to them. It is time we gave our children regular doses of indoor play, outdoor play, free play, guided play, and playful teaching and learning—and "deeper play," which is our term for the high-quality, high-order forms of play characterized by a child's self-direction, intrinsic motivation, positive emotions, process orientation, and use of the imagination. It is time we gave play to all our children in school—rich and poor, from preschool to high school.

Every moment of play that is abolished from school, every recess that is cancelled, every machine that replaces a caring, qualified teacher, and every unnecessary, high-stress standardized test that is forced upon a child represents a theft from children who yearn for movement, creativity, discovery, joy, warmth, encouragement, and friendship as they learn and grow.

We have piled onto our children stress upon stress, pressure upon pressure, standardized test upon standardized test. There is no evidence that this has helped our children's learning or their futures, but we keep doing it, year after year, to millions upon millions of children the world over.

We have done this helplessly, almost involuntarily, like the victims of some sort of hypnotism, like people in a dream, like lemmings heading for the sea.

This world without play is wasting the talents of its teachers, the potential of its schools, and the destiny of its children.

This is not a way of life at all, in any true sense, for any society or any child—it is childhood hanging on a cliff of sorrow.[19]

* * *

Someday soon, our children will play.

They will play at school, they will play at home, and they will play in our neighborhoods.

Someday soon, our children will no longer be overstressed, overworked, over-tested, shamed, and ordered to sit still for 6 to 8 hours a day in bleak indoor environments, spending their school time and free time drilling for low-quality tests given by faceless electronic screens. All schoolchildren, rich, middle-income, and poor, will have several safely supervised outdoor recess breaks per day between classes, even in the rain and snow—on top of lunch and gym class.

Every school will build its curriculum in part on a solid foundation of playful learning and experimentation, and individual differences and diversities will be celebrated, not punished.

Schools will be energized by an atmosphere of playful curiosity, creativity, and discovery. All children will feel free to fail, try again, and imagine in the pursuit of success. Mistakes by students and teachers will be analyzed, shared, and showcased, not branded as sources of shame.

Every early childhood classroom will have a sand table, arts and crafts materials, a dress-up closet and wooden block zone, and children will learn many of the foundations of academics the way they learn best—through intellectual, social, and physical play, through play guided by teachers, and through "free play," chosen and directed by the children themselves.

Children will have regular access to nature whenever possible, to a wood and metal shop, and to musical instruments and lessons. Schools will teach long-forgotten subjects like life skills, cooking, ethics, home economics, gardening, field trips, and hands-on science. Every school will serve nutritious meals to all children, because healthy children are better learners.

Children will not shed tears over pointless, government-imposed standardized tests and grossly excessive, counterproductive levels of overwork and toxic stress. Children will often race to school in a state of joy, excited to play, to learn new things, to focus and concentrate, to work together, try their best, sometimes fail, and to succeed and help other children to do so.

Teachers will learn how to integrate play-based and playful learning throughout the school curriculum. Teachers will assess their students constantly—not with faceless screens and high-stress bubble tests, but with personalized attention, warmth, encouragement, and teacher-designed, age-appropriate quizzes, tests, portfolios, presentations, and other assessments. Teachers will help their students assess themselves and each other.

Several times a week, children will choose what they'd like to do in class. Recess periods will consist mostly of outdoor free play managed by the children themselves, with a trained adult nearby to keep things safe. Children will sometimes scrape their knee and get sweaty and dirty and wet, because that's what children naturally do. Schools will recognize that children have the urgent need, and the right, to play outside several times a day and to enjoy regular breaks outside the classroom. Schools will also recognize that children also have the right to decide not to play or engage in sports at recess, if they'd rather read a book outside, chat with friends, climb a tree, or just "chill out."

Teachers, parents, and communities will give children safe environments to play in and encourage children to take manageable, age-appropriate risks. After school, the backyards, playing fields, and playgrounds that once were empty after school, when children were condemned to endless hours of enforced overwork and sedentary screen time, will fill up with laughing, yelling, running, and tumbling 3- to 17-year olds.

Children will be encouraged to go outside, run fast, get dirty, play in mud, explore, and sometimes even whittle sharp sticks with a pocket knife. They will learn how to climb trees and build a campfire. Parents will volunteer together to create and monitor safe play areas for children in their neighborhood—then they will back off and let them play.

The world will see the Dawn of the Post-Digital Child. Children and their parents will be the masters of their digital devices, not the slaves of them. Many of the electronic screens that once cluttered our nation's classrooms will be put in storage or disposed of, screen time for children in school and home will be limited to a few hours a week, and our children will live much of the week in a screen-free, non-digital oasis.

Following the examples of pioneering parents like Steve Jobs, Bill Gates, Barack Obama, and many Silicon Valley executives, children's screen time at home will be managed down to a bare minimum. At home, parents will regularly shut down the family's electronic devices, talk and play and read books with their children, chase them to the park, and play gentle rough-and-tumble with them on the grass, the bed, and the living room floor. Parents and teachers will recognize that smart schools are schools where smartphones are often switched off.

In schools from the inner cities to the sprawling suburbs and rural heartland, children will be encouraged to wiggle, giggle, and fidget if they need to; to walk in uneven lines; and even to bounce, shake, and slouch from time to time, since that's what children (especially boys) are biologically engineered to do.

Children will be encouraged by their parents and teachers to sometimes be bored, stare out the window and "zone out," so they can rest their brains to prepare for a fresh burst of learning, expression, physical activity, playful discovery, inquiry, and creative thinking.

Every few weeks in school, our children will attend "Failure Academy." They will be encouraged to fail—through bold thinking, creative experimentation, and intellectual risk-taking as pathways to success and achievement. The students' mistakes will serve as lessons to be learned, and the failures and mistakes of their own teachers will be showcased and celebrated with the class in a spirit of collaboration, fun, and shared learning. Children will learn that success and failure are not opposites but often coexist side by side.

Rather than punishing children for naturally limited attention spans and regular movement, schools will accommodate and respect each child's needs as an individual and as a gifted learner, and each child's regular need for physical and intellectual play.

Someday soon, politicians and decision-makers will stop mass social experiments on children and build education systems based on what we already know—that education is a public service that values professionalism, collaboration, research, equity, well-being, and empathy.

Someday soon, adults will listen to children, very carefully—and we will give their childhood back to them. Someday soon, government officials, parents, and educators will carefully study the research on how children learn and grow best, and they will realize a powerful, life-transforming insight: The children must play.

Someday soon, adults will let children be children. Parents, teachers, policymakers, and children themselves will co-create the schools of today and tomorrow on a solid foundation of play—free play, guided play, physical play, intellectual play, indoor play, and outdoor play—from day care and pre-K all the way to high school.

When that day comes, we will see great things happen. Children's health and behavior in school will improve. Their academic, social, and emotional skills will improve. Their attention span, focus, and "executive function" will improve. Their future skills will flourish. Children will be much happier—and they will learn better. And their schools will thrive.

* * *

We stand on the edge of a potential Golden Age of Childhood, a new education era of creativity, exploration, deeper learning, and improved health and well-being for the world's children—if we build our schools of today and tomorrow on a foundation of play.

2

A Tale of Two Fathers

If we love our children and want them to thrive, we must allow them more time and opportunity to play, not less.

—Professor Peter Gray[20]

F ive years ago, we switched countries.

Pasi Sahlberg moved from Finland to the United States to teach and research global education best practices as a visiting professor at the Harvard University Graduate School of Education, and co-author William Doyle moved to Finland to study the world-renowned Finnish primary school system as a

Fulbright Scholar and to give university graduate school lectures on media and education. We brought our wives and young children with us.

We were both in for a shock.

In the United States, Pasi entered a childhood and education culture that was increasingly based on stress, standardization, the de-professionalization of the teaching profession, and the systematic elimination of play in childhood education, even in kindergartens.

In Finland, in sharp contrast, William encountered a world-renowned childhood education system based on a strong foundation of learning through play, and a system that provided for constant bursts of play and playful discovery in school all the way up to high school, under the leadership of highly professional, respected childhood educators.

Over those 5 years, in our work and as we wrote this book together, we traveled the world and talked with thousands of teachers, parents, students, researchers and policymakers about childhood education, education reform and innovation, play, and the "schools of tomorrow."

Since then Pasi has traveled some half a million miles to visit schools, address teacher conferences, and observe classrooms from pre-kindergartens to upper secondary schools in 30 American states, throughout Europe, and in Canada, Latin America, South Africa, the Middle East, South East Asia, Australia, New Zealand, China, and Southern Africa.

In that time, Pasi has also served as visiting professor at Harvard University, a visiting scholar at Singapore's National Institute of Education and at Arizona State University, as an advisor to the governments of Finland, Scotland, and Sweden, as a governing board member of the University of Oulu in Finland, and as a board member of The Beijing Academy, one of the leading public middle schools in China's capital. Pasi has also presented education recommendations before the U.S. Congress, the United Nations General Assembly, a number of U.S. state legislatures, and a variety of international conferences.

During that same time, William embedded himself in Finland's largest teacher training school, gave lectures on "the schools of tomorrow" to high school students, graduate students, and international transfer students from over 30 different nations at the University of Eastern Finland, and served as advisor to the Ministry of Education and Culture of Finland in Helsinki, during a time when Finland was ranked as the world's #1 school system by no less than three international organizations: UNICEF, the World Economic Forum, and the Organization for Economic Cooperation and Development, or OECD. [21]

Back in New York City, one of America's most influential—and shamefully, most racially segregated—big-city school systems, William visited dozens of public and private school classrooms, and periodically "embedded" himself in his son's public elementary school, a highly diverse, desegregated school with a majority of students who are black or Latino and a majority of students who live below the poverty line.

This book is based on our field work, our interviews, and experiences as classroom observers of education systems and advisors to governments and schools around the world, and on an intensive review of the historical literature and media reporting on play and childhood education. A review of over 700 articles published in peer-reviewed educational, medical, and other scientific journals formed a pillar of our research.

This book is also based on a series of wide-ranging, original one-on-one qualitative interviews conducted by the authors in person and online with a distinguished international panel of experts, a "brain trust" of over 70 leading education scholars, researchers, thought leaders, and practitioners. We asked them for their research, opinions, and ideas on the subject of childhood play in school.

One of our interviewees, Gloria Ladson-Billings, is president of the National Academy of Education, the most prestigious research-based education institution in the nation. Three of the experts, Sergio Pellis, Anthony Pellegrini, and Stephen Siviy, have conducted among the most significant original experiments and studies on play. The panel also includes scores of renowned educators from around the world. Additionally, the book is informed by additional conversations the authors held with thousands of educators, researchers, students, and parents from a very wide range of different nations and cultures.

And finally, this book is based on our experiences as fathers who have logged thousands of hours in the world's most advanced laboratory of childhood development—the playground—and watched our own children and countless others play, run around, collaborate, socialize, grow, explore, be creative, fall down, get dirty, scrape their knees, build teams, create new games and new worlds of imagination, be bored, succeed, fail, and learn, in the deepest sense, what it means to become a human being.

A NOTE TO THE READER

No matter how much research there is that indicates the educational benefits of play, no matter how many teachers, pediatricians, and researchers endorse it, we know the idea can strike some people as surprising, outrageous, or downright dangerous.

After all, you may think, school is for learning, not for playing, which sounds and can even look like the opposite. We understand how you feel. The problem is, in part, due to the broad, fuzzy, and imprecise nature of the word *play* itself.

If you are one of these people, we have a suggestion. Every time you see the word *play* in this book, strike the word from your brain. Just forget the word *play*.

Replace it with a phrase that is, in fact, a more exact definition of the process of play in the educational context of the child: "systematic exploration, experimentation, and discovery," or SEED. This is what a child is doing when he or she plays. It is a SEED for learning, growth, and happiness.

PASI SAHLBERG'S STORY

Last year, I was invited to speak to the annual meeting of teachers at the Wisconsin State Reading Association.

I was asked to talk about differences and similarities in school practices in the United States and Finland. Finland's schools have attracted a lot of attention in the last 15 years, because Finnish students have performed very well in the Program for International Student Assessment (PISA) tests, an international benchmark standardized test supervised by OECD. To many people's surprise, Finland's school system does much the op-posite of what schools do, for example, in the United States—no formal academic instruction until children are 7 years old, less school-related stress, less homework, no standardized tests (other than periodic testing of very small samples of students to check for trends over time) until the end of high school, teachers prepared and respected like professionals—and lots and lots of play throughout childhood education.

Ironically, for a nation that shuns the standardized testing of children, Finland's schools became famous because its 15-year-olds did well on the PISA standardized tests. But Finnish teachers will be the first to tell you that while the PISA data can be interesting and may be able to flag some overall interna-tional trends and efficiencies, it is an imperfect and highly in-complete attempt to measure only a few narrow categories of learning. There are a host of skills, talents, and competencies that PISA does not measure, and most of these skills cannot and should not ever be reduced to standardized test data—things like creativity, empathy and compassion, leadership, presentation skills, curiosity, teamwork, and a host of other skills.

My audience at the Wisconsin event was made up of scores of educators, ranging from early childhood to high school teachers, administrators and college students. Toward the end of the talk, I made some suggestions of ideas to consider on how to improve American schools. I made it very clear that we can't "export" one nation's education system and practices to another country, since cultures are so different, but I do believe that different nations have much to learn from and inspire each other.

My talk included suggestions like invest more in equity in education, encourage collaboration between schools rather than competition, and keep standardized testing to an absolute minimum. My next presentation slide was usually a crowd-pleaser. I've given nearly 300 keynotes and speeches around the United States in the last 10 years, and whenever the audience has lots of teachers in it, this slide almost always gets a very positive reaction. I knew that this audience was made up of passionate, opinionated, and highly professional American educators, from rural schools to big inner-city schools, and I expected a strong response.

I braced myself and clicked the button for the next slide. Big white letters on black background said simply, "Let the Children Play."

Boom. The room erupted in smiles, applause, and then scattered cheers. It was one of the loudest reactions I've ever gotten. I was used to a big response to this message, but this was going over the top! Apparently, this was a simple four-word message that nearly everyone in the audience understood and believed in, but rarely if ever heard in their daily educational routine—*"Let the children play."*

The cheers continued as I told the teachers, "In Finland, all children are guaranteed a 15-minute, free-play outdoor recess after each 45-minute lesson every day, all the way to high school. Day care and childhood education before age 7 is based on learning to take responsibility for one's own actions and behavior, learning to be with other children through play, with no stress or formal academic pressure to learn to read or write unless children want to. The absence of external high-stakes standardized testing leaves both Finnish teachers and children free to focus on essentials: learning and well-being. Play is one of the main means of instruction and learning."

More cheers. More applause. Even some whooping and hollering. I was starting to feel like a rock star. I said that Finnish government regulations require that each and every kindergarten and preschool are responding to the child's needs, listening to the child, taking into consideration the child's interests and responsible care, and are enabling learning through play as central aspects of early childhood education. The audience was amazed.

I continued by saying that when children take their regular 15-minute breaks after each hourly lesson, that is also a "recess for teachers," who meet in well-equipped teachers' lounges to relax and have a chat with colleagues and enjoy a cup of coffee or tea, often to informally collaborate over new teaching insights or discuss how to help a particular child with a learning challenge.

Before long, it seemed to me like half the American audience was cheering, and the other half was crying. The unhappy half seemed gripped by sadness or anger that American children did not enjoy these essential educational and professional ingredients that every school in Finland seemed to have. The harmful effects of pushing children to do too much too early, the one-size-fits-all approach in many school systems, and the erosion of play in children's lives were becoming hot-button concerns in the minds of many American educators, as well as parents.

After the talk, two preschool teachers, both women in their 30s, came up to speak with me. I'll call them Carol and Lisa.

Carol was in her seventh year of teaching in a small rural primary school. Her colleague Lisa was a preschool teacher in the same community. They asked if I had a moment to talk with them.

Carol looked shaken, and Lisa was actually in tears.

"What's wrong?" I asked.

"I knew it. I knew it!" Lisa said, tears in her eyes. "I knew what we are doing to kids is wrong!"

"Oh, no," I thought to myself, "not again."

I've had reactions like this so many times from American teachers in recent years that I thought I'd gotten used to it by now, but this teacher was so emotional that I practically felt like crying, too. Many teachers have told me they are afraid that what they are forced to do in school will hurt children. I've received emails and letters from scores of teachers in the United States, Australia, England, and other countries who tell me that their outrage at being forced to overstress and deny play to young schoolchildren had grown so strong that they had left teaching altogether.

Lisa explained that she had been teaching kindergarten and preschool for 8 years, and that in that time, all aspects of play and child-friendly learning had been eliminated in her work. She was now being compelled by state education officials to administer high-pressure standardized tests to children of 4 and 5 years of age and to apply grossly inappropriate, premature academic pressure on her little students, all in the name of "standards" and "rigor."

The political theory behind this, apparently, was that America needed to "catch up" to high-performing global education nations like Singapore, South Korea, and Finland,

and that the sooner we applied academic "rigor" to pre-K students, the better they'd do in the long run, the sooner they would be ready for college and career, and America would be #1 in the international school rankings one day. Never mind that there was no evidence to support this theory, and that nearly 20 years of such "test and punish" and "earlier is better" practices had resulted in little if any improvement in America's international test scores or in reducing domestic racial and economic "achievement gaps" in educational outcomes. Instead, they have accelerated in parallel with recent trends of declining childhood mental health and well-being.

Children in Carol's and Lisa's classes, and in thousands of other American schools, were being forced to handle concepts they are unprepared for and made to feel like failures, during a time in their lives when they should be socializing, learning to love school, and learning the foundations of literacy and other academics through play, teacher guidance, and an atmosphere of warmth and support. Both teachers said that their children need care, support, and love, not "tougher expectations, harder work" and external tests that often classify children as failures.

Carol explained, "When I hear you explain how children in Finland are taught, I realize how harmful the things we are doing to children are. Somehow, I knew that these things are not right. They're not good for kids!"

I told her, "I know your situation in school is complicated and there is not much you can do alone. But don't quit!"

I didn't tell Carol that I'd heard the same kind of thing hundreds of times before. Across America, and in many other parts of the world, educators often feel trapped in the same situation, where they feel they can't give their pupils what they need in school, and they feel they are being asked to do something that goes against their profession as educators.

An increasing number of parents were subjected to this pressure, too, as I experienced myself when I moved to the United States in 2013 for a 3-year teaching assignment at an Ivy League university.

One morning in Cambridge, Massachusetts, I took my 3-year-old son to have a look at a local preschool to attend.

It was a pleasant place, and after a warm welcome, the preschool director sat me down for a cup of coffee.

"How many words does he know?" the director asked.

"Excuse me—how many what?" I asked, flummoxed.

"How many words. How developed is his vocabulary? And how many numbers can he count to?"

I hadn't the slightest idea. My boy was barely 3 years old, and I hadn't planned on figuring these questions out for at least another 3 or 4 years. Without warning, I had suddenly come face-to-face with a stunning new concept in American education—"preschool readiness."

I had heard that in the increasingly hyper-competitive, stressful, and academically pressurized American childhood education system, the symbolic summit of which, Harvard University, was a few blocks away, the idea of "college readiness" had been pushed down as far "kindergarten readiness" for incoming 5-year-olds. But applying the idea to 3-year-olds seemed downright bizarre.

I looked over at my son, a boy for whom toilet training and breastfeeding were very recent memories.

"Why do you need to know this?" I asked.

"We need to be sure he is ready for our program," replied the director. "We need to know if he can keep up with the rest of the class. We need to make sure all children are prepared to make the mark."

In my home country of Finland, and in many other countries, this conversation would be dismissed as flatly absurd, as would the required per-child price tag of $25,000 per year. The idea of measuring a child's vocabulary at age 3 as an academic qualifier for entering preschool would be condemned as grossly inappropriate. In Finland, children learn largely through play, games, songs, and conversation until they are 6 or 7, as they did in the United States until fairly recently. In Finland, the main question isn't "Is the child ready for the school?" but "Is the school ready for every child, and ready to accommodate each child's differences?" That was the question that I wanted to ask potential schools for my son: "How are you prepared to welcome our son here, as he is, and what will you do to secure his well-being and happiness here?" I never had an opportunity to get that far.

Yet here it was, a stark academic challenge confronting a toddler standing at the very gates of the American education system.

The scene couldn't have been more different from my own childhood learning experiences growing up in rural Finland, which were rooted in outdoor and indoor play. By age 7, I was wandering the neighborhood forest and streams on my own, alone and with my buddies, getting dirty, managing risks, climbing trees and hills, digging up worms, communicating with nature, and learning how the world worked. For children, play wasn't just part of free time, it was a way of life.

As a boy, I lived inside a schoolhouse in the rural village of Vuohtomäki. My father was the head of the local elementary school, and back then, to attract teachers to remote parts of Finland, local authorities built homes for them attached to the school buildings.

The school building was really nice. Built in the 1920s, it was a white, wooden castle-looking house where we lived, a house that also contained the school. It sat on top of the highest hilltop of that small Northern Finland village. There was no church in the village, which was too small for one, but there was this school, which all the people valued highly, much like a church. The schoolyard was full of trees to climb, big rocks and hills to run up and down on. It was the perfect place to play.

When the pupils were gone at the end of the day, I took over the empty classroom and played at being the teacher, pretending to give lessons to imaginary children.

It was a wonderful feeling. I was 8 years old, and I was teaching elementary school! I had to do this without my parents knowing about it—the classroom, which was just next door to our living room and kitchen, was a no-go zone, so I had to sneak in secretly. This made the whole "play" much more exciting. I was putting on plays, with me starring as the teacher.

There was nobody else in the deserted building, just me and my dear, faithful dog Luru, a Lassie who watched over me when my parents were away and served as my audience. In the class-room, I talked to imaginary pupils, called them by name, and corrected their answers. But the most thrilling plays were the times when I used my imagination to teach magical things, and experiments with natural phenomena, like water and wheels.

I always wanted to surprise my "pupils" to see their amazed faces. During one episode, when I led the class in experiments with fire (I didn't do it for real) the fire got out of control and I ordered all the pupils to escape the classroom through the window and use the ladder to climb down. We were on the second floor of the old wooden school building. I called the fire brigade, and soon all pupils in the schoolyard stared up in amazement to watch how the firefighters and I stopped the fire. We then climbed back to the classroom and learned about safety with fire.

I grew up to become a high school math teacher, and later an education policy official and university professor. To be able to "play with my future" was critical to my adult life and career.

Back at the preschool in Cambridge, Massachusetts, the conversation fizzled out and I took my son's hand to beat a hasty exit to investigate other options in the neighborhood. We wandered the streets of Cambridge, visiting two other preschools.

The experience was much the same. I was baffled that about the only thing these preschools were concerned about was how much progress our small son had made in a narrow "academic path" defined by the technical abilities of recognizing letters and numbers. But my son was good at other things. He was very good at play, and he had a vivid imagination that he used in painting, music, and dance. He was very friendly and curious about meeting new people. On top of these skills, he was trilingual, being able to communicate in Finnish, English, and his mother's language of Croatian, depending on whom he was talking with. These are pretty impressive skills for a 3-year-old.

But none of them really mattered when it came to "preschool readiness."

After a conference with my wife, I shared our final decision with my son over an ice cream break.

"It looks like at-home day care for you." Community playgrounds and weekly music classes would have to do. We had fairly flexible schedules, so it was feasible. It was also the most affordable option for us.

This seemed perfectly fine with my son. But this experience left me wondering why the wealthiest nation in the world could not better care for all of its youngest inhabitants, especially those whose parents or guardians can't afford to pay for early childhood education and care or weekly arts and sports activities for their children.

In 2013, back in Finland, I hosted a group of educators from Virginia who had traveled to Finland to take a closer look at its education system. They had read that Finnish schools are very different places compared to their own—no standardized tests, a strong focus on the arts alongside academic subjects, a minimum of an hour a day that students spend outside engaging in free play, and teachers who were largely happy with their work and were trusted as professionals by society.

The visitors were having a conversation about these peculiar features of Finnish schools at the empty outdoor schoolyard of Aurora Primary School in Espoo, Finland, when suddenly the school doors slammed open and 400 children charged outside.

"Is it a fire drill?" asked a startled American school administrator.

"No," said Martti, the Finnish school principal, "it's the regular 15-minute recess break they get after every 45 minutes of study indoors."

A group of fourth-grade girls played an improvised ball game. Packs of girls and boys wandered around the yard, chatting. Some children played with digital gadgets, others raced around at random or took some time for moments of solitude just for themselves.

A 10-year-old boy ran past the visitors to the far end of the play yard, shimmied up a tall tree, and perched, monkey-style, on his favorite branch.

"Did you see what that boy just did?" a stunned primary schoolteacher from Alexandria, Virginia, asked.

"Yes, I know him well," said principal Martti, who was in his 15th year of leading the school. "That is his passion, to climb, to be in high places."

"But what happens if he falls down from that tree and hurts himself?" asked another American teacher.

"Well, he probably wouldn't do it again," replied Martti.

"This could never happen back home," declared the visiting teacher.

"I assume in winter when it's cold outside and this schoolyard is covered with snow, students stay indoors?" one of the other delegates asked.

"Well, not usually. The rule is that if the outside temperature is below –15°C (or 5°F) they don't need to go out. Fresh air is always good for little brains," Martti said. The thought of children being sent out to play in sharply subfreezing temperatures seemed to stun the Americans into silence.

These scenes illustrate how radically different the school environments and cultures can be in two friendly Western democratic societies, the United States and Finland. One is not necessarily better than the other, but these different cultures provide very different contexts for children in which to play in school, and different ways in how parents and teachers relate to their children's play.

In hundreds of meetings I have held with government officials and education ministers around the world, there is one question I am asked most often, in conversations that often go like this:

"How can we improve our schools?"

That depends, I tell them, on what your objectives are. If your goal is to raise scores on international standardized benchmarking tests, I have no suggestions. Such tests and rankings are of very limited value to children's education. But if, on the other hand, your goal is to raise the quality of your students' learning across the board and maximize their chances of a bright future, especially students from challenging backgrounds, I can offer five ideas to consider.

First, I suggest, prepare and treat teachers like professionals, with advanced graduate-level, intensely clinical training in teaching theory and practice, childhood development, educational research, and leadership; put these teachers in charge of your schools; and respect them as elite professionals.

Second, encourage schools and teachers to collaborate, not compete against one another.

Third, fund and staff schools fairly and equitably so that all schools have adequate resources and highly capable teachers to cope with the inequalities that children bring to school every day.

Fourth, give children a classroom atmosphere of warmth, support, and well-being, instead of stress, overwork, and fear.

And finally, I tell them, "*Let the children play*. Build your education system on regular periods of playful learning and discovery and indoor and outdoor physical and intellectual play, from preschool to high school."

This idea is usually met with cold, dead silence. When many teachers hear the phrase "Let the children play," they often tend to cheer or cry. But many politicians and administrators, by contrast, revert to a quasi-vegetative state. The look on their faces often registers one of two expressions: "We don't have the slightest idea what you are talking about" or "That would never work in a million years, not where I come from."

Then I think, "If only they could see what I've seen. I have seen things they wouldn't believe."

When I was a grade school math and science teacher, I sometimes saw my own students become gripped by anxiety or confusion. Then, after I stopped the class to play a math game or simply sing a song, I saw them relax and open their minds to new ideas and new challenges.

I have seen small children in playgrounds in Finland and around the world invent wonderful new games when their parents and teachers back off and let them play all on their own. I have seen 9-year-olds disappear into a thick forest in Finland with sharp garden shears to gather plant samples for a science class that turned into a playful adventure.

I have seen children in Scotland running around muddy fields in winter during school recess, getting dirty and soaking wet, with the full support of their teachers and parents. I have seen low-income children in public schools in Texas and New York state achieve striking improvements in classroom focus and "on-task behavior" by following the Finnish example of enjoying a 15-minute recess every single hour of the school day.

I have seen school children race through a New Zealand meadow in brilliant sunshine for nearly an hour before lunch and return to their classroom sharp, focused, and in a state of joy, ready to learn much more efficiently than if they had been imprisoned indoors all day.

I have been in schools in Australia where children learn traditional outdoor games from community elders, and I've marveled at how much the children love to learn how their parents and grandparents played before them.

I have seen little children in China walking nicely one after another to the school play yard with toys and balls, then enjoy an energizing tai chi session with their teachers before class.

I have seen a Japanese eighth-grade teacher give a math lesson that was so playful, passionate, and enjoyable that the children were reluctant to leave his classroom when the bell rang.

I have seen preschoolers in Asia, Europe, and Latin America learn the early foundations of academics through free play, with objects, with costumes, with water and sand, with songs, and by being with each other.

I have seen thriving black, Latino, Asian, and white students in a New York public school enjoy something almost unheard of in American education—two 20-minute recesses per day, on top of an optional 30-minute recess period at the beginning of every school day before the bell rings.

I have seen teachers all over the world who know when to teach through direct, formal instruction, when to teach through guided play, and when to step aside and let children "learn how to learn" all by themselves.

I have seen children learn happier, learn more, and learn better—all by learning, in part, through play.

* * *

LET CHILDREN BE CHILDREN: THE HOLY GRAIL OF EDUCATION?

When politicians and technology vendors talk about "schools of tomorrow," their ideas often do not penetrate far beyond familiar discussions of "21st-century skills" and "digital learning." Much deeper insights are needed, and the critical role of play in schools can help inspire our thinking.

While some technology platforms and products hold promise in helping teachers and students, this book is not about education technology or "blended learning" or screen-delivered "personalized learning" or "digital learning" or "bringing your own device to school." This is a book about play, the flesh-and-blood kind.

We propose a new global awakening by teachers, parents, and citizens to restore and expand the power of play in our schools.

A striking body of scientific evidence and breakthroughs produced in studies, experiments, and classroom experiences around the world strongly suggests that children learn best over the long term in environments that are rich in play, and that play is both the engine of childhood and the basis of effective childhood education and future academic achievement.

Play is how children learn, and how they form a foundation for life in society. Play is how children explore, discover, fail and succeed, socialize, flourish and thrive. Play is the foundation of childhood.

Play is one of the keys to giving our children the skills and habits of mind they need to succeed—skills like creativity, innovation, teamwork, focus, resilience, expressiveness, empathy, concentration, and executive function, to name just a few. Play is an essential means of enabling every child to unleash the power of imagination, innovation, and creative thought.

Children are biologically engineered for constant intellectual and physical play. They are designed to question, daydream, pretend, arrange block towers and doll houses, wiggle, fidget, run, jump, laugh, cry, be frustrated, be absorbed, be bored, be creative, and, above all, to be different. And they have much to teach us. The mathematician and researcher Seamour Papert (1928–2016), who spent most of his career teaching and researching at MIT, wrote that "rather than pushing children to think like adults, we might do better to remember that they are great learners and to try harder to be more like them."[22]

Play is not an aimless, random waste of time. When the power of play is properly harnessed and unleashed, it is, in fact, a basis of academic, emotional, and physical growth for a child.

The life of a child is to play, in and out of school. The life of a child is to play outdoors and indoors—to play with academic concepts, math and language, science, objects, drama, books, music, the arts, nature, sports, risk, tools, imagination, experimentation, trial and failure, with guidance from adults and completely on their own.

Yet we are, on a global basis, systematically destroying conditions for authentic play in childhood, in our schools, and in our homes and our society. We have created emotionally desolate, bleak, oppressive environments for our children.

In a quest to prepare children for the future, we are taking childhood away from our children. In the name of "education reform," we are standardizing and squandering our children's futures. None of this is helping the healthy development and learning of children. Instead, we are overwhelming many of our children with anxiety, toxic stress, wasted effort, and relentless, sedentary screen time.

We wrote this book for two main reasons. First, we have reviewed the evidence from around the world strongly suggesting that play is an essential element of children's learning, growth, and well-being, and that play benefits children in multiple ways, including improving their health and learning. We believe that we actually can save and improve our schools—with more play. Second, we have seen the power of play in our own children's lives and in the lives of millions of other children.

When you watch your own children at home, you can easily see that children are born curious and creative. Infants and toddlers are good proof of that if you watch them play. But what often happens is that children grow out of curiosity and creativity when they go to preschool, kindergarten, and elementary school.

Sir Ken Robinson has suggested that our schools are much to blame. Not the teachers, but the educational system's rigid architecture, stiff regulations, and incorrect policies. The global education race for "higher standards" at lower financial costs have turned many schools to factories that try to produce standardized products efficiently on tight schedules. We believe, however, that more play embedded in the daily life of every school is the best way to have not only healthier and happier children but also schools that are better prepared to solve the challenges our planet faces.

We wrote this book because we are alarmed that play, discovery, and experimentation, the natural language of childhood learning, is being systematically removed from our schools, and it is being replaced by fear, stress, and ineffective education policies. We are alarmed at the human costs of this, and by the fact that it simply does not work in improving our children's learning and well-being.

We wrote this book because we are worried about our children—all of them, everywhere. We are alarmed by statistics, surveys, and research about declining mental health, rising obesity, increasing stress, growing disengagement in school, lack of life satisfaction, and the overprescription of drugs to deal with childhood problems that may be caused by a variety of cultural and social stresses, including the lack of intellectual and physical play. School policies around the world have helped create a human crisis that is exploding the social costs of education through the roof. We are afraid that unless we change the course soon, many of our youngest and weakest children won't be able to take it anymore.

It doesn't have to be this way. It should not be this way.

Some day soon, we will give childhood back to our children. Some day soon, adults will listen to children, very carefully.

Some day soon, adults will *let children be children.*

Anyone who claims to have discovered the holy grail for educating children probably doesn't know what they're talking about.

Education is a mysterious, complex, imperfect, and exquisitely difficult process that is rife with paradoxes and unknowns, a process that requires extreme intellectual humility, constant renewal, collaboration, and innovation. Every child, teacher, parent, and culture is different. Children are exposed to a host of social, emotional, and physical pressures and stresses that can impact their learning. Every student is gifted and talented in their own way, but sometimes these gifts are hidden or take time to be discovered and flourish.

There are, in fact, big gaps in our knowledge of how play affects learning, and much of the research on the subject is new or incomplete, since it is notoriously difficult to perform research on children because of ethical issues. Like most research, it is open to debate. Often, sample sizes are small, children studied are heterogeneous, older children are studied less than younger children, studies are short term, and studies with negative or inconclusive results may not get published.[23] Studies sometimes contradict each other. Since most of the studies on play are observational, associations and correlations can be clearly observed, but cause and effect often cannot. Much of the available research on play focuses on children in the West, especially in the United States and United Kingdom, and play research reflecting global differences in global culture, gender, ethnicity, and economic status among children is rare.

But right now, around the world, as they piece together all the available experiments, experiences and evidence, teachers, researchers, and parents are discovering a provocative solution to the question of how to improve our schools: children should play more.

Having more time to play alone is not the solution to the world's education problems. But we do argue that play is an excellent—and very inexpensive—resource to improve the conditions for better learning and well-being and happier children and, therefore, a better future for the world.

How can we best help our children thrive in school—and in life?

One of the most powerful solutions is not an app. It is not a standardized test, or a computer tablet in the hands of every child, or an educational fad. It does not require turning kindergartens into first grades, or turning elementary schools into stress factories.

It is something that most children on Earth intrinsically know. It is an approach that is being pioneered by schools, teachers, parents, and children around the world.

It has the power to give your child, and all children, a rich portfolio of powerful academic, social, and emotional advantages that are critical to success.

What is the purpose of education? If the answer is to increase childhood stress, to provide low-quality or irrelevant data to politicians and administrators, to squander billions of dollars on unproductive or unproven learning interventions, and to make little or no sustained positive impact on childhood learning and on reducing achievement gaps, then we as a society are doing an excellent job with our schools.

But if you believe, as we do, that the chief purposes of education are to inspire children to discover their passions, to learn how to learn, to love learning, and to become active, productive, healthy, compassionate, creative, and responsible members of society, then we must radically rethink the way we organize our schools. And that begins with building our schools upon a solid foundation of the learning language of children—play.

The problem, simply put, is that our schools are not working as well as they should. One of the major causes for this is that we are pursuing ineffective education policies that are squeezing out play in school, a key foundation of learning, and replacing it with fear, stress, premature and excessive pressure, and national education policies shackled to the universal standardized testing of children. We are not blaming teachers. Quite the opposite. We admire the millions of teachers who regardless of wrong-headed education policies and directives are doing the best they can every day to help all children to learn and grow in school.

What is the solution? How can we help all our children thrive in school and in life?

A critical piece of the answer is inspired by the wisdom of our ancestors and confirmed by a striking series of recent breakthroughs in brain science and education research.

The answer can be found in one simple phrase: *Let the children play!*

3

The Learning Power of Play

Our children from their earliest years must take part in all the more lawful forms of play, for if they are not surrounded with such an atmosphere they can never grow up to be well conducted and virtuous citizens.[24]

—Plato, *The Republic*

That is the way to learn the most, that when you are doing something with such enjoyment that you don't notice that the time passes.[25]

—Albert Einstein, in letter to his son, 1915

What do children need to learn best?

The answer, in part, is play, and lots of it.

One of the founding fathers of modern education, 17th-century Moravian bishop Johann Amos Comenius, had a vision of schools as "gardens of delight" where children grow, play, and learn together in harmony and joy.[26]

In 2008, when a panel of early childhood development scholars reviewed the research on how young students learn, they concluded that "children need both unstructured free play and playful learning under the gentle guidance of adults," because "learning takes place best when children are engaged and enjoying themselves."[27] For a child, playing is learning.

Pediatricians agree, too—children should learn, in part, through play. A landmark clinical report published in 2007 by the leading professional association of over 67,000 children's doctors in the United States, the American Academy of Pediatrics, declared that child advocates should "allow each child to fully reap the advantages associated with play."[28]

The doctors' report added that "play is essential to development" and went on to detail the many critical benefits that children earn through play:

> Play allows children to use their creativity while developing their imagination, dexterity, and physical, cognitive, and emotional strength. Play is important to healthy brain development. It is through play that children at a very early age engage and interact in the world around them. Play allows children to create and explore a world they

can master, conquering their fears while practicing adult roles, sometimes in conjunction with other children or adult caregivers. As they master their world, play helps children develop new competencies that lead to enhanced confidence and the resiliency they will need to face future challenges. Undirected play allows children to learn how to work in groups, to share, to negotiate, to resolve conflicts, and to learn self-advocacy skills.[29]

Pediatrician Michael Rich, who leads the "More Play Today" program at the Center on Media and Child Health in Boston Children's Hospital and Harvard Medical School, has compiled the latest research, facts, and experiments to provide practical advice to parents and teachers on how to increase time and quality of children's play at home and in school. According to Dr. Rich, the evidence demonstrates that "play helps kids' brains and bodies develop, and helps them learn how to get along with others."[30]

The medical and scientific consensus in favor of childhood play is so strong that there is an international political recognition of play as a fundamental right of every child. Article 31 of the UN Convention on the Rights of the Child (1989), the most widely ratified treaty in history, recognizes "the right of the child to rest and leisure, to engage in play and recreational activities appropriate to the age of the child." Similarly, the European Parliament and Council of the European Union declared in 2011 that "all children have the right to rest, leisure and play" and recognized "the importance of play, which is also crucial to learning in the early years."[31] All the Nordic countries have adopted legislation that declares play as a human right for all their children, including in school.

Play seems to be a built-in biological imperative not only for people but also for animals. "Play is part of our evolutionary heritage, occurs in a wide spectrum of species, is fundamental to health, and gives us opportunities to practice and hone the skills needed to live in a complex world," notes the 2018 clinical report on play by the American Academy of Pediatrics. "Although play is present in a large swath of species within the animal kingdom, from invertebrates (such as the octopus, lizard, turtle, and honey bee) to mammals (such as rats, monkeys, and humans), social play is more prominent in animals with a large neocortex [the part of the brain involved with higher order brain functions]."[32]

We should not exclude play from the lives of children when they grow older. Recent calls for education systems to prepare more "innovation-ready" citizens are better achieved when aspects of play are a part of learning in later years of schooling and even in colleges and universities, too. Tony Wagner, who is an expert in Residence at Harvard University's Innovation Lab, a Senior Research Fellow at the Learning Policy Institute, and author of the award-winning book *Creating Innovators*, is also an advocate for more play, passion, and purpose in education. "Play is part of our human nature and an intrinsic motivation," he told us. Wagner noted that "we all are born with an innate curiosity and desire to explore, experiment, and imagine new possibilities, in other words, to innovate." Children can develop these skills through play.[33]

Mammals are especially playful. Why is it that so many young mammals engage in play? At the turn of the 20th century, German naturalist Karl Groos argued that play was an evolutionary mechanism that enabled the young to practice behaviors they needed in order to survive. This "practice theory" of play explains why zebra colts "rehearse" the actions of bobbing and weaving, while lion cubs play at stalking and chasing. Groos extended the theory to humans, noting that children observed grown-ups and then played at skills that their culture demanded for survival, like bow-and-arrow hunting in hunter-gatherer cultures.[34]

Play has evidently been a natural foundation of childhood since the dawn of civilization, in all lands and cultures. A Greek vase dating from around 440 B.C. shows an illustration of a boy playing with a yo-yo.[35] Play is common in many hunter-gatherer societies, and Native American cultures featured constant rugged outdoor play in the wilderness, as children mimicked the adult skills of stalking, hunting, and fighting. In some parts of Australia, children play a game called "weet weet," or throwing a play stick, that originates from long traditions of indigenous communities.

The 1560 painting "Children's Games," by Dutch Renaissance artist Pieter Bruegel the Elder, depicts a medieval village that has been taken over by scores of children and adolescents playing. At least 80 games, sports, and toys have been identified in the painting, including dolls, masks, tiddlywinks, bowling, rattles, swimming, bocce ball, a hobby horse, a spinning top, putting on a show, stilt-walking, pole-vaulting, hat-twirling, dice, a swing, marbles, blind man's bluff, pitch-and-toss, mumblety-peg, and a squirting water gun.

American slave children found ways to play, as did the children of European settlers and children in the new American cities and suburbs—even children facing the Holocaust.[36] Play is a constant companion of human beings through their lifespan.

Children play with objects, sounds, movements, ideas, and emotions from their earliest days as infants, and playful behavior can persist well into old age.

If you ask many experienced childhood development professionals, researchers, and classroom teachers what young children need to learn best, you'll likely get variations on these themes: They need schools filled with warmth, encouragement, active exploration, rich dialogue, hands-on activities, joyful discovery, blocks, paint, crayons, sand and water tables, dress-up costumes, choice time, some guided and direct instruction appropriate to their age level and individual skills, regular formative assessments by their classroom teachers (i.e., assessments "for" learning rather than assessments only "of" learning), lots of breaks and running around outdoors—and a strong academic foundation of social support, proper nutrition, engaged parents, qualified teachers, equitable access to resources, and learning through various kinds of play, including both free play and guided play. When children ask for more time to play, explained Christopher Brown, Professor of Curriculum and Instruction in Early Childhood Education at the University of Texas at Austin, they are not trying to get out of work. "They know they have to work in school," Brown wrote. "Rather, they're asking for a chance to recharge as well as be themselves."[37]

What is play? In the English language, the word *play* refers to a wide range of all sorts of activities, from football to Broadway productions, and from drums to Las Vegas gambling games. When it comes to play in school, there are as many definitions as there are play advocates, which is a lot. The problem that often occurs when we talk about the role of play in early childhood and later on in schooling is that the word *play* has so many different meanings.

Dictionary definitions of play are often unsatisfactory, and they are sometimes criticized as contradictory and inaccurate by play researchers. The founder of the National Institute for Play, Professor Stuart Brown, has described play as "anything that spontaneously is done for its own sake." He wrote that play "appears purposeless, produces pleasure and joy, [and] leads one to the next stage of mastery."[38] Another academic, Professor Evan Ortlieb of New York's St. Johns University, described play as "a minimally scripted, open-ended exploration in which the participant is absorbed in the spontaneity of the experience."[39]

According to the American Academy of Pediatrics 2018 clinical report on play,

> The definition of play is elusive. However, there is a growing consensus that it is an activity that is intrinsically motivated, entails active engagement, and results in joyful discovery. Play is voluntary and often has no extrinsic goals; it is fun and often spontaneous. Children are often seen actively engaged in and passionately engrossed in play; this builds executive functioning skills and contributes to school readiness (bored children will not learn well). Play often creates an imaginative private reality, contains elements of make believe, and is nonliteral.[40]

Twenty-four hundred years ago, Plato championed the idea of "play sanctuaries" for 3- to 6-year-olds, and he described children's free play as an automatic process of nature: "When children are brought together, they discover more or less spontaneously the games which come naturally to them at that age."[41]

Trying to define play is like looking for a universal definition of love—we know it when we see or feel it, but the more you try to define it, the more elusive it can seem. We know when children are playing by just watching them, and we see love between two people when they hold one another in the park. A group of teenagers building sand castles on the beach, primary school pupils doing jump-rope rhymes in the schoolyard, a child building a tower of wooden blocks, or a toddler driving around a toy car with his big brother on the floor are all scenes of play. In school, play can include activities as varied as the following:

- A pre-K child learning her ABC's by singing a song
- A first-grader and his classmates designing and building a sky-scraper with building blocks
- A fourth-grade class play-acting as time-traveling news reporters to interview great figures in history, like Albert Einstein, Confucius, and Martin Luther King Jr.
- A high school biology class led by a passionate teacher who uses hands-on experimentation and unexpected failures and wrong turns to illustrate the scientific method
- A recess yard filled with children running around in the fresh air with no adult interference
- An eighth-grader engrossed in a self-chosen, self-directed classroom "passion project" during a weekly free period for independent discovery

- A fun math game played by third-grade students and gently guided by the teacher toward a learning goal
- A child jazz band improvising on multiple instruments for 30 minutes after their formal music lesson
- A teacher who, sensing her class is bored, stops the class and sings her favorite rock ballad at the top of her lungs
- An eighth-grade algebra teacher whose classroom energy and passion ignite high levels of interest and joy among his students

Play can mean many different things to different people. In the Finnish and Swedish languages, for example, the words for the verb *play* in school, *leikkiä* and *leka*, refer to unstructured, imaginative, and enjoyable intrinsically motivated activity, not structured ballgames or guided training in musical instruments for children. In the Finnish language, substantive play, or *leikki*, translates as "action done for fun, especially among children." There are also different Finnish words for playing football (*pelata jalkapalloa*) and playing piano (*soittaa pianoa*).

Because of this linguistic diversity, the word *play* has very different connotations from language to language. In 2002, a UK advocacy group called the Hampshire Play Policy Forum offered this attempt at a definition of play: "a wide range of activities and behaviors that are satisfying to the child, creative for the child and freely chosen by the child."[42] Friedrich Fröbel, a 19th-century German educator and the father of the concept of "kindergarten," or "gardens for children," wrote, "Play, then, is the highest expression of human development in childhood, for it alone is the free expression of what is in a child's soul."[43]

For us, one good way of defining *play* in childhood educa-tion would be those engaging activities, both self-guided and guided by adults, that allow a child to use her or his creativity, curiosity, and imagination in a process that can have powerful intellectual and physical benefits for the child. Another way to define it would be regular periods of intellectual and physical freedom, choice, creativity, and playful teaching and learning, both structured and unstructured, and both indoors and out-doors, without fear of failure or punishment. In the broadest sense, play in school could even be defined as all those educa-tional activities that generate the emotions of interest and joy in a child. Play is a child's dress rehearsal for life. Play is a universal human condition.

We define play in school as both "free play" by children and "guided play" by adults for children, as both physical and intel-lectual, and as both indoor and outdoor. Five broad types of play are often identified by play advocates and researchers: physical play, play with objects, symbolic play, pretense or socio-dramatic play, and games with rules. Both teachers and parents should understand that play is not a product but a process. "There is a notoriously Puritan streak in American culture," noted Alison Gopnik, Professor of Psychology at the University of California, Berkeley. "We have a knack for taking what are simple pleasures in other cultures, from food to walks to sex, and turning them into strenuous work projects. So American parents often act as if play is only valuable if it will produce predictable outcomes."[44] Play in childhood often does not need to have measurable, test-able, specific adult-defined "outputs"; the act of playing itself provides the benefit and the learning.

The educational benefits of play are many, but the child is usually playing for fun, and out of his or her own intrinsic interest and motivation. To the untrained adult eye it can look like a child who is playing is being frivolous or wasting time. But to a child, play can seem like the best thing in life, and the very reason for being. It is, therefore, a natural and highly efficient learning language for children, if it is properly understood and harnessed.

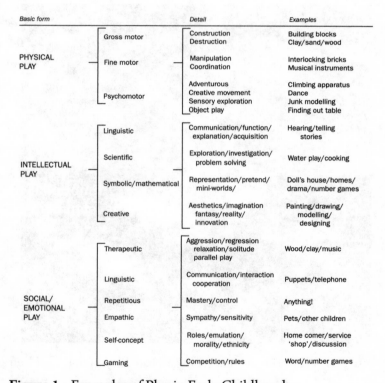

Figure 1. Examples of Play in Early Childhood.

Reprinted with permission from Moyles, J. *Just Playing? The Role and Status of Play in Early Childhood Education.* Milton Keynes: Open University Press, 1989.

Do you want your child to thrive in school and in life?

Then let them play—and make sure your school lets them, too.

In research studies, experiments and real-life school experiences around the world, various forms of play have been associated with many benefits for children (Figure 2). These benefits include cognitive development, social-emotional

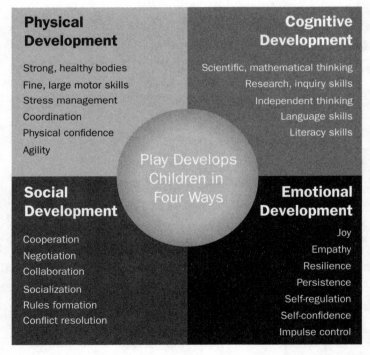

Figure 2. What the Science Shows: How Play Helps Children Learn and Grow.

Research summary by The National Museum of Play, 2013. Reprinted with permission of The Strong, all rights reserved.

health, physical health, improvements to attention, coping, memory, perspective-taking, cooperating, negotiating, helping, sharing, solving problems, dealing with trauma, planning skills, decision-making skills, motivation to learn, building friendships, school readiness, social skills and attitudes on sharing, turn-taking, self-restraint, working in groups and getting along with others, creativity and divergent thinking (generating multiple approaches to solving problems), healthy brain development, emotional stability and resiliency, empathy, feelings of well-being, motor skills, perspective-taking, early literacy and language development, self-regulation, child–parent attachment, science and math learning, and improvements in executive function.

Play in early childhood can deliver impressive long-term benefits, including for children who begin life with special challenges. This was the finding of the Jamaica Study, a long-term analysis of the effects achieved by a community health care worker visiting new mothers of children with growth retardation in the nation of Jamaica. The health care workers visited the mothers and children for 1 hour per week over the course of 2 years, and taught the moms parenting skills, including playing regularly with their children. The study followed the toddlers to childhood and found that those whose mothers received the visits caught up with more advantaged peers in their cognitive development, mental health, and social behavior, and showed less depression and violent behavior and better educational attainment over the long term into young adulthood.[45]

Do you want your child to thrive in the STEM (science, technology, engineering and math) subjects? Then let your child play.

Play with objects, patterns, blocks, sand, balls, art materials, crayons, and paper gives children many opportunities to experiment with the foundations of math and science concepts, like counting, computing, direction, distance, measurement, sequencing, physics, and architecture. Research has associated early object play with positive science and math outcomes. One study tracked a group of 37 children over 16 years and revealed that the complexity of their play with blocks as 4-year-olds was significantly and positively associated with their level of achievement in mathematics during middle and high school, even after controlling for gender and IQ.[46] "Even without specific adult guidance in the moment," wrote child psychologist Dr. Rachel White, "children's free play is rich with STEM lessons."[47] Curiosity, which is an integral ingredient of STEM learning, also flourishes and develops through independent and collaborative play.

According to a 2016 analysis by Cambridge University psychology and education researcher Dr. David Whitebread,

Neuroscientific studies have shown that playful activity leads to synaptic growth, particularly in the frontal cortex, the part of the brain responsible for the uniquely human higher mental functions. In my own area of experimental and developmental psychology, studies have also consistently demonstrated the superior learning and motivation arising from playful, as opposed to instructional, approaches to learning in children. Pretend play supports children's early development of symbolic representational skills, including those of literacy, more powerfully than direct instruction.

Physical, constructional and social play supports children in developing their skills of intellectual and emotional "self-regulation," skills which have been shown to be crucial in early learning and development.[48]

The evidence is becoming increasingly clear—physical play and physical activity boost academic performance. In 2013, the prestigious National Academy of Sciences issued a clinical report which declared that "time in the school day dedicated to recess, physical education class, and physical activity in the classroom may also facilitate academic performance," especially in mathematics and reading. "These topics depend on efficient and effective executive function, which has been linked to physical activity and physical fitness," the report found. It continued: "Executive function and brain health underlie academic performance. Basic cognitive functions related to attention and memory facilitate learning, and these functions are enhanced by physical activity and higher aerobic fitness."[49]

The potential benefits of play and physical activity to executive function are especially significant, as it is believed to be an early indicator of both school and career success. Executive function includes a broad range of higher-level cognitive processes, such as planning and decision-making, the management of information in memory, controlling negative feelings and actions, and smooth shifts from one task to another. Evidence from animal studies suggests that "play fighting" experiences, for example, benefit the synaptic growth and development of the prefrontal cortex, the area of the brain that influences executive function. The clinical report on children's play issued by the American Academy of Pediatrics in 2018 noted:

> Executive functioning helps children switch gears and transition from drawing with crayons to getting dressed for school. The development of the PFC [pre-frontal cortex] and executive functioning balances and moderates the impulsiveness, emotionality, and aggression of the amygdala [the section of the brain associated with emotions]. In the presence of childhood adversity, the role of play becomes even more important in that the mutual joy and shared attunement that parents and children can experience during play downregulates the body's stress response. Hence, play may be an effective antidote to the changes in amygdala size, impulsivity, aggression, and uncontrolled emotion that result from significant childhood adversity and toxic stress.[50]

In what may surprise some parents who pack their young children's schedule with highly structured, rigidly programmed activities, another possible booster of executive function is in fact the opposite—less structured activities. In a study of 70 suburban children ages 6 and 7 that was published in 2014 in *Frontiers in Psychology*, a team of researchers at the University of Colorado and University of Denver found that "the more time that children spent in less-structured activities [such as free play, spending time with family and friends, sightseeing and visiting zoos and museums], the better their self-directed executive functioning. The opposite was true of structured activities [like soccer practice, piano lessons, tutoring, and homework], which predicted poorer self-directed executive functioning." The researchers speculated that "structured time could slow the development of self-directed control, since adults in such scenarios can provide external cues and reminders about what should happen, and when."[51] Play, in other words, enables your child to practice and strengthen executive function.

"Executive function is extremely important for children," explained the study's co-author, University of Colorado Boulder psychology and neuroscience professor Yuko Munakata. "It helps them in all kinds of ways throughout their daily lives, from flexibly switching between different activities rather than getting stuck on one thing, to stopping themselves from yelling when angry, to delaying gratification. Executive function during childhood also predicts important outcomes, like academic performance, health, wealth and criminality, years and even decades later."[52] And according to the 2018 clinical report by the American Academy of Pediatrics, "play is not frivolous: it enhances brain structure and function and promotes executive function (i.e., the process of learning, rather than the content), which allow us to pursue goals and ignore distractions."[53]

After reviewing the research literature on play, researchers at the Lego Foundation, the charitable and research arm of the global toy company, identified five key characteristics of play. Learning through play, they concluded, "happens when the activity (1) is experienced as joyful, (2) helps children find meaning in what they are doing or learning, (3) involves active, engaged, minds-on thinking, (4) as well as iterative thinking (experimentation, hypothesis testing, etc.), and (5) involves social interaction." They added, "These five characteristics ebb and flow as children are engaged in learning through play and not all five are necessary all the time. But over time, children should experience moments of joy and surprise, a meaningful connection, be active and absorbed, iterate and engage with others."[54]

In our own analysis of the research on play, we see that different forms of playful activity are characterized by the *quality of play*. The key ingredients of higher-order, higher-quality play can be identified as self-directedness, intrinsic motivation, positive emotions, process orientation, and use of imagination. Teachers in school and parents at home can enhance the positive experience and overall impact of play by paying attention to these five dimensions of what we call "deeper play," which we discuss in chapter 7.

The 2007 report by the American Academy of Pediatrics stresses the importance of play in young children's school lives, noting, "Play is integral to the academic environment." The authors also note, "It has been shown to help children adjust to the school setting and even to enhance children's learning readiness, learning behaviors, and problem-solving skills. As they master their world, play helps children develop new competencies that lead to enhanced confidence and the resiliency they will need to face future challenges."[55]

In a large-scale, 5-year, longitudinal study of 3,000 3- to 7-year-old children, funded by the UK's Department for Education and published in 2004, researchers from the University of London and Oxford University found that an extended period of high-quality, play-rich preschool education made a significant difference in academic learning and well-being through the primary school years, including advantages for children from disadvantaged backgrounds. "Freely chosen play activities often provided the best opportunities for adults to extend children's thinking," the researchers found. "It may be that extending child-initiated play, coupled with the provision of teacher-initiated group work, are the most effective vehicles for learning." The researchers recommended that early childhood environments "work towards an equal balance of child and adult initiated activity."[56]

For over 30 years, Professor Sergio Pellis of the University of Lethbridge in Alberta, Canada, has studied the neuroscience of play in simple mammals, mainly rats and mice, and conducted experiments on the effects of play deprivation in animals, especially "rough and tumble" play, and play with objects. Pellis told us, "Based on the effects of free play on the development of social skills in rats and monkeys, I suspect that for many children interacting with peers in a playful manner is an important source for developing social skills that are mediated by the prefrontal cortex. Not only would play-induced improvements in social skills and the associated development of friendships make school participation more rewarding (who would feel good about studying if you are alienated from your peers?), but improved executive functions (e.g., attention, impulse control, emotional regulation, decision-making) arising from a more mature prefrontal cortex would also improve scholarly abilities more generally."[57]

Another pioneer in experimental play studies is Stephen M. Siviy, currently Professor of Psychology at Gettysburg College, who conducted some of the seminal animal research studies on the subject in recent decades with behavioral neuroscientist

Jaak Panksepp of Washington State University. "Children are highly motivated to play," he told us. Based on his observations of animals, Professor Siviy theorizes that when play is withheld, as is often done in school settings, two things happen: the desire to play keeps increasing, while the ability to concentrate and focus on the cognitive demands in the classroom go down. Withholding play, he argues, can also be detrimental to a child's social development.

Do you want your child to thrive in school, and in life? Send them outside to play. A report published in 2015 in the *International Journal of Environmental Research and Public Health* by researchers at the University of British Columbia (UBC) and at the Child & Family Research Institute at British Columbia Children's Hospital[58] found that "risky" outdoor play encourages creativity, resilience, and social skills. Children who participated in physical activity like climbing and jumping, rough-and-tumble play, and solitary exploration displayed greater physical and social health. Mariana Brussoni, lead author of the study, and assistant professor in UBC's School of Population and Public Health and Department of Pediatrics, said, "These positive results reflect the importance of supporting children's risky outdoor play opportunities as a means of promoting children's health and active lifestyles."[59]

Why should children get outside, take risks, and engage in lots of free, unstructured outdoor play, both in and out of school? Time spent playing in nature, it appears, delivers extra benefits for children, such as promoting children's sense of inventiveness, creativity, management of risk, and savoring the possibility of discovery and excitement. The UNICEF report, "The State of the World's Children 2012: Children in an Urban World" asserts that exposure to trees, water and the natural landscape "has positive impacts on children's physical, mental, social and spiritual health," and "has been found to restore children's ability to concentrate, which is the basis for improved cognition and psychological well-being." [60]

In 2015, a team of 20 Canadian public health researchers published the results of a major analysis of the benefits to children of outdoor play. In their words, their findings included the following:

- Access to active play in nature and outdoors—with its risks—is essential for healthy child development. We recommend increasing children's opportunities for self-directed play outdoors in all settings—at home, at school, in child care, the community, and nature.
- When children are outside they move more, sit less, and play longer—behaviors associated with improved cholesterol levels, blood pressure, body composition, bone density, cardiorespiratory, and musculoskeletal fitness and aspects of mental, social, and environmental health.
- Outdoor play is safer than you think. Risk is often interpreted as a bad thing, yet exposure to risk has been shown to be essential for healthy child development.
- Broken bones and head injuries unfortunately do happen, but major trauma is uncommon. Most injuries associated with outdoor play are minor.
- There are consequences to keeping children indoors—is it really safer? When children spend more time in front of screens

they are more likely to be exposed to cyber-predators and violence and to eat unhealthy snacks.

- Air quality indoors is often worse than outdoors, increasing exposure to common allergens (e.g., dust, mold, pet dander) and infectious diseases and potentially leading to chronic conditions.

- In the long term, sedentary behavior and inactivity elevate odds of developing chronic diseases, including heart disease, type-2 diabetes, some forms of cancer, and mental health problems.

- Hyper-parenting limits physical activity and can harm mental health.

- When children are closely supervised outside, they are less active.

- Children are more curious about and interested in natural spaces than prefabricated play structures.

- Children who engage in active outdoor play in natural environments demonstrate resilience and self-regulation and develop skills for dealing with stress later in life.

- Outdoor play that occurs in minimally structured, free and accessible environments facilitates socialization with peers, the community, and the environment, reduces feelings of isolation, builds interpersonal skills, and facilitates healthy development.[61]

Could more outdoor time boost your child's executive skills? Researchers in Norway think so. A 4-year longitudinal study of 562 students in 28 day care centers in Norway, published in 2017, found that children who were given high levels of outdoor time during childcare showed consistently higher levels of executive functions like attention and short-term memory, and fewer inattention-hyperactivity symptoms at ages 4, 5, 6, and 7 than the children with low levels of outdoor time. The researchers concluded that "outdoor time in the early childhood years may support children's development of attention skills and protect against inattention-hyperactivity symptoms." They also suggested that "placing day care centers in high vegetation areas and affording more outdoor time may be an effective and environmentally friendly way of supporting and enhancing children's self-regulatory capacities and cognitive development."[62]

An added benefit of outdoor time for schoolchildren may be eye health. Myopia, or nearsightedness, has reached epidemic levels in parts of Asia, for example, and there is no known effective intervention to prevent it, but several recent studies suggest that outdoor playtime may offer real promise. The results of the Guangzhou Outdoor Activity Longitudinal Trial, a randomized trial of close to 2,000 first-graders from 12 primary schools in Guangzhou, China, and published in 2015, found that the addition of 40 minutes of outdoor activity at school resulted in a reduced incidence rate of myopia over the next 3 years. Similar results were found in the 2003–2005 Sydney Myopia Study of over 4,000 6-year-olds and 12-year-olds.[63]

The more that child's play is truly free and unstructured, the greater the benefits can be. That's the conclusion of researchers who assert that the physical, cognitive, social, and emotional benefits for children are higher with less structured, less supervised play that involves dimensions of risk, challenge, and adventure. According to Michael Patte, Professor of Education at

Bloomsburg University in Pennsylvania, unstructured play, the kind of play dreamed up by children, benefits the "whole child" with a wide portfolio of advantages and strengths:

- It provides opportunities for children to master elements of the world on their own terms.
- It develops self-determination, self-esteem, and the ability to self-regulate—all vital elements of emotional development.
- It fosters social competence, respect for rules, self-discipline, aggression control, problem-solving skills, leadership development, conflict resolution, and playing by the rules.
- It stimulates the senses and allows children to discover the different textures and elements in the world.
- It provides fertile ground to cultivate creativity and imagination.
- It enhances cognitive understanding.
- It builds strength, coordination, and cardiovascular fitness and moderates childhood obesity and its associated health complications.
- It sees boredom as a vehicle for children to create their own happiness, enhance inventiveness, and develop self-reliance.[64]

RECESS IS THE RIGHT OF EVERY CHILD

Two things must be built into every child's school experience: daily recess and regular physical education.

These are two different things—recess should be, in the words of the Centers for Disease Control and Prevention (CDC), "regularly scheduled periods within the elementary school day for unstructured physical activity and play," and physical education,

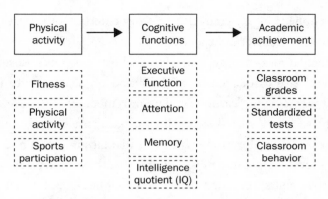

Figure 3. How Physical Activity Boosts Academic Achievement.
Reprinted with permission from Howie, E., & Pate, R. (2012). Physical activity and academic achievement in children: A historical perspective, *Journal of Sport and Health Science, 1*(3), 160–169.

by contrast, should be moderate-to-intense physical activity and structured instruction conducted by physical education professionals. Both of them are critical to a child's healthy development and academic achievement (Figure 3).

How do we know this? There are, in fact, gaps in our knowledge, and much of the research on the subject is new or incomplete, since it is notoriously difficult to perform research on children because of ethical issues. Few of the studies have been of the "gold standard" type that's considered the most reliable—randomized controlled trials conducted longitudinally over a substantial period of time. You simply can't "randomize" hundreds or thousands of children in primary school, deny half of them regular movement for 10 years, and follow both groups through college and adulthood to compare their life outcomes. But when you piece together and add up all the research that has been done, a highly compelling theory emerges—to succeed in school and in life, *children have got to move.*

Regular movement gives children a host of benefits. Research studies have associated daily childhood physical activity with improvements in cardiovascular and metabolic disease risk profiles, decreased risk of cardiovascular disease in adulthood, decreased risk of developing type 2 diabetes in childhood and adulthood, improvements in bone health and development, improvements in mental health and well-being, improvements in cognitive and academic performance, and improved motor control and physical functioning. Physical activity is believed to stimulate the growth of new neurons, leading to better cognition and memory and reduced likelihood of depression, as well as triggering the release of brain-derived neurotropic factor (BDNF), which can enhance cognition by boosting the neurons' ability to communicate with one another. Exercise may increase catecholamines, or brain chemicals such as norepinephrine and dopamine, which typically serve to energize and elevate mood.

In 2013, one of the world's most prestigious scientific bodies, the National Academy of Sciences, published what amounted to a plea for children to move more in school. The report, issued by the Academy's Institute of Medicine [now called the National Academy of Medicine], presented the findings of a committee panel of 14 leading medical and scientific experts convened to study the science of children and movement. The report found:

Extensive scientific evidence demonstrates that regular physical activity promotes growth and development in youth and has multiple benefits for physical, mental, and cognitive health. Physical activity is related to lower body fat, greater muscular strength, stronger bones, and improvements in cardiovascular and metabolic health, as well as to improvements in mental health by reducing and preventing conditions such as anxiety and depression and enhancing self-esteem.[65]

The report estimated that only about half of youth meet the current Physical Activity Guidelines for Americans' recommendation of at least 60 minutes of daily vigorous or moderate-intensity physical activity, and recommended that it is the job of schools to help children meet more than half of this target every day, through recess, physical education, and classroom-based movement and activity.

The report stressed the potential academic advantages of movement in school and pointed to a "growing body of evidence" suggesting a connection between vigorous and moderate-intensity physical activity and the structure and functioning of the brain. "Children who are more active show greater attention, have faster cognitive processing speed, and perform better on standardized academic tests than children who are less active," the report found.[66]

According to the American Academy of Pediatrics 2018 clinical report, "children pay more attention to class lessons after free play at recess than they do after physical education programs, which are more structured." It is little wonder, the report stated, "that countries that offer more recess to young children see greater academic success among the children as they mature." Additionally, according to the children's doctors' organization, physical play "decreases stress, fatigue, injury, and depression and increases range of motion, agility, coordination, balance, and flexibility," and play is well documented to provide "improvements in executive functioning, language, early math skills (numerosity and spatial concepts), social development, peer relations, physical development and health, and enhanced sense of agency."[67]

In a 2010 Gallup survey, nearly 2,000 elementary school principals were asked about recess in the first such nationwide report of its kind. The results were striking:

- Four out of five principals reported that recess has a positive impact on academic achievement.
- Two-thirds of principals reported that students listen better after recess and are more focused in class.
- Virtually all believed that recess has a positive impact on children's social development (96 percent) and general well-being (97 percent).[68]

In one study of physical activity among a group of 9- and 10-year-old boys and girls conducted at the University of Illinois and published in 2009, a single 20-minute bout of moderate-intensity walking was followed by significantly better performance on the ability to focus on a single task. Using "electrode caps" placed on the children's heads to measure neuroelectric activity in the brain, the researchers made an intriguing finding. After the period of physical activity, the intensity of one type of neuroelectric pattern thought to be related to aspects of executive function, known as "P3," was significantly higher while doing an "incongruent," or more complex, task, compared to the control group that didn't walk. A follow-up study by members of the same research team, published in 2013, demonstrated similar benefits for both mathematics and reading performance in healthy children and in children diagnosed with attention deficit/hyperactivity disorder.[69]

According to the CDC, students who are physically active tend to have better grades, school attendance, and classroom behaviors like on-task behavior. Additionally, both time spent in recess and brief classroom breaks of 5 to 10 minutes have been associated with better student cognitive performance such as attention and concentration, better on-task behavior, and improved educational outcomes like reading literacy scores. As a long-term bonus, regular participation in physical activity in childhood is associated with a decreased cardiovascular risk in youth and adulthood.[70]

How does physical activity help children perform better at school? There are several theories that point to likely physiological, physiological, neurological, psychological, and social factors that may lead to better brain function and improved academic achievement. They include effects that improve brain function, such as boosting blood and oxygen flow to the brain, increasing levels of norepinephrine and endorphins that reduce stress and improve mood, increasing neuroelectric activity, and increasing growth factors that help grow new nerve cells and support synaptic plasticity, which in turn improves learning and memory. In a 2012 article in the *Journal of Sport and Health Science*, researchers Erin Howie and Russell Pate of the University of

South Carolina's Department of Exercise Science stressed that "the most consistent positive findings, and most commonly-measured outcome, have been with executive functions (EF), particularly inhibition and working memory." Executive function, which the researchers said, "have shown to be highly predictive of academic achievement with early assessments of executive functions predicting later academic success,"[71] include the ability to organize, prioritize, plan, and rapidly shift between different activities.

According to a report issued in 2017 by the CDC and SHAPE America,[72] recess in schools benefits students by:

- Improving their memory, attention, and concentration.
- Helping them stay on-task in the classroom.
- Reducing disruptive behavior in the classroom.
- Improving their social and emotional development (e.g., learning how to share and negotiate).

The report called recess "an essential part of students' school experience that contributes to their normal growth and development," which helps students practice social skills (such as cooperation, following rules, problem-solving, negotiation, sharing, and communication), engage productively in classroom activities (such as being on-task and not disruptive), and enhance cognitive performance, such as attention and memory. And if these benefits aren't enough for you, consider this—recess not only helps students be more physically active, but may also improve their behavior and attention level in class, may reduce bullying and exclusionary behavior among students, help students feel safe and more engaged in the classroom, and contribute to higher levels of school connectedness and a positive school climate, all of which have benefits for attendance, engagement, and academic achievement.[73] While much of the scientific evidence is focused on elementary schools, the report noted that middle and high school students can benefit from recess featuring physical activity periods in addition to physical education and classroom physical activity.

Physical play and physical activity may be one of the strongest foundations of a child's potential social, emotional, and academic success.

PLAY IS THE ULTIMATE 21ST-CENTURY SKILLS BOOSTER

What does your child need to succeed in life?

No one knows for sure.

The world is filled with prognostications about "21st-century skills," and one thing is certain about the future—no one knows what it will be.

But in a world economy that is being rapidly reshaped by automation, digitalization, robotics, and artificial intelligence, there is a wide range of knowledge and skills that employers and researchers are identifying as increasingly important. These competencies are not best cultivated in school systems where play is eliminated and scripted teaching and standardized testing are the governing mechanisms of education, as is becoming largely the case in the United States.

We may, in other words, be giving our children largely the opposite of the education they most need for their future: a chance to flex their curiosity, collaborative exploration, and imagination to create new ideas that add genuine value to the world.

There is no question that children need to learn foundational skills and content knowledge, and they need to learn the basics of subjects like math, language, science, and the arts. But they also need to learn how to apply this knowledge in new combinations, patterns, insights, situations, and visions, and in collaboration with a wide range of other people—as leaders, followers, and teammates. A 2017 article in *Inc.* magazine reported that the rise of robots may mean that it is "the very things that make you human—your willingness to cover for a coworker whose mother is sick; your desire to help two radically different teammates work together; your heartfelt appreciation of a manager who had our backs—that will make you the most valuable."[74]

The knowledge and skills most needed in our ongoing "Fourth Industrial Revolution" will likely not be the ability to remember content knowledge, which Google already does quite well, but the more complex human skills of critical thinking, creativity, problem-solving, people management, and social skills—skills that are all developed by various forms of deeper play, in and out of school. As Ian Goldin, Oxford University Professor of Globalisation and Development and Director of the Oxford Martin Programme on Technological and Economic Change told us: "When you encourage kids to play, you're preparing them for how the real world works, in an age of rapid change and unpredictability, of surprises, uncertainties, sharp turns, risks and shocks. Play develops resilience, adaptability, improvisation, dexterity, agility, and the ability to adjust course and bounce back in the face of adversity, and to encourage others and give them hope and courage to change the world for the better."[75]

"We're trying to train our kids to be better computers, but our kids will never be better computers than computers," noted Temple University Psychology Professor Kathy Hirsh-Pasek in a 2018 *New York Times* article. She contended that we should not only teach children content, but strengthen their skills of creativity, exploration, and innovation through play, as early preparation and practice for their future work. "These are things humans do better than computers," she said, "and play helps us develop that."[76]

Additionally, Professor Hirsh-Pasek told us, "The place where most ministries and education systems went wrong is in their definition of success. If you define success as merely outcomes on a narrowly defined test, then teaching to the test is fine. But you just do not need that knowledge in a 21-century global economy—you need to know how to use the knowledge you have and to embrace a breadth of skills approach with a wider definition of success."

The world's business leaders agree. In 2016, the World Economic Forum, a global non-profit organization of business leaders and policymakers, surveyed 350 executives across 9 industries in 15 of the world's biggest economies to determine what skills would be most sought after in the year 2020. The top 10 skills were complex problem-solving, critical thinking, creativity, people management, coordinating with others, emotional intelligence, judgment and decision-making, service orientation, negotiation, and cognitive flexibility. Other

skills that are likely to be valuable in the near future are conflict resolution, divergent thinking, self-advocacy, management of failure, stress management, enthusiasm, empathy, and
self-reflection.

According to Professor Hirsh-Pasek and her colleague Roberta
Michnick Golinkoff, all of these critical skills can be developed
by play. They write:

> Children graduating from the K–12 system are largely
> unprepared for workplace challenges. CEOs across the
> world look for strong communicators, creative innovators,
> and expert problem solvers. Yet, formal schools remain
> narrowly focused on a definition of success that includes
> only outcomes in reading, writing, and arithmetic with
> little attention to the needs articulated by the business
> community.
>
> The American education system must move from the
> more traditional definition of success as good test scores in
> reading, writing, and mathematics (with a little science and
> social studies thrown in) to one that prepares our children
> to become competitive business leaders, entrepreneurs,
> and scientific pioneers. Success should be best judged by
> outcomes that nurture happy, healthy, thinking, caring, and
> social children who will become collaborative, creative,
> competent, and responsible citizens.
>
> With few exceptions, nations are preparing children
> to do well on tests that are not predictive of life success.
> Indeed, scholars in Taipei recently questioned why the
> United States educational system persisted on teaching

narrowly construed outcomes at a time when Taiwan and mainland China are transforming their education to build creators rather than memorizers![77]

* * *

The idea that play is essential in school can seem like a startling, counterintuitive concept.

We all want our children to be smart and successful. The world can be a tough and uncertain place, and it's reasonable to think that you can set children up to succeed by minimizing play in school and working them really hard, especially if they are from a poor, minority, or immigrant population or other groups with structural disadvantages.

One day not long ago we were both having breakfast together at an academic conference, preparing to give a talk on learning through play. The room was full of professors and researchers. Coffee and opinions were flowing freely. Hearing about the topic of our talk, one of the people at our table leaned over the scrambled eggs and offered a spontaneous critique. He was not a childhood educator, but an accomplished scientist from a nation known for harsh discipline, a highly competitive learning culture, and long hours in and out of school.

"Children should not play in school," he declared to us. "They are in school to learn, and learning is hard."

"Play in school is a waste of time," he announced. "When I was young I had to work hard in school. I spent evenings and weekends doing homework and preparing for exams. That's how I got to where I am. A friend of mine hired a math tutor who tutored her son every single day starting at 6:30 in the morning, starting at 6 years old. Now he is at the top of his university engineering class. You look at schools in the United States or in Finland—they are fun. In Asia, school is a serious business. It has to be. Children need rigor, and practice, and homework—not play."

"It is a tough, competitive world," he continued. "Maybe you can get away with it in Norway, or Sweden, or Finland, but that's because they're Scandinavian, with a totally different culture. My advice is not to waste your time on play in school. More play will never work for children in most other cultures. It's not what children need, and it's not what parents, especially Asian parents, want."

We wrote this book for him, and for others who share his opinion. We understand it. We wrote this book for parents and adults who believe, as we do, that school is a very serious business, and that children should be diligent, work hard and smart, learn a lot, embrace challenge and difficulty, learn to be disciplined, and achieve their highest potential.

But we believe all of this can and should be enhanced through the correct use of regular periods of intellectual and physical play in school, including both "free play" and "guided play," and that a wide range of research and experiments being conducted all around the world supports this. We believe that this is a better way than overworking and overstressing children, a way that creates better outcomes by channeling joy and well-being, and learning through play, as foundations of school.

We reject the notion that improving learning through play is impossible for certain nations because of their "cultural differences." This is a dangerous fallacy. Children are children the world over, and in order to learn, children need to play. Play is helping improve the learning of children all around the world.

In China, right now, a radical new experiment in play-based preschool, called "Anji Play," is proving so successful in one province that it is being widely expanded and becoming the national model of early childhood education.

In Singapore, an entire nation of high-achievers is shifting away from an elementary school model of childhood stress, academic ranking, and over-testing, toward a new vision of childhood exploration, experimentation, and discovery.

In north Texas and Oklahoma, where thousands of low- and middle-income children are now given *four separate 15-minute outdoor free play breaks every single day regardless of the weather,* principals and district leaders are reporting sharp improvements in academic performance and behavior from what is called the LiiNK Project. In suburban Long Island, New York, a similar new play intervention, the PEAS program, is achieving similarly striking results in a district of over 8,000 schoolchildren, a majority of whom are economically disadvantaged.

In Finland, where children don't start primary school before they are 7 years old, the government requires that all children must be given opportunities to play, have a voice in what and how they will learn, and must have at least 1 hour for physical activity every day, mostly outside, in addition to physical education classes.

In Scotland, regular periods of outdoor play are revolutionizing the school system, transforming the lives of children, teachers, and parents, and providing inspiration to the rest of the UK and the world, in a program called Active Scotland.

In Kenya, Uganda, Tanzania, and Bangladesh, the world's largest and most respected non-governmental organization, BRAC, is pilot-testing an early learning-through-play experiment that is achieving impressive results that strongly suggest that play can provide a key to learning for children in the developing world.

We are not arguing that the main point of school is to have fun, or that if school isn't fun, children won't learn. We are not arguing against all homework or against periods of direct instruction for children in elementary schools. We are not arguing against diligence and practice, or math drills and worksheets for elementary and secondary school students. We are not arguing in favor of 100 percent play-based schools.

We are arguing that in many nations, the counterproductively high levels of childhood stress, overwork, and excessive standardized testing are eliminating learning through play, hijacking childhood education, and undermining it by causing massive inefficiencies and wasted effort and money.

The point of this book is that play—including playful teaching and learning, play guided by teachers, and free play conducted largely by children themselves—must be an important part of learning for each and every child on Earth.

It is our job, as parents, teachers and citizens, to let the children play.

A PLAYFUL SIMULATED ARGUMENT BETWEEN TWO FATHERS

We wrote parts of this book in the mountains of Lombardy, Italy, one of the most beautiful places on earth to work and play.

We come from two very different cultures and countries, where the central themes of this book also exist with very different meanings and manifestations. Writing a book together is a journey, where learning and compromise often go hand in hand.

After months of research, interviews, site visits, writing, conversations, and debates over meals and walks in the Italian hills, we decided to sit down over a pot of coffee and think of questions that readers might have about children and play. This is how our afternoon break went as we play-acted a debate on play.

Question: Look, I plan on getting my children into an Ivy League school. The sooner they get on track, the better. What's wrong with that, and why should they waste time playing?

Answer: I recently taught at an Ivy League school, and I can tell you one thing: these schools are changing, too. Slowly, perhaps, but new expectations regarding "smart students" are already emerging. It is very hard to be successful in any top university or college anymore if you are not able to think outside of the box, solve real problems in a group of other people you don't necessarily know, or if you are terribly afraid of making a mistake when you try to accomplish your goals. These are exactly the qualities that your child develops when she or he explores the world through deeper play in and out of school. I am sure that by the time your young child gets to high school, what they've learned through play before that will make them a hot commodity in the college admissions market, and in the job market.

Think of play as the ultimate competitive edge for your child. It is the ultimate collaborative and compassionate edge, too.

Question: Let's get real. We're talking about children. Outdoor play is dangerous! Why are you promoting situations where children can get hurt?

Answer: The bigger risk to their health and long-term development is to imprison them indoors. We should understand and listen to parents' concerns about their children's safety. Many places are not safe to let your children hang around alone. But there are safe places in most cities and towns, parks and playgrounds where it's quite alright to go and play with your children, and also to back off from them and read the paper while they're in the sandbox, making new friends, or going the wrong way up the slide. Let them play—on their own. Hazards are bad, but risk is good.

We have to change our mindset about outdoor play. Dirt, mud, risk and constant movement are normal, natural features of a child's life. To keep them imprisoned indoors for fear of a stray germ or scraped knee is abnormal. As UK play advocate Neil Coleman has said, "Many schools will deliberately 'kettle' children within a small area of tarmac, unnecessarily preventing them access to their field during the winter, placing clothing priorities before children's health and increasing the likelihood of negative behavior and sedentary habits occurring, deploying nonsensical excuses about contaminated mud or dirty clothing."[78]

Children will fall when they run or climb a tree. They may get hit by a ball. They need to learn to understand the dangers and risks that are out there when they play with other children. Of course, we adults need to provide them all safety that we think is necessary but we shouldn't overprotect them by putting in place all the safety that is possible. Learning from mistakes, including being hurt a bit every now and then, is an important part of growing up. We remember from our childhoods that some of the best lessons were those when something unexpected happened, like hurting a leg when trying to climb a tree.

Question: Every politician, bureaucrat, think-tanker, and technology salesperson says they are building schools and creating education reforms to deliver "21st century skills." What's wrong with that?

Answer: The phrase "21st-century skills" is often more of a marketing slogan. Many of these so-called "reforms" are initiated by for-profit operators or political interest groups funded by them. Life and career skills, learning and innovation skills, and information, media and technology skills that constitute 21st-century skills emerge from traditional views of education. This is so complex a set of skills that when these are turned into standards that are "delivered" in schools, much of the art of teaching and learning will vanish. Many teachers know that one of the best ways to learn these and other essential knowledge and skills is for children to have more time for high quality play in and out of school.

Question: Are you arguing for 100 percent play-based schools? That is a recipe for pure chaos!

Answer: No. We are arguing for a balance between play and more formal teaching methods. There are many things in school that are obviously hard to learn through play alone, especially in the older years of childhood. Math and science, language arts and social sciences, for example, have a great many components that simply require that teachers teach that material directly, and children practice it in school and at home.

What we want to see, however, is that all schools—from preschool to high school—help children to learn and grow in part through free play, playful discovery, guided play, experimentation and exploration, the freedom to fail, and a school atmosphere energized with a playful spirit and passion for learning and collaboration. Give every child the academic advantage of SEED—systematic exploration, experimentation, and discovery. Give every child at least an hour of free outdoor play every day, and give them up to 20 percent of their indoor time for intellectual free play and self-directed "passion projects" of their own.

School learning is often over-controlled by teachers, to the point where children feel they are subjects of learning, without any control over their own educational path. Too many children feel disengaged in schools and therefore lose interest and motivation to learn. If they felt they had a voice, and influence over their own education, they would be more committed to do their best in school.

We can learn a lot about how children learn by watching them play, particularly when play is unstructured and there is minimum intervention by adults. Children will take the responsibility for their own actions, including play and learning, if we adults just let them do it.

Question: Come on—Finland, Singapore, Scotland, and the United States are completely different cultures. Don't bother with play in school in most places. It's not going to work. Don't you understand, you can't change culture?

Answer: We are different, but there is also a lot we can learn from one another. Children are children the world over, and a great many parents, researchers, doctors and educators around the world know that children need to play.

Schools must take into account the cultural realities. What seems to be a good idea in Finland won't necessarily be easy or appropriate to achieve in the United States or in Singapore. What is interesting when we look at how educational ideas travel from one country to another is that research, practical models and innovation regarding early childhood education, classroom teaching or school leadership in the United States during the last century or so has inspired educators and policymakers in many parts of the world to the point that some American models have been adopted. The unwillingness or inability among many American decision-makers and some educators to take a closer look at what more successful education systems do is a sign of an adult learning problem rather than a wide cultural gap between the countries.

Question: Without tests, how do you measure school success?

Answer: We are in favor of high-quality tests—assessments designed and administered by children's classroom teachers, not lower-quality standardized tests delivered by remote, for-profit testing companies. Beyond teacher-designed assessments and quizzes, there are many other highly sensitive and accurate teacher-led methods of evaluation of children's learning and development, like learning records, lab work, essays, portfolios, work sampling systems, performance-based tasks, project and group work, roundtable presentations of student work to a panel of judges, and even self-assessment and peer assessment by children. A well-trained teacher knows how to use all these assessments to help children learn and play. The training and professional development of teachers should improve and also include assessment of play-related skills on an ongoing basis.

At the school-system level, schools do need some common high-quality, low-stakes, sample-based measures of progress to monitor trends, which only requires testing a relatively small number of children. What we don't need is punitive, high-stakes standardized testing of all the children all the time. It does not help a child's individual, authentic learning, warps the educational experience and squanders billions of dollars that could be used for much more urgent education priorities. School policy should be "data informed," not "data driven." The values and judgment of educators and parents should always be paramount, and a sharp focus should be on ongoing, formative "assessments for learning."

Measuring school success is a bit like checking your own health. You need multiple measures. You need to have a conversation with your doctor. That doctor needs to be well prepared and experienced in understanding what constitutes health. Similarly, schools need to have different ways to measure what they do. Student achievement in language arts and mathematics is just one area of concern. Health, well-being, engagement, attendance, behavior, and the opinions of students, teachers and parents are other important aspects of school success.

Teachers should orchestrate assessments of their students' progress, not standardized test operators. It is hard to measure much of what counts most in education into "big data" or a data sheet—qualities like compassion, curiosity, teamwork, persistence through failure, passion for learning, critical thinking, entrepreneurial skills, flexibility, presentation skills, leadership, higher-order thinking, self-regulation, problem-solving ability, social and emotional competence, imagination, initiative, essay writing, and play.

Question: Isn't this whole play thing just a utopian hippie idea from socialist countries like the Nordic nations? What makes you think it would work anywhere else?

Answer: Don't take our word for it. Ask the 67,000 doctors in the American Academy of Pediatrics, which is strongly in favor of play in school, including high-poverty schools. Ask the scientists and researchers at the National Academy of Sciences and the Centers for Disease Control, both of which have taken strong stands in favor of play in and out of school. Ask the Association of Childhood Educators International, the world's largest professional alliance of childhood educators, which sees play as a critical foundation of school.

Play is not a culture-specific quirk exclusive to rural China, or Singapore, or Scotland, or Nordic countries. It is as American as apple pie and baseball. And it is as global as the air we breathe.

Cultures are very different. You can't export Finnish, Chinese, American, or French educational practices "in a box." But there is much we can learn from each other and much inspiration we can gain from each other. Don't forget, cultures change. The United States, for example, in barely one generation, 20 years, went from a nation that respects teachers to a nation that demonizes, shames, and punishes them on the basis of standardized tests, and incorrectly blames teachers for the horrific, real-life, flesh-and-blood consequences of generations of poverty, neglect and segregation in inner-city schools.

By the way, Nordic countries are some of the most competitive free-market economies in the world, who have succeeded in balancing capitalism and strong social safety nets and excellent public services, including childhood education.

Question: Don't you believe in choice and accountability when it comes to school?

Answer: Absolutely yes. We believe politicians should be held accountable to give all parents and children the choice of high-quality schools that are free from toxic stress and fear, that are safe and well-resourced, and are run by professional educators who give children a high-quality education based on research and evidence, with regular periods of play and physical activity to boost their health, well-being, happiness and learning.

Children should play because it is an integral part of human nature. Play is the right of every child. There is now a solid evidence base that demonstrates that play has critical benefits for children's well-being, physical and social health, individual and social development, self-esteem, empathy and academic progress. The great play experiments around the world reveal that play, and the values, habits and principles associated with it, can help to build more effective schools.

Play is good for schools because of its positive effects on health, well-being and happiness of those who play. When children play more in school, it reflects playful values, norms and expectations of adults in school. Playfulness is often linked to risk-taking, creativity and innovation in an organization, things that business leaders, for example, say they want more of from their employees.

Play should have a central place in ongoing campaigns to reform public education. In the United States and England, for example, public schools are required to follow standards that with given resources are often impossible to achieve by all students. Failure to meet these standards leads to privatization and closing of "failing" schools. If public schools were assessed using metrics that include well-being, health, engagement, and happiness, many public schools that are labeled as low-performing now would do much better in other dimensions of education. Therefore play, physical activity and character-building can serve as an effective means to strengthen public education.

Question: Children get bullied and have conflicts in the playground. Why do you want more recess?

Answer: Children get bullied in the classroom and in the cafeteria, too. No one is suggesting that we abolish lunch, or abolish classrooms. A trained adult should always be on hand during recess, to provide safety and security, and to resolve conflict or bullying situations when necessary.

Question: How about more rigor in education?

Answer: That depends what you mean by "rigor." Teachers should be clinically trained in research universities, with a graduate-level education in a subject matter specialty, extensive supervised classroom experience, and a solid understanding of educational research. In other words, we believe in rigorous preparation of teachers as we do for scientists, engineers, airline pilots, doctors and other professionals, the way teachers are trained in Singapore, Canada and Finland. We also believe in leadership rigor that requires that school principals should be experienced teachers with leadership capabilities, and that system leaders should have deep experience in teaching and leadership in school. That is where "rigor" should be applied.

This educational "rigor" would help make teachers respected and rewarded professionals. They should be in charge of our schools in partnership with parents and the community, with minimal interference from politicians, bureaucrats and technology vendors. This will help restore teaching to a highly competitive, selective career path, which is what it should be in all nations. Well-trained childhood education professionals know the critical importance of play in school. This level of standards and rigor is the critical minimum requirement upon which any attempt to improve schools must be based.

Question: No matter how hard I try, I just can't wrap my head around the idea of children spending time playing in school or at home when they should be doing homework and studying. What do you suggest?

Answer: Don't think of it as play. Think of it as systematic exploration, experimentation, and discovery. SEED. Think of it as nourishing brain and body food for your child.

And it's one of the most wonderful gifts we can give children— and they can give us.

DOCTOR'S ORDERS: THE CHILDREN MUST PLAY

And now—a word from America's children's doctors.

The American Academy of Pediatrics (AAP) is the leading professional organization of children's doctors in the United States, representing some 67,000 physicians. It is the group that establishes pediatric policy on a wide range of critical children's health issues like immunizations, screen time, car safety, and breastfeeding.

Like other doctors, upon embarking on their medical career, pediatricians take the Hippocratic Oath, in which they "swear to fulfill, to the best of my ability and judgment, this covenant: I will respect the hard-won scientific gains of those physicians in whose steps I walk, and gladly share such knowledge as is mine with those who are to follow."

In a series of landmark research-based clinical reports issued from 2007 to 2018, the AAP strongly recommends that in order to learn, children must have plenty of play—in school, at home and in the community. The doctors stress that these recommendations apply equally to children in poverty, as they are often the victims of play deprivation in school and society. We thank the AAP for giving us permission to summarize here these key points from their historic clinical reports on play. We urge readers to read the original reports in full, and to share and discuss them with teachers, administrators, politicians, and fellow parents.

This is what America's pediatricians say about learning and play.[79]

1. Play is integral to a child's education. The importance of playtime for children cannot be overemphasized to parents, schools, and community organizations.
2. Play, in all its forms, is the ideal educational and developmental milieu for children.
3. The benefits of play are extensive and well documented and include improvements in executive functioning, language, early math skills (numerosity and spatial concepts), social development, peer relations, physical development and health, and enhanced sense of agency.
4. Play provides rich opportunities for adults to help children develop the critical motor, social-emotional, language, executive

functioning, math, and self-regulation skills needed to be successful in an increasingly complex and collaborative world. Pretend play develops self-regulation, as children collaborate on imaginary environments and roles, which improves their ability to reason about hypothetical events.

5. The implications of play deprivation may be substantial, because play is essential to the social, emotional, cognitive, and physical well-being of children, starting in early childhood.

6. The most effective ways for parents to prepare children for a happy, successful adulthood are not shuttling them between numerous activities or scheduling multiple extracurricular or academic commitments but showing unconditional love; spending pleasurable time together; playing with children; listening, caring, talking, and reading to children even at very early ages; and guiding them through effective and developmentally appropriate discipline.

7. The most effective way of developing children's academic preparedness may be low-cost time spent reading with parents.

8. Children's creativity and imagination are enhanced with the most basic and least expensive toys, blocks, balls, buckets, jump ropes, dolls, and art supplies. More expensive toys can make play a more passive and less physically involved experience.

9. Free play is an essential part of childhood. All children should be given ample non-screen free play time to be creative, reflect, build resiliency, and decompress. Much play should be child driven instead of adult directed, and active play rather than passive entertainment like TV and computer games.

10. Parents should use love and understanding to encourage children to try again even when at first they fail. Positive

reinforcement goes further than negative responses when children engage in play alone and with others.

11. Unstructured play outdoors in nature—among dirt, trees, grass, rocks, flowers, and insects—offers children creative inspiration and physical and emotional benefits.

12. Children should have an academic schedule that is challenging and balanced based on their unique needs and skills, not on pressurized, competitive community standards or the perceived need to gain college admissions. Child care and education programs should offer more than "academic preparedness" and should also develop social and emotional skills.

13. Early learning is better fueled by facilitating the child's intrinsic motivation through play rather than extrinsic motivations like test scores.

14. The most effective educational model is to engage the student to promote skills within that child's zone of proximal development [a concept developed by psychologist Lev Vygotsky describing the distance between the actual developmental level of the learner as determined by independent problem-solving and the level of potential development through problem-solving under adult guidance, or in collaboration with more capable peers], not through drills and passive rote learning, but through free play, guided play, dialogue, guidance, active engagement, and joyful discovery.

15. Recess is a necessary break in the day for optimizing a child's social, emotional, physical, and cognitive development. Recess is a child's personal time and should not be withheld for academic or punitive reasons. Recess should never be withheld as a punishment, as it is a fundamental component

of development and social interaction. Reducing or canceling recess can negatively affect academic achievement.

16. Recess is a complement to, but not a replacement for, physical education. Only recess, especially unstructured recess, provides the creative, social, and emotional benefits of play.

17. Recess is fundamental to the school experience and develops lifelong skills of communication, negotiation, cooperation, sharing, and problem-solving.

18. After recess, for children, or after a corresponding break time for adolescents, students are more attentive and better able to perform cognitively.

19. Less physical activity may have even greater implications for boys. Sedentary school environments may be harder for boys to succeed in and may contribute to the discordant academic performance of boys and girls.

20. Children pay more attention to academic work after free-play recess than after physical education, which is more structured.

21. Academic and cognitive performance depends on regular breaks from classroom work, and this applies equally to both younger children and adolescents. The frequency and duration of breaks should be enough to allow the student to mentally decompress.

22. For economically disadvantaged children, play in schools, communities, and homes must be preserved and supported.

23. School should be safe and enjoyable for children. To decrease failure in school, which can lead to depression, entry into the juvenile justice system, and continued poverty, school engagement should be promoted through play, creative arts, physical education, and social and emotional learning.

24. We should consider the possibility of linkages between early, high-pressure, intense preparation for a "high-achieving" adulthood and rising mental health issues like anxiety, stress, and depression among children and adolescents.

25. Schools should be the kind of places that children and adolescents want to be in. All children, including lower-income children, should receive recess, physical education and the arts so they can achieve their highest potential for cognitive, physical, and social development—and so they will like school.

In other words, America's pediatricians are telling us to provide school and home environments to our children that are much the total opposite of what we are giving them now!

We listen to our children's doctors when it comes to children's check-ups, medicine, and flu shots.

Why wouldn't we follow their guidance when it comes to our children's learning and emotional, mental, and physical health in school?

What gives any politician, or any school, the right to ignore the clear recommendations of America's pediatricians?

It is time that we design the learning, emotional, and health environments of schools not mainly on the ideas of politicians, bureaucrats, or technology vendors, but on the perspectives and visions of parents, teachers, pediatricians—and children themselves.

THE PLAY STAGES OF A CHILD'S SCHOOL LIFE

This chart shows how play can be delivered to effectively boost learning across a child's years in school. But in many schools today, this chart is a blank slate.

Age	4	5	6	7	8	9	10	11	12	13	14	15	16–17
Sand/water play	x	x	x	x	x								
Dress-up play	x	x	x	x	x	(transitioning to drama)							
Object play	x	x	x	x	x	x	x	x	(transitioning to STEM)				
Musical play	x	x	x	x	x	x	x	x	(transitioning to lessons)				
Art free play	x	x	x	x	x	x	x	x	x	(transitioning to specialties)			
Outdoor free play	x	x	x	x	x	x	x	x	x	x	x	x	x
Guided play*	x	x	x	x	x	x	x	x	x	x	x	x	x
Deeper play**	x	x	x	x	x	x	x	x	x	x	x	x	x

* Playful teaching and learning, discovery, and experimentation with adult guidance.
** Regular periods for free play, choice, and passion projects that offer self-directedness, intrinsic motivation, positive emotions, process orientation, and use of imagination.
Source: the authors.

4

The GERM That
Kills Play

The importance of playful learning for children cannot be overemphasized.[80]

—American Academy of Pediatrics, 2018

The world is in a war against play.

For schools and children under intense government pressure to achieve high scores on standardized tests, play—and many other absolutely critical educational foundations like the arts and physical education—is dismissed as a disposable, unnecessary luxury.

Play is being eradicated from childhood education.

In schools across the United States and around the globe, childhood play is being decreased, devalued, eliminated, and forgotten. Play is being replaced by incorrect, counterproductive education practices that can lead to excessive stress, disengagement from school, fear of failure, lack of motivation to learn, and declining well-being and life satisfaction for millions of children around the world.

Discovery and dialogue for children is being replaced with age-inappropriate instruction and worksheets for 4- and 5-year-olds. Pre-K and kindergarten classrooms are cutting out hands-on play and banishing building blocks, dress-up costumes, and sand tables. Children are being denied daily recess and sometimes even natural toilet breaks. Digital screens are replacing qualified flesh-and-blood teachers. Trained teachers who can customize learning are being replaced by "temp" teachers who are ordered to teach from pre-packaged scripts. Schools are being turned into stress factories.

One educator, New York University Associate Professor of Applied Psychology Joshua Aronson, has worked with hundreds of schools as part of his ongoing research on how to help culturally disadvantaged students, and what he sees in classrooms appalls him. He told us, "Both structured and unstructured play are critical for healthy development and learning. But I think the biggest problem is that schools prioritize the kind of academic learning that requires students to sit at desks and not move their bodies."

The state of play in schools, said Aronson, is "abysmal, and we should know better." He continued,

> When I sit in classrooms in America I see children deprived of exercise, who have to be yelled at, bribed, or threatened or drugged to make them focus in class and complete their academic work. A staggering percentage of the kids I meet are obese and are palpably uncomfortable in their bodies. They need to play and run around about 500 percent more than they currently do and I suspect that one day, we will look back in shame at how deprived we allowed this generation of kids to be, in the name of academic accomplishment.
>
> My conviction of how needlessly awful our lack of play in school is comes from my observing children in all kinds of schools. I have learned that American kids don't suffer from "Ritalin deficiency"; they suffer from a lack of the nature, play, and freedom that their hunter-gather ancestors enjoyed. Play and exercise demonstrably boost academic achievement. Most principals should know this. But they ignore it.[81]

Many schools have become outright hostile to play, and a false dichotomy has defined childhood play and work as two separate things. According to educational psychologist and professor Gene Glass of the National Education Policy Center at Arizona State University, "the puritanical attitude toward play is widespread to the detriment not only of schooling but to all of life." He told us, "Virtually everything is wrong with this way of thinking. And it is a crime that it permeates all levels of the education system." Play, said Glass, "can lead to cognitive development of many kinds, but the prejudice against play is shot through the education system and it is just getting worse."[82]

Gloria Ladson-Billings, the president of the prestigious National Academy of Education and professor emerita at the University of Wisconsin-Madison, told us, "Play allows children to build, imagine, role play and in essence become fully human. Most U.S. schools do not understand the importance of play. In them we spend an inordinate amount of time attempting to discipline and manage bodies, which is a losing proposition. Too much of what we do in school is mind-numbing."[83]

Psychology professor Stephen Siviy of Gettysburg College, who has helped conduct some of the most important animal studies on the subject of play,[84] is equally amazed by the lack of play in schools. He told us he believes that "providing ample opportunities to engage in free play should be considered an integral part of the curriculum for young children." However, he reported,

It is crazy to see what has happened to the state of play especially in elementary schools—and even in pre-schools. Educators and administrators have become so obsessed with test scores that they have systematically removed more and more recess time from the school day. Now that I have grandchildren in elementary school, I have been shocked to hear that first-graders in my grandson's school get only one 30-minute recess a day! Even crazier is using removal of recess as a punishment for bad behavior in the classroom. So, a 7-year-old acts out in class—probably because they need to run around and play for a little bit—and the way this is addressed is to take away the opportunity for them to go out and play. Hence the problem can get worse.[85]

Play deprivation may lead directly to children disconnecting from school, especially poor children. That's the view of Pedro Noguera, Professor of Education at UCLA, who explained to us,

> Too many schools deprive kids of time for recess and the opportunity to learn through play. This is especially true for poor kids, who are frequently denied time for play because it is seen as coming at the expense of learning time that promotes achievement. This view toward play adds to the alienation many children experience in school.[86]

Play in childhood education is becoming an endangered concept, agreed education researcher professor Jeanne Goldhaber of the University of Vermont: "I've spent many years observing early childhood programs, kindergartens and primary grades and have watched the slow demise of play in children's educational lives. Their days are chopped up into arbitrary curriculum segments with days that involve 6–10 transitions and leave little room for children to explore, invent, and interact."[87]

For renowned education historian and research professor Diane Ravitch of New York University, the problem of play deprivation is one of colossal government mismanagement. She told us,

> Our education system today is guided by very bad federal law that imposes standardized tests as the measure of children, teachers, and schools. Children are expected to master academic goals that are not age-appropriate. Our policies and laws today are actively hostile to children. We discourage play by leaving no time for it. Children need time to blow off steam. In play, they can develop their thinking, inquiring, creating, and imagining. It would be wonderful to see a general recognition of the importance of play, for people of all ages.[88]

DAWN OF THE DARK AGE OF GERM

The war against play is largely an unintended consequence of inept political attempts to "raise standards" and "close the achievement gap" by increasing "rigor" and forcing academic demands on younger and younger children. It is a war being waged by an alliance of politicians, administrators, and ideologues, many of whom have one glaring weakness in common—they have little or no knowledge of how children actually learn. It is, in effect, a conspiracy of ignorance, misguided policies, and misinformation.

You can call it the "Global Education Reform Movement," or "GERM," as we do, and instead of supporting proven global best practices like teacher professionalism, education research, system-wide collaboration, equity of resources, a whole-child approach, physical activity, and learning through play, it is pushing failing education policies into our schools. They include pitting schools against each other in a Darwinian race for higher standardized test scores, one-size-fits-all teaching, the universal standardized testing of children, punishing schools and teachers based on testing data, forcing young children to prematurely absorb academic material at the expense of other critical subjects like the arts and physical activity, the elimination of teacher credentials—and the crowding out and elimination of play, all of which are becoming epidemic in the United States.

This "GERM" is, in other words, a virus spreading around the world, infecting school systems, and it is killing play in our schools.

Excessive standardization in education does not benefit teachers and students in the long haul. A major example of this is the case history of England, which launched a system-wide education reform in 1988 that for the first time brought tight external control to what and how teachers taught in the country's public schools. The reform was based on the assumption that "school choice" for parents would work as it does in a marketplace and would enhance efficiency by raising the quality and lowering the cost. This brought along the standardization of education services. Data from frequent standardized tests were supposed to provide parents with information they needed to make their choice of the best school for their child. Research evidence shows that this logic didn't improve either the quality or equity of public school education in England.[89] School inspection that is intimately linked to externally mandated instructional strategies and standardized test scores has instead narrowed the freedom that schools and teachers used to have to choose the best strategies and tactics for their children to thrive.

The danger of basing schools on high-pressure standardized teaching and high-stakes standardized tests is that they violate the very essence of how children, especially younger children, learn. Every child is unique. "Children learn skills and concepts at different times, rates, and paces," argues the advocacy group Defending the Early Years in a 2014 *Washington Post* opinion piece.

> Every child possesses a unique personality, temperament, family relationship and cultural background. Each has different interests, experiences and approaches to learning. Each child perceives and approaches the world differently, often taking different routes to reach the same ends. Thus, all children need learning experiences that take into account, support and build onto who they are as individuals.[90]

Standardization is not the same as having high standards in education. Just as airplanes, hospitals, and restaurants operate under strict sets of standards, our schools need standards, too. The popularity of the "standards-based" movement that became fashionable in the 1990s in the English-speaking part of the world was first based on giving priority to learning (outcomes) rather than teaching (inputs). That makes some sense. These reforms therefore aimed to have a stronger emphasis on how schools performed instead of just inspecting the content and structures of schooling. It remains unquestioned today within the education community that the presence of clear and sufficiently high performance standards for schools, teachers, and students is a precondition to improved quality of teaching and betterment of schools. However, the enforcement of external standardized curricula, and teaching scripts, and aligned testing protocols to judge how these standards have been attained have been an evident offspring of these standards-based education policies.

Strict standardization narrows the freedom and flexibility in schools and classrooms to do things that are truly meaningful to them, like experimenting with new ideas or letting children learn through play. It also restrains teachers from local experimentation, reduces the use of alternative approaches, and limits risk-taking in schools and classrooms. The consequence is that the more that teaching gets standardized in schools, the less freedom teachers and children have to take risks and think creatively.

Despite the wide consensus in favor of learning through play among many researchers, pediatricians, and teachers, the United States, which is the world's biggest victim of the "GERM," is leading the world into a Dark Age of Childhood Play Deprivation in education.

In fact, if you ask the average American politician, policymaker, administrator, or self-styled education reformer who suffers from GERM what they think children need in order to learn better, their answers can effectively be boiled down to variations on these themes: Children and schools should be "data driven,"[91] constantly computer measured and assessed; teaching should be standardized; and children and schools that don't hit arbitrary data targets should be shamed, punished, and retested. All children will then be ready for school, college, and career at ages 4,

5, 8, and 12, they can acquire the skills necessary to compete in the world economy, no child will be left behind, every student will succeed, and the United States can race to the top and be #1. In other words, children will learn best from an evidence-free stew of recycled PowerPoint clichés. GERM is an idea that combines all the efforts to transform education that have failed since the 1980s, including punitive accountability measures tied to standardized test data—and the evidence demonstrates that no successful nation has used GERM-related policies to achieve major improvements in their school system.

The focus of education policy in many parts of the world has shifted to more use of frequent standardized tests, investing in educational technologies, and searching for more efficient ways to measure and deliver teaching and learning to students. Sometimes these reforms are designed by applying solutions from other countries and occasionally by applying educational ideas from international development organizations. The transfer of educational solutions across country borders has become so frequent that it is now a global movement. Some of the consequences of this movement have benefited schools, such as increased attention to achievement gaps and inequities, but others have not been beneficial for teachers or students—for example, the narrowed focus on curriculum, the overreliance on test scores, and the decline of play in schools.

The use of the phrase "Global Educational Reform Movement" to refer to these trends was first used in a 2006 journal article about educational reforms for raising economic competitiveness.[92] The initial idea was inspired by Andy Hargreaves, research professor at Boston College, and his research on how standardization affected teachers' work in schools in the 1990s when the "standards-based reform" movement began gaining international popularity among policymakers. Since then, in education systems that have been heavily "infected" by GERM, such as the United States, the United Kingdom, and Australia, data derived from the universal standardized testing of children have become the Alpha and Omega of education, the governing "metric" for judging the success or failure of schools, teachers, and children. GERM is not just about high-stakes standardized testing; it is an intellectual and political paradigm that is an offspring of global competition that manifests itself in policies and practices in perverse ways.

GERM has many other manifestations that vary from one education system to another. The first, and perhaps the most visible common feature, is increased *competition* between schools for student enrollment. Many education systems within the Organization for Economic Cooperation and Development (OECD), an intergovernmental organization of 36 nations, have enhanced mechanisms that require schools to be competitive against other schools in their geographic area. The school choice experiment in Chile in the 1980s, school voucher system in Sweden in the 1990s, charter schools in the United States in the 2000s, and secondary school academies in England more recently are examples of how market-like competition is believed to function as an engine of system-wide educational improvement. But there is little to no evidence that this has worked.

The second feature of GERM is the *standardization* of teaching and learning in schools. Shifting the focus from inputs to outputs in education in the 1990s led to the popularity of "standards-based" education policies, especially in the English-speaking part of the world. These reforms initially aimed to have a stronger emphasis on learning outcomes and school performance instead of content and structures of schooling. The Common Core State Standards in the United States, National Curriculum in England, Curriculum for Excellence in Scotland, New National Education Standards in Germany, the Australian Curriculum, and the New Zealand Curriculum are examples of efforts to standardize teaching and learning in all schools within an education system. Again, there is little evidence that these forms of standardization improve the performance of national education systems. There are, by contrast, two forms of standardization that can be highly effective in public education— *standardizing teacher training* to an extremely high level of quality and intensity, as, for example, Singapore does, and *standardizing school funding* so that resources are fairly distributed to each child and each school, as done in Finland.

A third common feature of GERM is the *de-professionalization* of the teaching profession and school leadership. Teaching in school is incorrectly seen as a job that can be done by anyone who understands the procedures or scripts of effective instruction, or any recent graduate from a top university who can attend a 7-week training program that then anoints them as a "teacher." Various fast-track, non-academic, "quickie" pathways into teaching offer an alternative route to teacher education degree programs that universities and colleges typically offer. Similarly, in many American school districts, public school leadership has been opened up to anyone with management or leadership experience.

In a thoroughly bizarre turn of events, many American schools are now increasingly being run and taught by non-teachers and non-educators—people with no professional education qualifications to teach. It is as if our nation's medical, dentistry, legal, architecture, accounting, aviation, engineering, and aerospace professions were run and staffed by people with no relevant professional qualifications.

The fourth global trend of GERM is the *large-scale high-stakes standardized testing* of children as young as 4 or 5, a wave of data collection that supposedly holds teachers and schools accountable for students' achievement. School performance—in the form of standardized test data—steers the processes of evaluating, inspecting, and rewarding or punishing schools and teachers. Merit-based pay, data walls in teachers' lounges, and school scores in newspapers are examples of accountability mechanisms that often draw their data primarily from external standardized student tests and teacher evaluations. When school accountability relies on high stakes for schools and low stakes for students on low-quality standardized tests, accountability becomes what is left when responsibility is subtracted. In other words, strengthening accountability for student achievement is weakening the responsibility that students take for their own learning and shrinking the space for authentic learning and playful learning.

The fifth trend of GERM is *market-based privatization* of public education. A theory developed by Nobel Prize–winning economist Milton Friedman in the 1950s held that parents should be given the freedom to choose their children's education and thereby encourage healthy competition among schools so that they better serve families' diverse needs. School choice and vouchers that often facilitate parental choice have led to privatization of public education through private schools and various types of charter schools (United States), academies (England), and free schools (Sweden) around the world. School choice ideology maintains that parents should be able to use the public funds set aside for their children's education to choose the schools—public or private—that work best for them. Here again, however, there is little objective evidence that market-based privatization improves education systems overall, or even for the students it serves.[93] Education systems do not behave much like markets. This should come as no surprise, since the chief organizing principle of a business is to generate profit and return on investment for owners and shareholders by maximizing sales, profits, and market share, often at the expense of competitors. The organizing principle of a public education system, in sharp contrast, is to deliver high-quality education to all its students in all its schools. Additionally, most teachers are motivated not chiefly by the profit motive or bonus pay but by civic duty, professional pride, and the love of helping children learn.[94]

In fact, a wide range of evidence shows that GERM has not been successful in improving student learning or well-being anywhere it has been a dominant education policy framework. Instead, cooperation, creativity, professionalism, trust, and equity are the education policy priorities that underpin successful education systems like those in nations like Singapore, Canada, and Finland.

Who is behind GERM, and who, in effect, are the anti-play warriors? Incredibly, in the George W. Bush, Barack Obama, and Donald Trump eras of American politics, they include the leadership of all three administrations, a wide spectrum of Democratic and Republican Senators and U.S. Representatives, national and state elected officials and decision-makers from both political parties, several liberal and conservative think tanks, and several of the large, powerful philanthropies that have dominated the education discussion in recent years. Their combined efforts to "raise standards, accountability and rigor" in schools through the large-scale standardized testing of children have done little to improve schools and have managed to largely squeeze out and eliminate play from childhood education.[95] They do not appear to have intentionally set out to destroy play in school as an explicit policy objective, but the net effect was the same, and an undeclared War on Play was unleashed to make room for testing and test preparation, and the "pushing down" of age-inappropriate academic pressure to younger and younger children.

In 2001, Republican President George W. Bush, Democratic Senator Edward Kennedy, and other American politicians championed the No Child Left Behind Act, which helped shackle schools to evaluations based on the large-scale, high-stakes, mandatory standardized testing of children, tests designed and run by distant testing companies and not by children's classroom teachers. Barely a decade later, the act was widely considered a failure. It helped spotlight problems in the education system, but it did little to nothing to solve those problems.

Then, President Barack Obama doubled down on this failure by championing, with wide bipartisan support, both the "Common Core" curriculum standards and the massive "Race to the Top" federal competition for over $4 billion in grants, which continued the role of the large-scale and high-stakes standardized testing of children, while effectively ignoring a multitude of root causes for educational problems, like poverty, inequitable funding, and uneven teacher training and quality. These federal education schemes, too, however well intentioned, were widely seen as major disappointments. None of these efforts made a significant overall positive impact on the learning outcomes of American children or on reducing achievement gaps. What they did, however, was intensify the de facto War on Play in American schools.

In the War on Play, our children are the victims. They are losing authentic learning time; they are losing the opportunity for joy, discovery, and experimentation; they are losing the chance to build a solid foundation for their future skills; and they are losing their childhoods. It is a war that has achieved no measurable results except childhood stress, school inefficiency, and the squandering of billions of precious taxpayer dollars. It is a war that makes some children hate school and disengage from learning in school, and it is therefore a war that threatens the future of our society.

Understanding the nature of problems in education is a necessary condition to successfully solving them. Most school reform efforts have been directed at symptoms, not the root causes of educational problems. "After many years of covering education and educators," wrote former PBS education journalist John Merrow, "I am convinced that we as a nation are 'hooked' on what we hope will be quick fixes for deep systemic problems."[96] We need to understand these basic problems. The educational problem that this book addresses is not that children don't have enough time to play in school. It is far from the only educational problem we face, and it is only a symptom, a consequence of deeper issues that trouble education systems around the world.

The problem in the United States, simply stated, is that decades of neglect, racial and economic segregation, poverty, and political mismanagement have devastated many schools, especially those in inner city and poor areas. To address this, misguided education policies are turning all public schools into standardized test factories. Play and other critical school components are being removed to make room for the testing, and a critical foundation of childhood education is being demolished, putting the entire structure at risk of collapse.

The anti-play warriors believe that in order to "catch up" with nations that achieve higher scores on international benchmark tests, to reduce achievement gaps, and to equip children with "21st-century skills" necessary for future workforce and individual career success, American children as young as 4 years old need to sit still in class and be subjected to near-total play deprivation, constant direct instruction, drilling, penalties for failure attached to test data, hours and hours of excessive homework, and chronic sleep deprivation, all the way through to high school. The anti-play crusaders call this "academic rigor necessary to get kids on track for college and career with 21st-century skills." Childhood development experts, by contrast, consider it other things—"developmentally inappropriate," "educational malpractice," and even "borderline child abuse."

Play historian Joe Frost, professor emeritus at the University of Texas, noted that against all the evidence, test-obsessed officials are eliminating play, recess, physical education, and the arts, and parents have allowed it to happen. He wrote:

Parents who fear their children will fail standardized tests, be held back a grade, and not get into college willingly go along with this absurdity. All these things—adult anxiety, organized sports, tech-play, and high-stakes testing—collectively and independently reduce children's opportunities for creative, absorbing play in natural contexts and negatively affect their physical and emotional health.[97]

As education reporter Andrea Gordon of the *Toronto Star* put it in 2014:

> Here's what kids at play have always liked to do: Race, climb, wrestle, hang, throw, balance, fence with sticks, jump from heights and gravitate toward sharp objects. Ideally, while escaping the watchful eye of grown-ups.
>
> Here's what today's kids hear when they're even flirting with such pursuits: Slow down, get down, put that down, no throwing, no sticks allowed, don't jump from there. Don't touch, that's too dangerous, be careful.[98]

Unfortunately, in the United States and United Kingdom and elsewhere, adults have come to the misguided view "that children must somehow be sheltered from all risks of injury," in Frost's words. "In the real world, life is filled with risks—financial, physical, emotional, social—and reasonable risks are essential for children's healthy development."

Instead of learning that includes play, outdoor recess, vocabulary-rich conversations with highly qualified teachers, and hands-on exploration and discovery combined with the correct balance of formal instruction, American children are being imprisoned indoors for most of the day with little if any recess or free time for themselves, prepared for screen-delivered bubble tests and data collection, and subjected to stress, behavior modification, rote memorization, and academic pressure years before many are ready for it. After school, young children who should be outside playing, exploring, and enjoying free time and family time are instead shackled to hours of homework, plus more and more screen time for learning and entertainment. According to one recent estimate, the average American young person spends 6 to 9 hours consuming screen-based media every single day, and 45 percent of American teenagers say that thay are online "almost constantly."[99]

A cross-cultural research study of 2,400 mothers in 16 countries published in 2008 by Jerome Singer and Dorothy Singer of Yale University found that 72 percent believe that children are "growing up too quickly," and in the United States the number was the highest of all countries studied, at 95 percent.[100] According to a recent global survey, 54 percent of mothers said that "playing outside at a playground or park" made their children happiest, more than watching TV or videos (41 percent).[101] Another global survey, sponsored by the IKEA Corporation, found that over 80 percent of 7- to 12-year-olds would rather play with friends than watch TV or use the Internet.[102]

But play, which once was a key foundation of American early education, is being killed off. Millions of American children are being subjected to unfriendly, even hostile school environments that are the opposite of what many parents, teachers, and childhood development experts recommend. One Florida mother was recently stunned to learn that her daughter's first day of kindergarten, her introduction to elementary school, which should be a day of joy and wonder for a child, was devoted almost exclusively to testing. Five different strangers asked the girl to perform tasks to be evaluated. "By the time I picked her up," the mother reported, "she did not want to talk about what she had done in school, but she did say that she did not want to go back. She did not know the teachers' names. She did not make any friends. Later that afternoon, as she played with her animals in her room, I overheard her drilling them on their numbers and letters."[103]

Politicians are forcing elementary and secondary school students, especially those in poor and minority neighborhoods, into "no excuses," boot camp–style drilling-and-discipline schools, with harsh workloads, relentless standardized test prep, and screen-delivered teaching, testing, and data collection, enforced with stress- and fear-based "rigor." Dr. Lawrence Rosen, a New Jersey pediatrician, said he sees more children come to his office throughout the spring standardized testing season with headaches, stomach aches, and other stress-related symptoms than at any other time of the year. "I have kids as young as first grade, second grade, who are being subjected to these tests, coming in with migraine headaches and ulcers, and not eating well," he reported, "to the point where parents are really thinking about pulling their kids out of the school for that week and just saying, Enough. I'm not going to get engaged in this."[104]

Politicians are usually forcing these policies on other people's children, not their own. "These officials don't even send their children to public schools," said Dao Tran, then the PTA co-chair at the public Castle Bridge Elementary School in New York. "They are failing our children, yet they push for our children's teachers to be accountable based on children's [standardized] test data. All while they opt for their own children to go to schools that don't take these tests, that have small class sizes and project-based, hands-on, arts-infused learning—that's what we want for our children!"[105] To attract children of privileged families in New York City, for example, many of the most elite private preschools stress their play-based, research-based philosophies, available with annual tuitions of up to $25,000 or more.

As Concordia University Associate Professor Isabel Nunez put it,

> One of the most destructive consequences of having non-educators running our districts and schools is that we have forgotten the fundamental principles of human development. Any developmental psychologist will tell you that young children learn through play. There is no debate on this within the discipline. [Educators] Maria Montessori, Johann Pestalozzi and Friedrich Froebel were scientists. Their vision for education is based on research, not a touchy-feely desire to let the children play just because they enjoy it. A play-based curriculum for early childhood classrooms is developmentally appropriate, because play is the way children learn.[106]

Former PBS education correspondent John Merrow has argued, "Non-educators who are not versed in child development shouldn't be deciding how three- and four-year-olds spend their days. And under no circumstances should those days involve testing." He added,

> Early childhood programs and kindergarten are for growth, exploration, acculturation, and fun. Of course, teachers should be observing children and learning about them, to help them grow, but there's no place for standardized, machine-scored tests in the early years. Unfortunately, many of the people in charge of education place value on what they know how to measure, perhaps because we have failed to articulate what matters to us—what we value.[107]

The national Common Core academic standards promoted by the U.S. federal government and some philanthropies from 2009 until 2015, when they suddenly became politically toxic and were widely (and often only cosmetically) "rebranded," were apparently developed without the significant input of a single K–3 classroom teacher or childhood development expert. "The promoters of the standards claim they are based in research," assert Professors Nancy Carlsson-Paige and Edward Miller in a 2013 *Washington Post* opinion piece. "They are not. There is no convincing research, for example, showing that certain skills or bits of knowledge (such as counting to 100 or being able to read a certain number of words) if mastered in kindergarten will lead to later success in school."[108]

The result, in the words of childhood development experts at the non-profit group Defending the Early Years, has led to a set of education standards that "list discrete skills, facts and knowledge that do not match how young children develop, think or learn; require young children to learn facts and skills for which they are not ready; are often taught by teacher-led, didactic instruction instead of the experiential, play-based activities and learning young children need; devalue the whole child and the importance of social-emotional development, play, art, music, science and physical development."[109] The very idea of one-size-fit-all standards, with school and teacher penalties connected to them, ignores the fact that children develop at different speeds, and that one child may "decode" the basics of reading at age 5, and another may do it at age 7. It is a natural, normal reality of childhood.

Thanks to the anti-play crusaders, right now, across the United States and in several other nations, in many schools, children as young as 5 and 6 are given little to no time to move and explore naturally, and are forced to endure up to 6- or 8-hour days of what some teachers call "drilling and killing," far beyond the probable points of diminishing returns for authentic learning. They are doing this with few short breaks or transition times, and little or no recess to have time for themselves and move their bodies.

The grim statistics unfold in a spectacle of cruelty to American children, a real-life, flesh-and-blood, slow-motion horror movie affecting millions of girls and boys over the years. According to the American Academy of Pediatrics 2018 clinical report on play, "because of increased academic pressure, 30% of US kindergarten children no longer have recess,"[110] a truly shocking statistic by any measure. In 2016, the *Washington Post* reported that only 5 percent of public and charter schools in Washington, DC give children the required amount of physical education.[111] As incredible as it may seem, in the giant school district of Chicago, safety and logistical concerns led school administrators to deny recess to most children for at least 7 years, until furious parents and teachers finally rebelled in the mid-2000s and began bringing it back.[112]

According to a 2003 study by Jodie Roth and her colleagues at Columbia University and the University of Maryland, 83 percent of American children above the poverty line had recess, but only 56 percent of American children living at or below the poverty line did. A similar gap was reported between white and black children.[113] When it comes to recess, poor and minority students suffer from two curses—their schools are more likely to have unsafe or substandard facilities for physical activity, and politicians and administrators are more likely to consider recess as a disposable luxury in the quest for better standardized test data.

In 2015, in a bipartisan pro-recess move that is exceedingly rare in the United States, the state legislature of New Jersey passed a law requiring public schools to give children a bare minimum of 20 minutes of outdoor recess every day. Then the bill landed on the desk of the state's governor, Chris Christie. He vetoed the bill, calling it an example of "crazy government run amok." He did not cite any research, educational, or scientific basis for his veto. "Part of my job as governor is to veto the stupid bills," he declared. "That was a stupid bill and I vetoed it."[114] He told a reporter, "With all the other problems we have to deal with, my legislature is worried about recess for kids from kindergarten to fifth grade?"[115] In 2018, after Christie left office, the New Jersey legislature finally passed a bill requiring 20 minutes of recess per day for K–5 students, outside when feasible, to be implemented in 2019.

Inside many American schools today, play is an endangered species, and often extinct. One Chicago public school mom, Cassie Creswell, parent of a first-grader, said, "The lack of play is only made worse by the narrow academic focus. There's an overemphasis on reading and math skills and little else starting very rigorously in kindergarten and even pre-K. This year, my daughter's class will have seven standardized tests administered to them in total 20 times during this school year. It is simply insanity."[116]

The United Nations Standards of Human Rights recommends that prisoners have at least 1 hour of outdoor exercise daily. But we don't give the same right to our own children. In 2016 in the United States, only 5 states out of 50 had a recess requirement, and only 8 more had general physical activity requirements for schools.[117]

Subjects that were once standard in American elementary schools—like music, the arts, metal and wood shop classes, foreign languages, even history and social studies—are being squeezed out of the curriculum in order to make room for drilling for standardized tests. "One of the practical effects of the trend is decreased time left during the school day for other academic subjects, as well as recess, creative arts, and physical education," noted the 2007 clinical report on play issued by the American Academy of Pediatrics. "This trend may have implications for the social and emotional development of children and adolescents. In addition, many after-school child care programs prioritize an extension of academics and homework completion over organized play, free play, and physical activity."[118] When learning becomes mastering facts to pass a standardized test, play will decrease, as there's only so much time in the school day. If "higher expectations" for what children should learn don't include risk-taking, creativity, problem-solving, and teamwork, for example, play will have very little room in a school's repertoire.

Tests—those designed and administered by a child's classroom teacher—are an essential way to track a child's progress in school subjects, in combination with other measurements. And standardized "sample-based" tests given to small, representative samples of students can act as an important and statistically accurate diagnostic tool for a school or district to flag trends and monitor overall progress.

But the mandatory, universal, high-stakes standardized testing of younger and younger children in a few academic subjects, used to generate data to reward and punish teachers and schools, is an unnecessary, invalid, outdated, counterproductive, and incredibly expensive process, the total costs of which may approach the tens of billions of dollars each year in the United States.[119] Australia's version of a national testing system, called NAPLAN, or the National Assessment Program—Literacy and Numeracy, is a series of annual standardized tests focused on basic academic skills in literacy and mathematics. According to some estimates, the annual total cost of NAPLAN is at the scale of 100 million Australian dollars. Many educators, and politicians as well, question whether this is money worth spending.

Standardized testing is a huge time-waster and energy-diverter. And standardization, by definition, also works against risk-taking, creativity, imagination, and innovation in schools, the very traits that education should be promoting. Standardization overemphasizes direct instruction in whole-class settings rather than small-group learning and independent study. It gives priority to teaching in the same way, to all students, while crushing creativity, personal expression, diverse talents, and imagination. Standardization promises efficiency, assuming that when teaching processes are standardized they can be repeated in a lower cost. If it's not in the standardized-tested curriculum, it is not seen as necessary. And play, increasingly, is not in the curriculum, and neither are subjects once common to American schools, like civics and the arts.

The average student in a large American urban school district took a total of 112 standardized and often high-stakes tests from kindergarten to graduation, according to a 2015 analysis, up from only a handful in earlier decades.[120] According to some teachers, many weeks of class time are set aside to make time for test preparation. Stanford education emerita professor Linda Darling-Hammond wrote, "There is a saying that American students are the most tested, and the least examined, of any in the world. We test students in the U.S. far more than any other nation, in the mistaken belief that testing produces greater learning."[121] As a result, by as early as 2007, according to one survey, fully 44 percent of school districts had cut time spent on social studies, music, physical education, science, art, recess, or lunch so they could increase time devoted to tested subjects. "Standardized tests produce results normed on a bell curve," explained historian Diane Ravitch. "The students who cluster in the bottom half of the bell curves are predominantly poor, children with disabilities, and children of color. The bell curve, by design, never closes. That is why it is fundamentally wrong to rank students, teachers, and schools by a measure that favors the most affluent."[122] Standardized tests only partially reveal what students learn in school, they almost entirely focus on measuring only routine knowledge and memorization rather than deeper understanding, and they divert valuable class time from authentic learning to test prep. Standardized tests do not measure most of the skills and future skills most valued by employers and society, like critical thinking, teamwork, empathy and compassion, confidence, leadership and communications, presentation skills, tolerance of ambiguity, and global citizenship.

The standardization and over-testing in schools has come to affect public education policies and practices in many states and countries. International student assessments, especially the OECD's PISA, or Program for International Student Assessment, have driven much of the global education reform discussion, and while the tests can be helpful in the sense that they provide a benchmark in some school subjects to national policymakers and can flag some overall trends, they can take on far too much importance in defining educational success. Students have been the losers, sentenced to often mind-numbing schooling. As comparative international standardized tests increase pressure on policymakers to improve their national scores, critical pieces of childhood education are being pushed out. Teachers who care about their craft have also lost out.

A 9-year study by the National Research Council, published in 2011, found that the national program of large-scale standardized testing of children in the United States had resulted in little learning progress.[123] The test results are of dubious relevance and validity, especially for younger children. Kindergartners, for example, are unreliable test-takers, and the scores of children below third grade are highly variable and unstable. Depending on the day of the week, they could score in the 99th percentile or the 65th percentile of a standardized test.[124]

Worse yet, standardized tests are largely invalid for the purposes of authentically assessing the learning of individual children, and they don't reflect the quality of instruction, other than instruction in standardized test preparation. "In fact, our [research] results demonstrate that standardized tests don't really measure how much students learn, or how well teachers teach, or how effective school leaders lead their schools," reported Christopher Tienken, Associate Professor of Education Management and Policy at Seton Hall University, further adding:

> Such tests are blunt instruments that are highly susceptible to measuring out-of-school factors. Though some proponents of standardized assessment claim that scores can be used to measure improvement, we've found that there's simply too much noise. Changes in test scores from year to year can be attributed to normal growth over the school year, whether the student had a bad day or feels sick or tired, computer malfunctions, or other unrelated factors.

The tests, according to Tienken, are simply overall system monitoring devices and not designed to diagnose the individual learning of a child, and assessments made by teachers are better measures of student achievement than standardized tests. He noted, "For example, high school GPA [grade point average], which is based on classroom assessments, is a better predictor of student success in the first year of college than the SAT [a widely used college entrance standardized test]."[125]

Despite some modifications mandated by the federal Every Student Succeeds Act (ESSA) of 2015, the universal high-stakes standardized testing of children starting in grade 3 remains a major foundation of American federal and state public education policy, and in many states it influences policy and funding decisions, as well as teacher rewards and punishments. It has also become a vast, lucrative business for a few testing companies. "The purpose of tests is to figure out how kids are doing," said education journalist John Merrow in 2017. "We use tests in this country to figure out how teachers are doing, and to punish teachers."[126]

Standardized tests have become an important part of most of American public school life, down to the third grade and even lower. Teachers and children spend many weeks each year to prepare for and take the tests. Teachers train children on how to answer the questions that are most often multiple-choice ones and practice strategies to maximize the number of right answers. This has very little to do with what children should learn in school today. The United States, Australia, and England are among the most tested school systems in the world, but children in these countries don't learn any better than children in countries with much less testing and with student assessments that teachers design and use.

The 2007 position paper of the Association for Childhood Education International, or ACEI, called for a complete ban on standardized testing in the early years of schooling and stated that "standardized testing, as it gets more all-encompassing, has become a nightmare of huge proportion in the United States." A thorough review of the research reveals, in the words of these experts, that "although those in power would have us believe that increased [standardized] testing motivates children to learn more, research indicates that the correlation is weak at best and non-existent at worst. [Standardized] testing does virtually nothing to support or increase student learning."[127]

It's little wonder that a wide range of other experts have cautioned against the overuse and misuse of standardized tests, including the American Educational Research Association, the National Association for the Education of Young Children, the International Reading Association, the National Council of Teachers of English, the American Evaluation Association, the Association of Childhood Education International, the National Parent Teacher Association, the American Psychological Association, and the American Statistical Association, among others.

But still, the educational malpractice persists, and it is growing. On any given day, according to education professor Lindsey Russo of the State University of New York at New Paltz, you can now walk into a classroom in New York City and not know whether you're in a kindergarten or a first-grade classroom. "I have experienced classroom environments where 5-year-old children are sitting in rows completing worksheets while their teacher models handwriting skills on an overhead projector. There is no sign of a rug or dramatic play area, both of which were staples of the kindergarten classroom. In contemporary scripted classrooms, children must follow a highly regimented routine where lessons are linked to standardized tests designed to measure children's progress in learning discrete facts and skills."[128]

In school systems governed by standardized testing, children can suffer in a vicious cycle without a solid foundation of play skills upon which to build academic skills. "We drill more because they can't pay attention, but they can't pay attention because they don't have these underlying play skills, so we drill more," said Elena Bodrova, Professor Emerita of Psychology at Metropolitan State College of Denver. "It's pathetic."[129] Sometimes, the drilling and measurements can make little to no sense. As Microsoft founder Bill Gates marveled in 2015, "In one Midwestern state, for example, a 166-page Physical Education Evaluation Instrument holds teachers accountable for ensuring that students meet state-defined targets for physical education, such as consistently demonstrating 'correct skipping technique with a smooth and effortless rhythm' and 'strike consistently a ball with a paddle to a target area with accuracy and good technique'. I'm not making this up!"[130]

There are some 100,000 schools and nearly 4 million teachers in the United States. They all have their own cultures, traditions, and ways of doing things. But most scholars agree that learning is an active process where the learner (child) has the key role, not the teacher. We also know that social interaction between the student and other students is a powerful force behind productive learning. Furthermore, we know that emotions are very important in enabling as well as preventing children learning in school. And physical activity, being engaged, and play are all associated with positive learning experiences and outcomes for children.

Beyond the effects of excessive standardized testing, the War on Play has also been intensified by a wide range of social trends affecting the lives of children. Historian Howard Chudacoff considers the first half of the 20th century to be "the golden age of unstructured play in North America,"[131] when free play among children flourished. Back then, children often filled their free time with self-chosen and self-directed play—group play, solitary play, horsing around in their backyards and neighborhoods, and organizing outdoor games. Today, children are lucky if they have any free time at all.

A culture of parental overinvolvement and overprotection and overscheduling of children is feeding the War on Play. One study published in the *Archives of Pediatrics and Adolescent Medicine* found that children's free-play time dropped by a quarter between 1981 and 1997, and "this change appears to be driven by increases in the amount of time children spend in structured activities."[132] "We are literally scheduling their lives away," wrote Colorado mother Joelle Wisler in an essay published on the popular parenting website, Scary Mommy. "We sign them up for soccer and music and karate and Spanish lessons and every other freaking thing because we really think these things are important. I am guilty. We are all guilty. And not only are we scheduling their lives away, they are also spending way too much time on electronics."[133]

5

Why Don't Children Play in School Anymore?

Play is not a luxury but rather a crucial dynamic of healthy physical, intellectual, and social-emotional development at all age levels.[134]

—David Elkind

The sooner a child starts reading, the better.

Who's got time to play?

Children must learn to read in pre-K or kindergarten or they will be left behind, never catch up to their peers, and suffer life-altering consequences.

This is how many adults think. "The stress is palpable," wrote early childhood educator Erika Christakis. "Pick the 'wrong' preschool or ease up on the phonics drills at home, and your child might not go to college. She might not be employable. She might not even be allowed to start first grade!"[135]

We adults often think that children today need more education in order to succeed in life. We therefore assume that instruction in reading, writing, and mathematics must start earlier in life than when we were young. Free play and physical activity outdoors seem to fit poorly into this new agenda of education. For many parents today, one of the central concerns is where to find an early childhood program that would guarantee access to a good preschool and then to great primary school. Some moms and dads will do anything, if they can afford it, to give their children only "the best" possible education, and that can translate into the earliest and most academically intense education possible.

More and more, these ideas are considered basic, obvious truisms of life, not only by politicians but also by many parents, eager to give their children a head start by unlocking their children's language decoding skills at younger and younger ages, through "academic" preschools and kindergartens, apps, educational tablet games, enrichment classes, and tutors. The truth, however, may be far more complex. "Many young children are not developmentally ready to read in kindergarten and there is no research to support teaching reading in kindergarten," declared the childhood advocacy group Defending the Early Years. "There is no research showing long-term advantages to reading at 5 compared to reading at 6 or 7."[136] According to Professor Nancy Carlsson-Paige, "The research is clear. Faster is not better when it comes to early education; young children need play and hands-on interactions for genuine learning to occur."[137]

There is, however, an intriguing body of international research to suggest that the "earlier is better" or "push down" strategy of childhood learning is, for many children, unnecessary or even counterproductive, and by killing play in order to fit in excessive formal academic instruction for 4-, 5-, 6-, and 7-year-olds, a "backfire effect" may occur. Some research indicates that early instruction in reading and other areas may help some students, but these boosts appear to be temporary and "wash out" by fourth or fifth grade.[138]

One study published in 2015 found a strong mental health benefit to a later school starting age, and a likely academic payoff as well. The study, titled "The Gift of Time? School Starting Age and Mental Health," was published by the National Bureau of Economic Research and authored by Stanford Graduate School of Education Professor Thomas Dee and Hans Henrik Sievertsen of the Danish National Center for Social Research. The study used data on tens of thousands of students across Denmark and other nations and found a striking effect beginning at age 7 on inattention/hyperactivity, a measure of self-regulation with strong negative links to student achievement. The researchers reported, "We found that delaying kindergarten for one year reduced inattention and hyperactivity by 73 percent for an average child at age 11 and it virtually eliminated the probability that an average child at that age would have an 'abnormal,' or higher-than-normal rating for the inattentive-hyperactive behavioral measure."[139]

A 2009 study by German education researcher and developmental psychologist Sebastian Suggate looked at about 400,000 15-year-olds in more than 50 countries and found that early school entry provided no long-term advantage.[140] Another study published in 2013 and co-authored by Suggate examined a group of over 300 students over several years and reached the counterintuitive, tentative finding that "equal, or even greater, long-term reading achievement can result despite delaying reading instruction by nearly two years," or from 5 to 7 years of age.[141] Among two samples of English-speaking students, by about age 10, children learning to read at age 7 had caught up to those learning at age 5. Additionally, "later starters had no long-term disadvantages in [language] decoding and reading fluency," and "for whatever reason, the later starters had slightly better reading comprehension."[142]

According to Suggate, there are no studies that definitively show that early reading instruction confers a long-term advantage in either reading or in overall academic success. "Regardless of whether the research uses international data or looks at different approaches such as play-based preschools, Montessori or Steiner, the balance of the evidence clearly indicates that early reading advantages wash out in the first years of primary school," he said. "Of course, on average, children who learn to read in kindergarten can have a small advantage later, but this is not likely due to their having learnt to read earlier. Instead, it seems that they enjoy some natural ability or perhaps a home environment that fosters educational achievement. Because these factors remain throughout childhood, they, not early reading, lead to both better earlier and later success." Suggate has warned that policymakers may be engaging in a "dangerous game with children's futures"[143] by overemphasizing academic skills, when playful learning is essential for physical, language, social, motor, explorative, cognitive, and intellectual development.

One long-term study, the longitudinal High/Scope Preschool Curriculum Comparison Study, found that a group of 61 lower-income children had distinctly better life outcomes when they had a play-based early education[144] instead of a more formalized and "academic" one. In another analysis, Rebecca A. Marcon, a psychology professor at the University of North Florida, studied 343 children who had attended a preschool class that was "academically oriented," one that encouraged "child initiated" learning, and one in between the two approaches. "What we found in our research then and in ongoing studies," reported Marcon, "is that children who were in a [play-based] preschool program showed stronger academic performance in all subject areas measured compared to children who had been in more academically focused or more middle-of-the-road programs."[145] These findings correspond with the position expressed by the American Academy of Pediatrics in its 2018 clinical report on children and play. "It has been demonstrated that children playing with toys act like scientists and learn by looking and listening to those around them," the children's doctors declared. The report went on:

> However, explicit instructions limit a child's creativity; it is argued that we should let children learn through observation and active engagement rather than passive memorization or direct instruction. Preschool children do benefit from learning content, but programs have many more didactic components than they did 20 years ago. Successful programs are those that encourage playful learning in which children are actively engaged in meaningful discovery.[146]

Why aren't children being given periods of intellectual and physical play in school to enhance their health and learning?

There are four main, interrelated problems, all of which are symptoms of GERM: the misuse and overuse of standardized testing, one-size-fits-all teaching, narrowed curriculum and conceptions of learning, and seeking success by demonizing failure. All of these problems must be understood, confronted, and addressed in order to save our schools and help children thrive, by unleashing the learning power of play.

PROBLEM #1: THE MISUSE AND OVERUSE OF STANDARDIZED TESTING

In the United States and several other nations, the standardized testing of children has become the governing management mechanism of school systems, and test data are often used to punish and shut down schools and to reward and punish teachers. This represents a misuse of standardized testing, and one of the destructive consequences is the crowding out of critical untested subjects and the elimination of periods of recess and play.

Standardized tests in education are assessments that meet two criteria: (1) all students answer the same questions, or a section of questions from a common question bank, in the same way, and (2) students' answers are scored in a consistent or standardized way. Standardized testing is designed to measure a student's knowledge base in an academic subject—usually limited to reading and mathematics—and these data can be used to compare the relative achievement of individual students or groups of students. Educational testing companies are now marketing standardized tests for preschoolers and kindergarteners, promising to enhance school readiness for children.

Standardized tests can be either census based, which measures all students, or sample based, which only tests randomly selected representative sample of students. The rationale for regularly testing all children is that test scores are used to "hold teachers and schools accountable" for students' progress in schools. As a consequence, in many education systems today, data derived from the large-scale, high-stakes standardized testing of children have become the sole criteria of performance. The excessive and inappropriate use of standardized tests increases time spent on preparing for these tests, counterproductive competition between schools and teachers, the narrowing of curriculum, and disengagement in teaching and learning in schools. All of these consequences together are serious obstacles to play in schools. "If it's not tested, it is not important." In other words, if it is not tested, don't teach it.

Standardized testing remains a highly controversial topic in many countries. Proponents claim that standardized measurements are the best—and for many the only—way to objectively determine whether children learn in school what they are supposed to learn. Opponents argue that standardized tests tell only partially what students learn in school, waste staggering amounts of time and money, focus on measuring only routine knowledge and memorization rather than deeper understanding, and, worst of all, pervert and corrupt the entire education system while yielding little to no apparent benefits.

A big part of the standardized testing debate is about what one does with the data generated by these tests. Policymakers and politicians are attracted to having such data because it is, they believe, an efficient way to control the performance of the publicly funded education system.

The misuse of standardized tests can have negative effects on children and their learning. Student stress to perform, teaching to the test, narrowing curricula, and the increased likelihood of corruption are among the most common negative consequences. There is no strong evidence to support the claim that using universal high-stakes (meaning they are connected to major potential punishments and rewards), standardized tests is positively associated with improved learning outcomes, student well-being, or better quality of education overall. American scholars have made similar conclusions based on extensive educational research since the emergence of the mass-standardized testing culture in the U.S. school system in the 1990s.[147]

When the stakes of testing get higher, as is the case in many parts of the world, so does the emphasis on those academic subjects that are measured by these tests. The obsession with success and avoidance of failure become the name of the game. This means that both time and space for play decreases.

PROBLEM #2: ONE-SIZE-FITS-ALL TEACHING

A common education objective in many countries is to "prepare students for the global economy." This has led to the adoption of government-mandated curricula that are supposedly "aligned to global standards," and teaching methods that are highly scripted and inflexible and tied directly to the generation of standardized test data for bureaucratic review and analysis. This trend of standardizing teaching into one-size-fits-all instruction is becoming evident all the way down to the preschool level, and a net effect is the elimination of play in school.

Globalization has affected education in many ways. One major trend is that international student assessments like the OECD's PISA test are used in more countries around the world as a main measure of the quality of education. These global tests serve as education policy and reform beacons for administrators and education leaders in guiding their decisions. They are also used as global metrics in a growing competition between education systems trying to race to be the best in the world. The hierarchy of subjects taught in schools is looking increasingly similar across nations as they adjust their policies and practices to those on the top of the global testing "score cards." At the top are language arts and mathematics. Then come natural sciences and technology. At the bottom of the list are social sciences, art, music, and physical activity. Play is rarely even mentioned in educational programs that aim to deliver "world-class education."

Standardization—and using standardized student assessments to compare school performance with district or national performance and with that of other schools—has become a common solution to these developments. When government officials aim for economic efficiency in education, they think that arranging teaching and learning according to similar routines and procedures makes it cheaper to deliver and monitor. This is certainly true in industrial production like car manufacturing.

In childhood education, detailed national curricula, teacher-proof manuals and guidelines, and standardized assessments to control the outcomes are becoming common elements of education systems around the world. In the United States many teachers are required to teach from predetermined "scripts" to guarantee that the "products" of schooling are as similar as possible. In some African countries that are used as sites for large-scale social experiments by Western for-profit educational firms, low-cost private schools promise high-quality learning through tablet-based lesson plans that anyone can deliver in the classroom; highly trained and qualified teachers supposedly aren't needed. Standardization, by definition, also works against risk-taking, creativity, and innovation in schools.[148] The irony is that even highly standardized industries like automotive products today are being customized to the needs of clients. But childhood education marches backward toward obsolete industrial practices.

Excessive standardization narrows the freedom and flexibility in schools and classrooms to do things that are truly meaningful to them, like experimenting with new ideas or learning through play. It also prevents teachers from experimentation, reduces the use of alternative approaches, and limits risk-taking in schools and classrooms. The consequence is that the more teaching gets standardized in schools, the less freedom teachers and children have to take risks, think creatively, and learn through play.

PROBLEM #3: NARROWED CURRICULUM AND CONCEPTIONS OF LEARNING

The learning sciences have changed the way we understand how children learn. Three decades of systematic research has revealed that productive learning is often constructive, cumulative, contextual, cooperative, self-regulated, and goal oriented. These features of learning also appear in many of the contemporary learning theories. The standardization movement that focuses on enhancing efficiency and accountability of mass education systems has, to a large extent, ignored these findings and instead accepted a mechanistic or instrumental view to learning that typically means the linear transmission of information and the assimilation of externally motivated, isolated knowledge. All of these consequences together are serious obstacles to both authentic learning and play in schools.

Perhaps the most serious negative consequence of ineffective, GERM-driven school reforms in the United States and other countries is the belief that children need to spend more time on academic instruction, assigned tasks, and homework. Many states and districts have reduced or removed altogether recess in schools' schedules. More schools are requiring children to work for multiple hours into the night. But there is little to no evidence that these beliefs and practices actually benefit children's learning or well-being.

PROBLEM #4: SEEKING SUCCESS BY DEMONIZING FAILURE

The strategy known as "trial and error" is a basic component of engineering, innovation, research, science, and the arts—and real life. It is also an innate skill that all of us have when we are very young.

But in many places, as soon as children go to school, or even to preschool, they learn—or are taught—to avoid failure and pursue success. Failure is demonized. Children learn early on that failure in the classroom, or on a standardized test, is one of the worst things that can happen to you. This creates a perception that failure and success are extreme opposites of the continuum: The further you are from failure, the closer you are to success. In real life, however, failure often precedes or accompanies success; in other words, failure and success are close to one another, not the opposites. Driven by high-stakes standardized testing, the culture of many schools now prefers safe and "results-proof" teaching and learning practices that demonize trial and error and devalue new ways of learning or problem-solving. All of these consequences together help solidify the barriers against play in childhood education.

Children in school should learn how to fail, how to make mistakes, and how to "fail well"—how to turn failure and mistakes into learning opportunities. In real life, at home, and in the workplace, the courage to fail and take lessons from failure is a valuable asset. Success is often the result of "good failures" that become learning experiences, trial runs, and building blocks for success.

Taken together, the GERM-driven trends of the standardization of teaching and learning, the frequent use of standardized tests to determine whether these standards have been accomplished, the narrow conception of learning, and the demonization of failure have all combined to help crush the learning power of play in schools (see Figure 4 and Table 1).

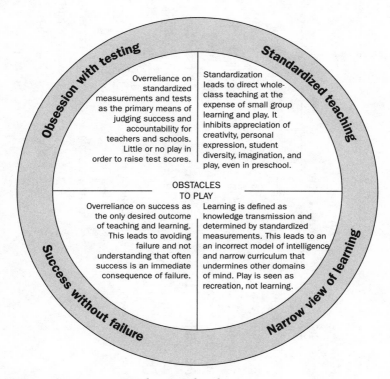

Figure 4. Barriers to Play in Schools.

Source: Authors.

HOW SCHOOLS ARE BECOMING PLAY-STARVED STRESS FACTORIES—AND THE DAMAGE IT IS DOING TO OUR CHILDREN

Not long ago, American kindergartens were places of joy, laughter, singing, playing, and discovery, as teachers gently welcomed young children into the world of education through conversation, games, songs, and child-friendly group activities,

Table 1 Barriers to Play in Schools

	What do we know?	How do we know it?	How does it impact play?	Solutions
Misuse and overuse of high-stakes standardized tests	Inappropriate use of standardized tests increases teaching to the test, competition between schools and teachers, narrowing of curriculum, and disengagement in teaching and learning in schools.	Research shows that children spend more time drilling and getting prepared for standardized tests and the cost of testing and test-prep increases.	Recess in many schools has been reduced or deleted in order to add instruction time to subjects of highest stakes for schools. As a consequence, there is less time for music, arts, and play.	Put teachers in charge of testing individual children, replace unnecessary universal high-stakes standardized testing with sample-based testing to monitor system trends and quality. Let the children play.

| Standardization of teaching | Standardization of teaching provides externally designed "scripts" that determine content and methods of teaching. It favors direct instruction in whole-class settings over small-group learning and independent work. | Evidence shows that there has been a clear move toward direct instruction, a focus on literacy and numeracy, and a decrease in child-initiated activities. | Standardization narrows teachers' and schools' freedom and flexibility to do things that are personalized and meaningful to students, such as experimenting with new ideas, creative problem-solving, and playful learning. | Give schools professional flexibility and the freedom to innovate. Teach children not through undue stress, pressure, and fear, but through warmth, encouragement, and professionalism. Let the children play. |

(continued)

Table 1   Continued

	What do we know?	How do we know it?	How does it impact play?	Solutions
Narrowed learning	We know the basic principles of children's learning. We are much less certain about how teachers teach in schools around the world.	Teachers devote more time than before to test-taking skills, teach more often according to tightly scripted, uniform lesson plans, and have experienced reduced free time for students during the school day.	If we want all children to have more time to play in and out of school, one way to do this is to make sure that teaching in school is built upon evidence of how children learn. Narrowing ideas of learning lead to excessive direct instruction and the devaluation of play.	Give children a rich curriculum that includes the arts, science, math, languages, hands-on activities, civics, life skills, and physical activity. Let the children play.

Pursuing success by demonizing failure	Overreliance on being successful without failure leads to avoiding trying different ways to get things done and learning from one's own trials.	Evidence from school systems around the world suggests that teaching in schools primarily aims at finding the right answer by preparing students for the tests that only value success.	Time spent on test preparation and drilling to succeed in tests and exams reduces the time available for play. Incorrect beliefs about the role of play in learning and growth hinder use of playful learning.	Teach children not only how to succeed but also how to experiment, innovate, question, and learn through failure as a pathway to success. Let the children play.

all of which lay the foundation for formal academic formal learning in grade school.

Today, many preschools and kindergartens have turned into stress factories for children. If you peek into the average American preschool classroom today, according to early childhood educator Erika Christakis, you're likely to see "every surface festooned with alphabet charts, bar graphs, word walls, instructional posters, classroom rules, calendars, schedules, and motivational platitudes—few of which a 4-year-old can 'decode,' the contemporary word for what used to be known as reading." Over the last two decades, she writes, much of the day is now devoted to "seat work" and highly controlled, scripted "direct instruction" teaching, a method that used to be largely confined to older grades.[149]

Nancy Carlsson-Paige is an early childhood development expert and Professor Emerita of Education at Lesley University who is a leading advocate for research-based approaches to childhood learning (as well as being actor Matt Damon's mother). Not long ago, she paid a visit to a kindergarten and pre-K school in a low-income community in North Miami. What she found was a child's dystopian nightmare. "There were 10 classrooms," she reported. "The program's funding depended on test scores, so, no surprise, teachers taught to the test. Kids who got low scores, I was told, got extra drills in reading and math and didn't get to go to art. They used a computer program to teach 4- and 5-year-olds how to 'bubble' [fill in the blank circles in a bubble test]. One teacher complained to me that some children go outside the lines."[150]

The walls of one kindergarten classroom visited by Professor Carlsson-Paige were barren, as was the entire classroom. On the chalkboard were the Orwellian commands: "No talking. Sit in your seat. Hands to yourself." Scared and disengaged-looking children in the class were writing the words at their tables. One little boy sat apart from the rest, softly crying. At the side of the room, a teacher who was testing a boy at a computer shouted, "Be quiet! No talking!" Carlsson-Paige said she would never forget the feeling of watching children "suffering" in an environment "that was such a profound mismatch with their needs." She explained, "It's in low-income, under-resourced communities like this one where children are most subjected to heavy doses of teacher-led drills and tests."[151] Carlsson-Paige added that many normally developing children won't be able to read books on their own until age 7. "When we require specific skills to be learned by every child at the same time, that misses a basic idea in early childhood education," she explained, "which is that there's a wide range to learning everything in the early years."[152] Walking, for example, might be mastered by one child at 9 months and another at 14 months. Most children wind up walking equally well.

According to a 2016 study titled "Is Kindergarten the New First Grade?," co-authored by Daphna Bassok, Assistant Professor of Education and Public Policy at the University of Virginia, the percentage of kindergarten teachers who expect children to know how to read by the end of the year rose from 31 to 80 percent during 1998 and 2010, a shift probably triggered by pressure from both policymakers and parents.[153] At the same time, kindergarten curricula have been narrowed and play has been steadily eliminated.

"Almost every dimension that we examined," notes Bassok, "had major shifts over this period towards a heightened focus on academics, and particularly a heightened focus on literacy, and within literacy, a focus on more advanced skills than what had been taught before." Bassok and her colleagues found that while time spent on literacy in American kindergarten classrooms went up, time spent on arts, music, and child-selected activities (like station time) significantly dropped. Teacher-directed instruction also increased, revealing what Bassok described as "very large increases in the use of assessments.[154]

The researchers were surprised by how drastically the kindergarten experience had changed in 12 years and found the following:

> Overall, our results suggest that kindergarten classrooms became increasingly similar in structure and focus to typical first grade classrooms of the late nineties, but that first grade classrooms have also shifted away from art, music and science instruction and increased their emphasis on assessment. Finally, our findings indicate that while changes to kindergarten classrooms were pervasive, they were particularly pronounced among schools serving high percentages of low-income and non-white children."[155]

The impact of such changes on children's learning is not known, the study reported, since some experts think they could help close achievement gaps, while others think they are "potentially harmful."[156]

In the wake of decades of play deprivation and, to be sure, other major trends in education and society, American children have suffered a startling drop in creativity, according to one widely used "creativity test," the Torrance Tests of Creative Thinking (TTCT), which is based on samples of U.S. schoolchildren in kindergarten through to twelfth grade.

In 2011, Professor of Creativity and Innovation Kyung-Hee Kim at the College of William & Mary reported on her review of 300,000 Torrance scores of children and adults and found that creativity scores had been constantly increasing until the 1980s, then fell steadily ever since, especially among young children from kindergarten to sixth grade. Kim reported in her November 2011 article, "The Creativity Crisis," published in the *Creativity Research Journal,* that "children have become less emotionally expressive, less energetic, less talkative and verbally expressive, less humorous, less imaginative, less unconventional, less lively and passionate, less perceptive, less apt to connect seemingly irrelevant things, less synthesizing, and less likely to see things from a different angle."[157]

Declining creativity among children and youth is alarming given that many researchers emphasize creativity and innovation as key skills for the 21st century. Employers around the world look for people who are able to think creatively and initiate new ideas with other people. Many experts on creativity agree that we cannot teach creativity per se, but we can instead create conditions for children to develop their habits of minds and skills that are necessary in creative thinking and action. Play is a natural and effective way to do just that.

The magnitude of the academic pressure now being put on children can come as a shock to some parents. One Boston mother, Leslie MacKinnon, who has two young children attending public schools, said of her 5-year-old kindergartener, "He's so overtaxed. He's having the worst year ever." She added, "He comes home with this giant backpack full of homework every night. I don't make him do it. I feel like it's just going to add to his discipline problems at school. He's 5. He wants to be moving and doing art projects and playing with Legos."[158]Another Boston-area parent, Jennifer Debin, saw similar academic stress being applied to her son's kindergarten class. "It came as a surprise to me, during my observations of the classroom. There were a lot of work sheets, a lot of seat time, and it was all very teacher directed," Debin said after volunteering as a class parent. "There wasn't as much joy in learning, laughter, excitement, and just the noise and playfulness you'd expect in a place trying to get kids excited for that first voyage into school."[159]

From 2012 to 2014, the large, ethnically diverse Lincoln Unified School District of Stockton, California, launched an unusual kindergarten experiment. District administrators made the decision to integrate play as a central component of the curriculum by adding an hour of open-ended, child-initiated "free play" in the morning and an hour in the afternoon. In other words, instead of making kindergarten the new first or second grade, they began restoring it to the correct academic foundation of play that kindergarten has meant for decades, much of the world over.

During the 2013–2014 school year, 71.4 percent of the students in the test district qualified for free and reduced lunches, and 49 percent spoke a language other than English in their homes. The school district was located in a city that is one of the most violent in California and in the nation. Many students witnessed violence firsthand in their neighborhoods. According to the teachers, the results of the play-intervention experiment were impressive. The children were better behaved. They exhibited better "self-regulation" skills, considered a key predictor of future academic achievement. They enjoyed a boost in both academics and social-emotional development. But in 2014, funding priorities changed in the district and the experiment vanished onto a research shelf.[160]

By then, in many American public school classrooms, play had largely been systematically eliminated, especially for low-income children and children of color. The United States had in effect conducted a vast, uncontrolled experiment in play deprivation, affecting tens of millions of children.

Though correlation is no guarantee of causation, some experts believe the sharp decline in play over the last few decades may be one of several contributing factors to various mental health problems among our young, along with other factors like social isolation and economic stresses. "Over the past half century, in the United States and other developed nations, children's free play with other children has declined sharply," wrote psychologist and Boston College research professor Peter Gray, a leading play researcher and advocate. He noted, "Over the same period, anxiety, depression, suicide, feelings of helplessness, and narcissism have increased sharply in children, adolescents, and young adults."[161]

Since the 1950s, for example, the suicide rate for U.S. children under age 15 has quadrupled, and the rates of what today would be diagnosed as generalized anxiety disorder and major depression are five to eight times higher.[162]

By 2009, there were mounting reports of "stressed-out kindergartners, behavior problems including uncontrollable anger and aggression, and expulsion of young children from school, a problem that is particularly severe for young boys,"[163] according to a report by the Alliance for Childhood. According to a recent National Survey of College Counseling Centers, 94 percent of counseling directors said they were seeing growing numbers of students with severe psychological disturbances.[164]

Between 2008 and 2015, the number of children aged 5 to 17 who visited children's hospitals and emergency rooms for suicidal thoughts or attempts nearly doubled.[165] A striking research finding revealed that year after year, the visits peaked in the middle of spring and the middle of autumn, and plunged to the lowest number in the lowest point in the summer. Researcher Gregory Plemmons, a pediatrician at Vanderbilt University in Nashville, Tennessee, told National Public Radio, "We knew there was an association with school seasons, but actually seeing that mapped out was surprising." Dr. Robert Dicker, associate director of Child and Adolescent Psychiatry at Zucker Hillside Hospital in Glen Oaks, New York, said, "It really speaks to the stress and the strain at school." He added that children appear to be under much more academic pressure to achieve.

Saint Louis University School of Medicine professor and pediatrician Stuart Slavin agrees. "My personal feeling is that we are conducting an enormous and unprecedented social experiment on an entire generation of American children, and the evidence of a negative impact on adolescent mental health is overwhelming," he said, as quoted in Vicki Abeles's book, *Beyond Measure*. "This is particularly disturbing given the fact that having mental health problems in the teen years predisposes to mental health problems in adulthood. It is even more profoundly disturbing when one considers that there is absolutely no evidence that this educational approach actually leads to better educational outcomes."[166]

You may wonder what is behind the widespread obsession to *over-academize* early childhood education and thereby reduce children's playtime in school and at home. One apparent reason is the increasingly common assumption that starting formal academic learning earlier will pay off later in higher achievement scores in school and better-paid jobs in adulthood. But while many policymakers and parents may assume this is true, there is little compelling evidence to support this theory.

Believe it or not, the world's 5-year-olds will now be the subject of a new global testing competition. The OECD has come up with a new global testing instrument that would generate data about how much progress 5-year-old children have made in literacy and numeracy skills. This pilot test, the International Early Learning and Child Wellbeing Study (IELS), has been colloquially dubbed "Baby PISA." The OECD asserts that "Baby PISA" will "provide robust empirical data on children's early learning through a broad scope of domains that comprise cognitive and social and emotional development," but it creates yet another standardized global learning metric that will eventually rank countries on how well young children—at age 5, no less—are prepared for reading and mathematics in primary school.

"Baby PISA" will likely accelerate the international educational "race" between nations for higher test scores, and now at the very earliest years of education. As the stakes get higher, as happened with the "mother" PISA test of 15-year-olds, the movement to start age-inappropriate academic instruction in reading and mathematics—and squeeze out play—will affect tens of millions of young children around the world. While the Association for Childhood Education International welcomes more comparative research to understand the importance of child development and learning, it has concerns about IELS: "The greatest concern from early childhood scholars and practitioners is how the standardized assessment of young children across countries will account for cultural and historical contexts."[167] The impact on childhood may be disastrous: Early childhood education may be narrowed down to what is measured: literacy and numeracy. Even more play will disappear from the school and home lives of children when governments are pushing parents to send their children to school younger and to replace play with age-inappropriate homework and literacy and numeracy drills—for the world's post-toddlers.

According to one highly provocative theory, the rise of standardized testing and school stress, which has taken place in parallel with the growing epidemic of play deprivation, may even be triggering increases in diagnoses for attention-deficit/ hyperactivity disorder, or ADHD, a condition where children are hyperactive and tend to have difficulty staying focused and controlling behavior.

The sharp rise in ADHD diagnoses and in the number of children under medication in recent years may result from improved awareness and detection, but the question arises as to whether it may also be in part due to overdiagnosis triggered by excessive childhood academic pressure and play deprivation. A stunning 6 million American students are now labeled with the condition of ADHD, or about 15 percent of all children, and 20 percent of boys.[168] "Shockingly, it's almost certain that kids misdiagnosed with ADHD outnumber those with the legitimate, clinical problem, leaving the disorder so muddied that no one quite knows what to make of it at all," according to *New York Times* reporter Alan Schwarz, who authored a major investigation of the issue.[169]

Stephen Hinshaw, a professor of psychology at the University of California, Berkeley and editor of *Psychological Bulletin*, studied the impact of the federal No Child Left Behind Act of 2001, which rewarded states that achieved high standardized test scores. He found that children with an ADHD diagnosis often get more time to complete the tests, and in some schools they are not included in the overall average. "That is," said Hinshaw, "an ADHD diagnosis might exempt a low-achieving youth from lowering the district's overall achievement ranking,"[170] a process that might be leading to an overdiagnosis of children with ADHD.

In one study of the early roll-out period of the No Child Left Behind Act from 2003 to 2007, ADHD diagnoses among children between ages 8 and 13 jumped from 10 percent to 15.3 percent, a jump of 53 percent in just 4 years.[171] By 2011, fully 20 percent of high school boys were diagnosed with the condition. A 2015 study published in the academic journal *Psychiatric Services* found that in the years after No Child Left

Behind began, ADHD diagnoses among low-income children attending elementary and middle school rose especially sharply in states that had recently attached rewards and punishments to standardized test scores. The tests, concluded the researchers, "provide incentives for teachers to address and refer children having academic difficulties"[172] for ADHD treatment.

Dr. Allen Frances, Professor Emeritus at Duke University School of Medicine, and former chairman of its Psychiatry Department, believes ADHD is a real issue, but has become overdiagnosed because the definition has "been watered down so much in the way it's applied that it now includes many kids who are just developmentally different or are immature." He said, "It's a disease called childhood."[173] In a 2010 article in the *Journal of Health Economics*, a team of researchers analyzed several major health and treatment databases and found that kindergarten students who are relatively older than their classmates "have a significantly lower incidence of ADHD diagnosis and treatment compared with similar children born just before the [kindergarten] cutoff date, who are relatively young-for-grade."[174] The researchers reasoned that since ADHD is a physiological condition where incidence rates should not vary so sharply from one birth date to the next, their findings suggest that a child's age relative to classmates, and the resulting behavioral differences, directly affects the child's probability of being diagnosed with and treated for ADHD. In other words, some incorrect ADHD diagnoses may be triggered by a child's natural reaction to developmentally inappropriate academic pressure.

As behavioral neuroscientist Jaak Panskeep has controversially speculated, "Although there are more serious problems with a small minority of children, most diagnosed with ADHD have no clinically relevant brain disorder. Many merely have problems with social-compliance behaviors when their urges to play are thwarted." Panksepp wrote, "For grades K–3, at the very least, the first class of each day should be recess, where joyful physical activity and positive socialization are encouraged." He explained, "Our postmodern societies have stolen natural play away from our children, to be replaced, all too often, with regimented activities and medications that reduce the urge to play. Preclinical evidence suggests that if we learn to restore the power of PLAY to our preschoolers' educational diet, in new and creative ways, we may dramatically reverse the rate at which ADHD is proliferating."[175] Adding support to this theory is a 2003 study published in School Psychology Quarterly which found that "levels of inappropriate behavior were consistently higher on days when participants did not have recess," and recess periods "may potentially promote academic achievement by increasing on-task behavior or academic engaged time."[176]

One of us was an eyewitness to how easily a diagnosis of ADHD can appear, and possibly incorrectly. Pasi was attending an education conference in New England, with his wife and then 2-year-old son. It was a beautiful August morning. While Pasi attended a meeting, his wife and son took a long walk with an American psychologist and education expert who was there to accompany her husband. At lunch, she approached Pasi cautiously.

With a grave look on her face, she asked, "Do you know your son probably has ADHD?" Pasi was stunned by her question, and asked her what she was talking about.

During the entire morning, she explained, she noticed that his son couldn't stand still or sit down. "He was wildly running around without focusing on any one thing," she reported.

But he is just a 2-year-old boy, thought Pasi. *He is designed that way!*

"If he was my son," the psychologist declared, "I would take him to a specialist right away, to check for early signs of ADHD."

"Back home in Finland, we have ADHD too," said Pasi, "but we usually have a different term for it." "What's that?" asked the psychologist.

"We call it childhood," Pasi said. "It often goes away when children turn 18 years old or so, though with some people it can last longer."

When correctly diagnosed, ADHD is a serious issue that requires professional medical attention. But according to a 2017 Harvard Medical School report,[177] "ADHD is overdiagnosed." The authors noted that "experts estimate that 5% is a realistic upper limit of children with the disorder," but in many areas of the country, as many as 33 percent of white boys are diagnosed with the condition, with several states reporting over 13 percent of both boys and girls being diagnosed by 2011.

It is reasonable to ask if the possible overdiagnosis of ADHD in some children is the result, in part, of both premature and excessive academic pressure on children and a lack of sufficient play, recess, and physical activity in school. If American children were to play more, we believe there is a good chance that they would have less anxiety and attention deficits than they do now.

* * *

Across the United States, many of our most experienced and gifted teachers of young children are giving up in despair in the wake of the tidal wave of rushed academics, premature academic overpressure, universal standardized testing, and play deprivation. "They are leaving the profession," said Dr. Carla Horwitz of the Yale Child Study Center, "because they can no longer do what they now will ensure learning and growth in the broadest, deepest way."[178]

In a 2015 review of teacher online discussions, published in the *Journal of Play*, one teacher described misguided parental expectations as part of the problem. "So many preschools build up a lot of hype about how academic they are in an effort to entice parents to send their children to their preschool. They give parents the wrong message. It confuses parents when their children come into kindergarten and they see the kitchen area, blocks." The teacher concluded, "The parents think their children aren't learning if they aren't doing paper-and-pencil tasks."

Regrettably, some teachers and principals are adopting this "push down" strategy of applying more and more academic demands and pressure on younger children, and an increasing number expect 4- and 5-year-old children to have academic, social, and self-regulatory skills by the time they enter kindergarten. Pressured by politicians and policymakers to achieve higher standardized test scores, many teachers and administrators are abandoning play in kindergartens, and even in preschools. School principals who are untrained in early childhood education increase the pressure, and teachers often feel powerless to fight back. "So often the people who have the most power to affect your teaching have no idea what appropriate, best practice looks like,"[179] lamented one teacher.

Principals are sometimes part of the problem. One American principal was, in the words of a kindergarten teacher, "appalled" to see housekeeping centers and blocks in a kindergarten. The kindergarten teacher reported, "I got in trouble because I was completing mandatory individual testing on the sixth day of school and let my kids play with math manipulatives for twenty minutes." The teacher lamented, "I feel like my kids get no time for social development, and I certainly don't get to know them at all. I have kids who are failing, and there is nothing wrong with them. Making kids read and write at the age of five is just not realistic for all students, and telling students and parents that they are failing because they can't is unfair."[180]

Some teachers are even being punished for allowing children to play in school. Teachers in the 2015 *Journal of Play* article described being disciplined by administrators for allowing play in early childhood classrooms, like the day a group of children at one school were sitting on the floor in a circle and singing "The Farmer in the Dell," and one superintendent walked by and said, "You are going to stop singing and start teaching, right?" Teachers reported getting commands from "the system" to eliminate free play in their classrooms, because "there needs to be a purpose behind all play activities."[181]

The people behind such instructions clearly have no idea of the wide range of benefits offered by play in school, including creativity, self-regulation, collaboration, literacy, and communication, to name just a few. "Play is often perceived as immature behavior that doesn't achieve anything," noted Professor David

Whitebread, a psychologist at the University of Cambridge who has studied the topic for decades. "But it's essential to their development." As Whitebread has argued, children need to learn to persevere and to control their attention and emotions, and they learn these things through playing.[182]

Classroom teachers report that some elementary school principals have a background not in early childhood education but in middle school or high school teaching, or even have no teaching experience at all, so they may have little or no real knowledge of how children learn, especially younger children. One principal flatly announced to a teacher that children "are not in kindergarten to color and play."[183] Another teacher was "shocked" and "extremely upset"[184] to find her entire closet full of play-based kindergarten teaching supplies had been relegated to the garbage bin, on her principal's orders.

Even children's snack time is under assault. One teacher reported that it "takes at least ten minutes and with our new math mandated seventy minutes per day; there just is not time."[185] Another confessed her fear that snack time would affect her own job review, saying, "when they come to do my evaluations, they will consider it to be unnecessary and cutting into my teaching time."[186] Teachers lamented that there is "no more time for show and tell, no time for holiday and special craft projects, not enough time for daily music and movement activities and the list goes on."[187] Another teacher wrote: "We don't even have a housekeeping area or blocks any more—no time for that! Every minute, the kids are expected to be 'engaged.' "[188] In Connecticut, a teacher with more than 30 years of experience lamented: "Everything that is taught is taught [at] an earlier age. It is frightening to see what is expected of young students."[189]

In 2014, a teacher with over 25 years of experience, named Susan Sluyter, quit her job teaching pre-K and kindergarten in the Cambridge, Massachusetts public schools and released her resignation letter to the public. In her letter and in other public statements, Sluyter described a disturbing era of "testing, data collection, competition and punishment" that was hitting kindergartners with a barrage of "new academic demands that smack of 1st and 2nd grade, instead of kindergarten and pre-K." These "inappropriate and ill-informed pressures" on her young children of 4, 5, and 6 years old, she concluded, helped trigger frequent extreme behaviors by her children, including "tantrums, screaming obscenities, throwing objects, flailing, self-injury, and sadness and listlessness." Sluyter, who remembered a distant time early in her career when hands-on exploration, investigation, joy, and love of learning characterized the early childhood classroom, explained, "When adults muck about too much in the process of learning to read and write, adding additional challenge and pressure too soon, many children begin to feel incompetent and frustrated. They don't understand. They feel stupid. Joy disappears."[190]

In America, the overuse of standardized testing is literally making our children sick. Kathy Vannini, an elementary school nurse in Longmeadow, Massachusetts, reported that during the grueling springtime testing season, "My office is filled with children with headaches and stomachaches every day." The testing, she reported, "has greatly increased their anxiety level."[191] In 2013, a group of leading New York principals were so shocked by the spike in student stress that they wrote an open letter to parents: "We know that many children cried during or after testing, and others vomited or lost control of their bowels or bladders. Others simply gave up. One teacher reported that a student kept banging his head on the desk and wrote, 'This is too hard,' and 'I can't do this,' throughout his test booklet."[192]

By 2007, the American nightmare of standardized testing mania had already reached the point where one state, Ohio, included these official instructions for 8- and 9-year-old third-graders subjected to a mandatory standardized reading test: "A student who becomes ill and vomits on her or his test booklet and is able to continue the test should be given a new test booklet so that she or he can continue. Later, the student's responses and demographic information must be transcribed into the new test booklet, which will be the copy of the test to be scored. The soiled test booklet should be placed in a zip-lock bag and returned to the STC (school test coordinator) with the unused materials. Please alert the STC to this situation so that she or he can document it on the District/School Security Checklist."[193] The test data, in other words, was the precious commodity to be protected at all costs, not the sick child, who must endure the pain. No mention was made in the instructions about medical or emotional help for the stricken child.

In Florida, when a 9-year-old Florida boy failed the state's comprehensive assessment test by one point, then failed a retest, his mother reported that the child was "utterly crushed." When she noticed a sudden silence from the boy's room, she ran down the hall, banged on his door, and got no reply. She related what happened next: "I threw the door open. There was my perfect, nine-year-old freckled son with a belt around his neck hanging from a post on his bunk bed. His eyes were blank, his lips blue, his face emotionless. I don't know how I had the strength to hoist him up and get the belt off but I did, then collapsed on the floor and held [him] as close to my heart as possible."[194] Suicide has many causes other than standardized testing and school stress, but our high-pressure academic culture is ramping up pressure on young children to sometimes unbearable levels of magnitude.

In 2010, Milwaukee teacher Kelly McMahon reported that her kindergarteners were subjected to no less than 100 different state-mandated assessments, a testing overload that pushed her school and many others to the point of "data-drenched obsession." She lamented that teachers "have precious little time to spark a curiosity about the natural world, or to engage their artistic bents, or to inspire a love of learning, or to impart crucial life skills, such as being able to get along well with others." In many cases, reported McMahon, play was being removed from school to make room for more test preparation. "This is precisely the wrong thing to do if we're interested in the healthy development of our children."[195]

Lower-income children are especially feeling the impact. "Poorer children, because they are more likely to attend publicly funded programs, receive an education that is more inappropriate developmentally," reported the advocacy group Defending the Early Years in 2013. "They have less time for exploration, play, and active learning, and spend more time in direct instruction and with inappropriate testing. Put simply, it is our poorest children, those attending publicly funded programs, who are receiving the most inadequate early education."[196] Children who attend private preschools, by contrast, tend to enjoy schools better grounded in play-based learning, reported the authors.

Across the United States, a growing number of teachers, early educators, and parents are realizing that there is something terribly wrong about the way we are educating our children. The African American population, for example, is affected disproportionately by poverty, and the odds against black boys and girls in the American public school system, and in society, can sometimes seem overwhelming. Over 8,000 black 4- and 5-year-olds are being suspended from preschool every year, according to the U.S. Department of Education Office for Civil Rights.[197] Black children represent 18 percent of preschool enrollment but 48 percent of preschool children who are being punished with more than one out-of-school suspension.[198] Black K–12 students are nearly four times as likely to receive one or more out-of-school suspensions as white students,[199] putting them at greater risk of making lower grades, delinquency, dropping out, having contact with the juvenile justice system, and entering the "school-to-prison pipeline."

In an effort to improve the school performance of students of minority and high-poverty backgrounds, some American philanthropists, joined by politicians like presidents George W. Bush and Barack Obama, have supported policies that led to practices that critics decry as harsh, punitive, and counterproductive—like "no excuses" schools with military boot-camp atmospheres and draconian discipline policies, relentless preparation for high-stress standardized testing, extra-long hours, and little or no play or recess. By "raising standards," these policies were supposed to alleviate the black–white achievement gap and boost American international test scores. But after nearly 15 years of bipartisan doubling-down on such policies by the Bush, Obama, and Trump administrations and their allies, America's national and international test scores have remained largely flat, with little to no improvement in the achievement gap.[200]

In other words, a supreme irony of the dark age of childhood over-testing, over-pressure, stress and play deprivation in our public schools is that there is no evidence that it works, even when measured by the narrow metrics promoted by its own proponents—standardized test scores.

By 2011, some 8 years into era of the No Child Left Behind Act and its successor Race to the Top, the federal programs that sharply increased reliance on universal standardized testing and data collection, a National Academy of Sciences committee commissioned by Congress to review America's "test-based accountability systems" concluded that the tests "have not increased student achievement enough to bring the United States close to the levels of the highest achieving countries."[201] One of the authors of the report summarized the findings: "There are little to no positive effects of these systems overall on student learning and educational progress, and there is widespread teaching to the test and gaming of the systems that reflects a wasteful use of resources and leads to inaccurate or inflated measures of performance."[202] "It has been twelve years since No Child Left Behind became the law of the land," wrote Daniel Domenech, executive director of the School Superintendents Association in 2013. "The standards and accountability movement swept the nation, followed by an education reform agenda often driven by non-educators. Still today half of African-American and Latino students fail to graduate from our high schools. They drop out in disproportionate numbers from our schools. The numbers for attending and graduating from college are dismal."[203]

"Play deprivation has the greatest potential impact on populations already experiencing discrimination, challenges, and high levels of stress,"[204] contend Penn State educational psychologists Elise Belknap and Richard Hazler in a June 2014 article in the *Journal of Creativity in Mental Health*, citing the risk to children in minority groups, those of lower socioeconomic status, and children with disabilities.

Some fifteen years of standardized testing–based education reform has succeeded in eliminating play in school, but it has failed in its chief objective—closing the infamous achievement gaps between white and African American and Hispanic students and between affluent and low-income students, as measured by the National Assessment for Educational Progress (NAEP), a sample-based national student assessment program used to monitor the performance of American school system. Meanwhile, according to a 2016 report by the Government Accountability Office, American schools have become more racially segregated.[205] The child poverty rate in the United States has grown to reach 22 percent nationally, one of the highest rates in the developed world. Teachers are leaving the profession in droves—barely half of teachers stay teaching in school after 5 years in the career.

These dismal facts raise an intriguing question: What if high-poverty students are the children who are most urgently in need of the things that, for example, American parents of means obtain for their own children in private schools, including a play-rich early education? Why would high-poverty children deserve any less? At least one experienced educator and inner-city school expert strongly agrees with such an approach. Barbara Darrigo is a career special education teacher and the retired principal of P.S. 149, the Sojourner Truth School in Harlem, New York, a large pre-K through eighth-grade school with a high percentage of black, special-needs, and "free-and-reduced-price lunch," or economically disadvantaged, students.

In Darrigo's opinion, high-poverty children need many of the same things in school as other children do—including play. "All children need to be given the opportunity to be children," she says. "Play is an essential part of a child's development. There must be time during a child's school day to engage in play with other children. This includes time for creative free play and physical activity, as well as during recess time." For Darrigo, a warm teacher–student relationship is critical for any student, especially those with extra needs. "Children must feel that they are in a safe and supportive environment," she argues:

> This is not a function of mere personal safety. The adults in the educational setting must be aware of, and accepting of, the variations in each child's development. This is a key factor when considering and evaluating a child's social skills and academic readiness. Children must feel "safe" in that it is okay to make "mistakes." It is how these "mistakes" are handled by the trusted souls in the school that will have a huge impact on a child's development and self-esteem.[206]

Jamaal Bowman, principal of the Cornerstone Academy for Social Action in New York City's South Bronx, a public middle school that he founded in 2009 that serves mostly black and Hispanic and low-income students, considers standardized testing to be "a form of modern day slavery" that is "designed to continue the proliferation of inequality in our society."[207] In one essay, he argues:

> The state [standard test] exams do not measure creativity, verbal communication, real world problem solving, spatial intelligence, collaboration, initiative, or adaptability among other competencies. Only schools can do that. The intuitive brilliance of students is ignored by state [standardized tests] exams and I would argue that it is exactly intuitive brilliance of students that is widely needed to rescue our economy and humanity from the damage of old mindsets and policies that continue to facilitate inequality and despair.[208]

Play is a critical missing ingredient in our public schools, according to Bowman. He continued:

> Have we forgotten how play facilitates joy and how joy drives a love of life? The more we play, the less we are stressed, the less anxiety we feel, the more anger dissipates, the [fewer] crimes are committed. Imagine a school system in which play and sports were at the center? Or at the very least a part of a holistic approach to public education? Special education referrals would go down as would diagnoses for

ADHD and depression. I argue that the school-to-prison pipeline, and the disproportionate number of boys placed in special education and diagnosed with ADHD would cease to exist if movement and play were pillars of our curriculum. Why should public school students be left behind?[209]

6

An American Tragedy

The Death of Recess

Experience has shown that when children have a chance at physical activities which bring their natural impulses into play, going to school is a joy, management is less of a burden, and learning is easier.[210]

—John Dewey, *Democracy and Education* (1916)

I magine that you are a child.

You sit in a hard-backed chair with 25 other people in a box-like room bathed in fluorescent light, with a faulty ventilation system and closed windows.

The room is a constantly busy place where you must distinguish relevant information from distractions that erupt from multiple sources simultaneously. You must listen to the teacher, follow classroom procedures, and focus on a specific task. You must hold, recall, and manipulate information, and you must make connections between novel information and previous experiences.

You are just a child. You are ordered to sit still for most of a 7-hour shift, with a short break for food and liquids. All day, your body desperately wants to wiggle, twist, and stretch, but you are commanded: "Be quiet. Sit still. Be quiet. Sit still."

Every hour, you and your colleagues must shuffle in straight lines to another room just like the first one. You are given almost no transition time. If you want to go to the bathroom, you must ask permission from an overseer. If you're lucky, you might get a 15- to 20-minute break outside after a rushed lunch, but if the overseer thinks you are underperforming or goofing around, the break is canceled.

If you are one of millions of children in the United States and around the world today, this is your life in school, day in and day out, month after month for 12 years.

Recess, which was once a basic cornerstone of childhood education, has been slowly killed off for millions of American children. Until the 1980s, according to education professor Rhonda Clements of New York's Manhattanville College, American elementary school children typically got three 10- to 20-minute recesses per day,[211] but today it has become an endangered species. Some studies suggest that as many as 40 percent of school districts around the country have eliminated or reduced recess.[212] According to a report by the Centers for Disease Control and Prevention, about 95 percent of kindergartners have some form of recess, but the figure drops to about 35 percent of the elementary schools that offer sixth grade.[213]

Some American education officials have even expressed outright hostility toward the very idea of recess. In 1998, the *New York Times* reported that school districts in Atlanta, New York, Chicago, New Jersey, and Connecticut were eliminating recess, "even to the point of building new schools in their districts without playgrounds."[214] Atlanta Public Schools Superintendent Benjamin O. Canada (whose successor as superintendent, Beverly Hall, died while awaiting trial on racketeering charges for rigging standardized test results) was quoted as saying, "We are intent on improving academic performance. You don't do that by having kids hanging on the monkey bars."[215] One of his newly built schools, the Cleveland Avenue Grammar School, was constructed without a playground, leaving a 5-year-old kindergartener named Toya to ask a reporter, "What's recess?"[216]

The throngs of children in America's playgrounds, it seems, are fading away. "I have noticed that no matter what time I drive or walk by elementary or middle schools throughout my county or state, I do not see or hear children and youth on the playgrounds," lamented Jacqueline Blackwell, Associate Professor of Education at Indiana University. "The voices, laughter, screams, and running feet of children have faded into the playground surfaces and structures."[217] A Pennsylvania educator named Michael Patte added, "I will always remember the sheer joy of the screaming voices, the beaming faces, and the wild eyes of children engrossed in their unstructured outdoor play at recess. Just as striking is the deafening silence of the abandoned playgrounds that I witness too often today."[218]

The trend has extended directly into school, as recess has been cut in the face of often-exaggerated safety concerns and to make room for more instruction time, often in subjects measured by the wave of standardized tests that engulfed American schools in the 2000s in the wake of the federal No Child Left Behind and Race to the Top education eras. Recess has experienced a similar fate as physical education, says Francesca Zavacky, project director for the National Association for Sport and Physical Education (NASPE). "Competing priorities in schools for higher test scores have resulted in physical activities of all kinds being reduced," she said. "It comes down to dollars. The focus is not on the well-rounded student."[219]

Even if you are one of the lucky American children allowed outside for a 15- to 20-minute recess period, your movements may be carefully controlled and restricted. You are forbidden from swinging on your belly or spinning in circles, for fear you may get dizzy. "Fifteen minutes is not adequate for a child to acquire the benefits of recess," said Rhonda Clements, Professor of Education at the Manhattanville College School of Education in Purchase, New York, and former president of the American Association for the Child's Right to Play. "It's depriving them of the chance to get some of the benefits of physical activity and fresh oxygen to the sluggish brain."[220]

Children aren't the only ones to see the absurdity of life without recess. "Adults have coffee breaks for their jobs, but we expect kids to sit for several hours in the classroom," observed Rick Pappas, a physical education teacher in Kansas. "It's just crazy."[221] Beth Wieder, mother of a 12-year-old son in DeKalb County, Georgia, commented, "It's frustrating for the highly active kids to be told to sit still all day because they end up using all their energy trying not to move instead of learning," adding that it is "so counter-productive." When her son started middle school last year, he kept telling her he missed elementary school. When she asked him what he missed, the boy said wistfully, "Recess."[222] When a New Haven, Connecticut, mother named Tahnee Muhammad saw her son crying and declaring "I hate school," she asked "What are the tears coming from? What are you not liking?" He responded, "We don't have recess!"[223]

When a mother named Heather Mellet was told her children couldn't have more than 10 minutes of recess a day at their school in Winter Park, Florida, the school explained any more recess time would cause music and art classes to be cut. Besides, went the explanation, more recess was a bad idea since children might get bullied. "Kids get bullied in the cafeteria," said the mother. "Are you going to make them stop eating?"[224] She noted, "This started with the whole [standardized] testing craze. It's gotten so out of control."[225] Mellet and several other parents started a Facebook group of over 5,500 members who call for a daily 20-minute unstructured recess period for all elementary school students in Florida.

"I wonder how grown-ups would like it if their bosses took away their lunch hours and dictated how they spent it,"[226] said Anna Monroe-Stover, one of a number of American teachers who agree on the urgent need for recess, as expressed in an online discussion on the Scholastic website. A teacher named Brenda Johnson declared, "We need more time for exercise and fresh air to bring about more productive students." Rebecca Webster, a third-grade teacher, agreed, arguing, "Free play helps to develop problem solving and critical thinking skills. If we direct that time for students, how will they ever learn to do and think for themselves? Kids need to feel like they have some autonomy, or education feels more like a prison than a learning experience."[227]

"We need to recognize that children are movement-based," said Brian Gatens, the superintendent of schools in Emerson, New Jersey. "In schools, we sometimes are pushing against human nature in asking them to sit still and be quiet all the time." He added, "We fall into this trap that if kids are at their desks with their heads down and are silent and writing, we think they are learning. But what we have found is that the active time used to energize your brain makes all those still moments better."[228]

In a stunning case of mass child neglect, in 1991, after decades of crumbling infrastructure, safety and security problems, lack of manpower, and severely underresourced schools, Chicago public schools banned recess for most students for a full 7 years, and by 2005, 7 years after the relaxation of the ban, only 6 percent of Chicago public schools provided a recess of at least 20 minutes per day, according to one survey. Tens of thousands of Chicago boys and girls, many from high-poverty neighborhoods where after-school opportunities for safe play are rare, spent much of their childhood without any recess.[229] After years of protests by parents, teachers' unions, and community leaders, a daily recess period of a minimum of 20 minutes was finally reinstated in 2012 for all Chicago kindergarten through eighth-grade students.

One eighth-grader at Chicago's Caesar Chavez Elementary School, Alondra Nino, welcomed the change, explaining, "For me, it's always been a problem concentrating on work. And if it's all work, work, work, it's even harder. And now having an extra break, it's actually going to be easier for me." A fourth-grader at Emiliano Zapata Academy named Jose noted, "I want recess because we don't have any time to start having fun and get moving. The only time we get to do that is at gym, and that's only once a week. [Now] we'll be exercising more and we'll be playing nice things like tag and hide and seek and stuff like that." Julio Medrano, a fourth-grader at Stevenson Academy, chimed in, "Kids should be healthy, running. They should be doing something active during school."[230]

Today, precise data on school recess are hard to come by, and decisions on details like recess locations, activities offered, and duration are usually made at the local school level, with little uniformity in reporting or practices. But by the 2011–2012 school year, only 22 percent of American school districts required daily recess, according to an analysis by the Centers for Disease Control and Prevention, and less than half of those schools required a minimum recess of 20 minutes.[231]

Additional research has found that children in poverty and urban children also have less access to free play, less physical activity during the day, and the fewest minutes of recess in school. Physical education classes have also suffered—a 2013 study by the New York City Public Advocate found that 57 percent of the elementary schools surveyed offered physical education only once a week, violating state regulations mandating physical education every day in the lower grades.[232] A child is less likely to get recess if the child is African American, living below the poverty line, or struggling academically. According to one set of informal surveys, in approximately half the high-poverty schools with recess, individual children, primarily African American and Hispanic males, are regularly deprived of recess as punishment for a range of misbehaviors, including noise in the hall, talking back, tantrums, not finishing homework, and not finishing classwork.[233] In yet another alarming sign, a Gallup poll commissioned in 2009 by the Robert Wood Johnson Foundation found that 77 percent of school principals reported taking away recess as a punishment for disruptive behavior or underperformance. But in the same report, 8 in 10 principals acknowledged that time to play has a "positive impact on achievement," and two-thirds of principals stated that "students listen better after recess and are more focused in class."[234]

It could be argued that taking away recess as a punishment is educational malpractice. The Centers for Disease Control and Prevention cautions against taking away recess, stating that "withholding physical activity deprives students of health benefits important to their well-being."[235] The American Academy of Pediatrics warns against the cancellation of recess as well, declaring, "Recess is a necessary break in the day for optimizing a child's social, emotional, physical, and cognitive development. In essence, recess should be considered a child's personal time, and it should not be withheld for academic or punitive reasons."[236]

And while the New York City Department of Education policy, for example, forbids the practice, conversations with a wide range of New York City public school parents indicate that many schools may be ignoring the ban or not even aware the ban exists.[237] The use of recess as a punishment has become a mainstream practice in American childhood education.

Across the United States, teachers, parents, and children reported to us that the cancellation or reduction of recess is routinely used in schools as a punishment for academic or disciplinary reasons. Public school mother Christine Davis leads a group called Arizonans for Recess, a grassroots coalition that in 2018 helped win passage of a law requiring a minimum of two recesses per day for K–5 students in the state. She told us that recess-withholding has been rampant in Arizona, even after the law was passed. "Recess withholding is the modern-day paddling, knuckle-rapping, or dunce-cap corner-standing," Davis argued. "It is a knee-jerk, low-skill educator habit, against all multidisciplinary consensus and common sense. In Arizona, since 2009, our state Department of Education has an evidence-based professional standard against using recess to punish classroom behavior or for academic purposes. It is widely ignored."

According to Davis, the problem of recess deprivation becomes most severe when three conditions exist, all of which are rampant in Arizona public schools: (1) too many students per teacher, so individual attention is less, relationships are weaker, and teachers are highly stressed; (2) woefully inadequate and infrequent recess and physical education, resulting in highly stressed children; and (3), in her words, "developmentally inappropriate curriculum marketed for standardized test prep by commercial test makers that compels the impossible from teachers and students. It's a perfect storm." Davis and many of her fellow pro-recess activists believe that withholding a recess break from children with excess energy is akin to keeping medicine from a sick person.

Davis first became aware of the problem one day in 2016 when she passed by a schoolyard and was shocked to witness children at one K–4 school being subjected to a near-medieval style of punishment. During the short outdoor recess period of 15 to 20 minutes tacked onto lunch, she saw a group of six children who were forbidden to play, and instead ordered to sit down at metal posts along an outside wall to complete overdue classwork. She could barely believe her eyes. It was a truly sadistic form of public shaming and humiliation, as the children had to keep their heads down and try to finish their work as dozens of their classmates frolicked in the fresh air and sunshine a few feet away, in their direct line of sight. She remembered that the children at the posts "looked soul-drained and depressed as they watched their peers play, like drowning puppies." She saw the same punishment happening day after day to the same group of children.

When she confronted the school principal about it, she recalled that the response was that the procedure was legitimate "instructional support." She took the issue to the district superintendent, who, she recalls, said it essentially wasn't happening— that recess withholding was discouraged and rarely used. "It took a photo of children 'sitting on the wall' on front page of our local paper to crack that denial," reported Davis, a mother of three. "Some people commented that the photo looked like a correctional institution, or even Gitmo. That district now has a written policy against the practice. Still, it is widely ignored. In fact, in some schools recess-withholding was merely moved and relabeled from 'sitting on the wall' outside to indoors 'lunch detention' where it is less exposed to visiting parents."

During our research for this book, many other parents and educators around the United States reported cases of "recess punishment" to us, and most of them requested anonymity since their children or jobs were still inside the public school system. A long-time substitute teacher from Florida told us, "I've worked for districts in three states. I've seen many instances where the district teacher has left a list of names of the students who are [ordered to sit] 'on the wall' for recess. It has never made sense to me that a child should have to sit or stand near the school and watch as others get to run and play. Many times they have to finish an assignment at recess time. These are the children who NEED to run off some of the 'wiggles' and then they could concentrate." Another Florida teacher reported to us, "In every elementary school that I taught, recess was always used as a punishment. I personally never did this, as the kids who were being punished were the ones who needed recess the most!"

Yet another teacher from Florida told us that recess is not allowed at her high-poverty school because it was labeled by the state as a "failing" school.

Only schools with "A" grades in the area are allowed to offer recess to students. This was a shock to me as I was raised with the knowledge that play is super-important for the development of children. A co-worker and I would sneak our students a 15-minute recess behind our building right after lunch. With new legislation we are now required to give students a 15-minute recess. However, I notice that many of my colleagues do not use this time to let students play. Rather, they keep them inside to continue work or silent controlled activities. I am a teacher who still believes in the power of play.

A Florida mother added, "This tactic is used frequently in Pasco County public schools. Both of my children reported that due to excessive talking during class, lunch or outside hallways—recess would be removed for the whole class." Another mother said, last year at an Orange County, Florida elementary school, "My fifth-grader's class lost recess time because some of the students were goofing around while they were walking through the halls. The whole class had to practice walking in line around the playground instead of playing." Also in Florida, noted one mother, "The state law exempts charter schools. Kids at charter schools don't deserve a recess? The stupidity levels are astounding. My kids go to a public charter school in Lake County. Third grade and up are lucky to get one day of recess a damn week."

A mother in Georgia told us, "My kids have had recess canceled because they talked too loudly during lunch as a class, because it was too cold—in Georgia!—or too hot, or because the pollen count was too high. I've mentioned it to teachers and have heard them say that they can't afford to take the time for recess so they do [short, in-classroom] 'brain breaks' instead." According to an experienced elementary school teacher in Ohio, "In 15 years, I've never known a teacher who has no problem taking away recess from a kid. For behavior, not doing homework, for make-up work for being absent the day before."

One mother in northern Virginia told us that during the second week of classes in the new school year, "Already my sixth-grader complained that her teacher took time away from their class as a punishment. They had to stay inside with their heads on their desk for the 5 minutes that they lost of their recess." Tim Macdowall, the father of fifth-grade and ninth-grade boys in Long Island, New York, reported that his school district "routinely takes recess away from children." He told us, "Lunch aides also are authorized to practice collective punishment and keep the whole lunch period from going to recess due to the poor behavior of a few kids." Another Long Island parent said that when her daughter was in elementary school, in "what is considered a tony, leafy, supposedly progressive-upscale community, docking recess was definitely used to punish the entire class due to the 'misbehavior' of a few. I complained bitterly to the then-principal and told her that docking recess was THE LAST thing that should be done to children, especially those who were acting out, and argued that the kids were acting out because their growing bodies needed more, not less, recess. I was met with 1950s-like resistance."

Yet another Long Island parent, a mother with a 10-year-old daughter, told us that the child was punished by being kept from recess because she was not able to keep up with the rest of the class academically:

She had to do classwork on the ground while others played and socialized, though they only had 9 minutes to play.

I was shocked that this was happening. She is extremely sweet and her report card shows she gets along well with others. She only wanted to please her teacher. The effect of her being kept from recess was enormous. She suffered with depression and anxiety by the end of the school year. Of course, it didn't help that she also struggled academically. She is very angry at what happened to her. We hired an attorney and my daughter now attends a school where recess and outside play are common and encouraged. She's so much happier.

A parent in Michigan told us,

My son is in elementary school and has had recess taken away for behavior. He has ADHD. Despite the policy stating recess can't be taken away, one of his teachers did it anyway. When I brought this up to the teacher and principal it was denied. However, other parents confirmed this was happening to my son. I argued that children should have free play no matter what, but it fell on deaf ears. In the wintertime my son rarely has recess outside. He stays in his classroom with the rest of the kids. He also puts on a lot of weight during the winter from having to sit inside the classroom. It's really hurting him not getting to release his energy.

In the working-class and middle-class neighborhood of Canarsie, Brooklyn, in New York City, a public school teacher reported that canceling recess as a punishment has been common for 12 years. According to the teacher, one kindergarten class had its recess canceled for a full 2 months in 2016 because the lunch staff said they didn't behave, and the punishment was supported by the principal. "Kindergarteners not having recess was cruel," lamented the teacher. "It was bad enough they didn't have art or music in that school." Another teacher at a different school, in Queens, told us that children are "threatened daily by lunch staff about not going out [for recess] and when they do go out, after having to sit for 30–40 minutes in a hot, smelly, loud room, they may get to go out for 5–10 minutes."

At a rural school in the upstate New York town of Pennellville, the mother of a 5-year-old kindergarten student told us,

> My child on multiple occasions couldn't finish a worksheet or task in the allotted time frame of 15 to 30 minutes. He wasn't goofing off, he was on task, but recess would be taken away until it was complete. My child rightly felt that he was being punished for trying his best. Also in kindergarten, if the children didn't do their homework, recess would be taken away and they would be made to work on the home work sheet. The way my child was treated caused him to be diagnosed with anxiety.

A Pennsylvania teacher told us that canceling recess as a punishment "happened frequently between 2009 and 2018" at a kindergarten through fifth-grade elementary school in Pittsburgh. A mother from Burlington, Connecticut, reported,

> My son had to stand on a line at recess and was not allowed to get off it until recess was over because he was

having trouble completing a test. This happened on several occasions. When my daughter was in sixth grade, she left her completed social studies homework in her locker by accident. She lost 10 points on her "homework grade" as well as recess for the day. Mind you, she had done the work, but accidentally put it into the wrong folder.

A teacher at a high-poverty public elementary school in Cañon City, Colorado, told us, "The students are allowed only 10 minutes of recess before lunch, which is often shortened due to the need to clean up and to line up properly. By the time all is said and done, the children receive about 5 minutes of play each day." The teacher, who has 33 years of experience, reported that her fellow teachers "are completely stressed out by the extra planning, preparations, assessments, and meetings" required by the state to improve the school's performance on standardized tests.

At a school in Tucson, Arizona, the malpractice of using recess as a punishment is so common that the school created a form letter for it. "This is to inform you," the form states, "that your child stayed in for morning recess detention to complete homework, or in [sic] class assignments. We feel it's very important to notify you of this consequence so that your child understands that we are working together to ensure he/she realizes the importance of completing and turning in quality homework and class assignments on time."[238]

An experienced teacher in Pennsylvania told us:

I have been an elementary public school teacher for 21 years. During my 21 years I have taught in three states, four districts, one charter school, high-poverty schools, a solidly middle-class school, and one affluent school. The diversity of my experience has given me the privilege of noticing many things about education. In my years teaching K–5 I have seen many teachers, principals, assistant principals, etc. take recess away from students (individuals and groups) for behavior and lack of completing work. I'm sad to say this has included me on occasion, but I do not believe it is effective. Usually when it happens it is out of sheer frustration. Frustration is a much more common emotion in schools now than it used to be.

What I can tell you is this. Taking play out of school has led to serious consequences for our schools, but I'm not just talking about recess. The removal of play from the youngest grades and replacing it with "higher standards" has led to a significant snowball effect. Children are not developing the skills they need to attend to lessons and assignments later on down the road, and yet we expect more from them using narrow and scripted curriculum. I can tell you that when kindergarten teachers at my school advocated for an additional 15- minute afternoon recess for their students, the answer from administration was "absolutely not."

I truly believe policies in public education are responsible for many of the mental health issues we are seeing now in children and teens—the anxiety, the depression, the suicide. Many times when these problems are discussed in the media the focus is on technology and social media, but

I do not believe that is the whole story. Anecdotally, I have seen and many of my colleagues have also said that the severity of student behavior has increased in the past few decades. When I started my career in 1997, even as a brand new teacher in a high-poverty school, I rarely had to ask for help from administration with behavior problems. In my current school (also high poverty) it is a regular occurrence for me and the other teachers. Students are becoming more violent in the classroom and are acting out in unsafe ways, including frequently fleeing from the classroom (multiple students a day).

The crazy amount of pressure put on students and teachers to achieve at any cost has led to more exasperated educators taking away recess because they are at a loss for what to do. These behavior problems, in my opinion caused by the developmentally inappropriate curriculum driven by the emphasis on standardized tests, are a large part of what is causing a teacher shortage. I have seen many teachers just quit and leave their jobs mid-year because they could not do it anymore. I have had substitute teachers leave my classroom saying they need to go to the bathroom and instead leave the building never to return (not kidding). We do not have enough people speaking up.

They are expecting children to be robots, and when teachers speak up and voice opinions we risk being made an example of. It is so exhausting and unhealthy, for the children and adults.

There are some principals, teachers, and even parents who approve of the idea of canceling or reducing recess as a punishment for behavior or academic reasons, but it is critical to recognize the evidence demonstrates that the logic of this practice is completely backward, and that the practice directly violates the recommendations of medical authorities like the American Academy of Pediatrics and the Centers for Disease Control and Prevention. "It's the kids who have trouble concentrating that need recess more than anybody else—and they are the ones less likely to get it,"[239] notes Olga Jarrett, a leading researcher on recess and an associate professor of early childhood education at Georgia State University.

According to a survey by the National Parent-Teacher Association, 3 out of 4 parents believe recess should be mandatory.[240] They are correct. The medical and scientific evidence demonstrates that physical activity, in the form of high-quality physical education and regular, daily, safely supervised recess, outside whenever possible, improves children's academic performance, behavior, engagement, health, and well-being. When there are behavior or safety problems during recess, the solution isn't to cancel recess but to instead invest in adequate supervisory staff and in building group behaviorial awareness and management among children.

The denial of recess to American children makes the United States something of a global outlier. Many other nations offer breaks to children throughout the day, to give children a chance to recharge and refocus with sharper attention. Japanese children are given 10- to 15-minute breaks every hour or so, and in other East

Asian primary schools, children are typically given a 10-minute break every 40 minutes or so. In Finland, where regular recess is considered a right of every child in school, for decades children have been sent outside for an average of 15 minutes every single hour, even in the freezing cold, snow, and rain, to keep them energized and engaged. Children across Europe often have five to ten 10-minute breaks after each lesson. "Everybody needs breaks," argues Jarrett, "and the brain research shows that neither children nor adults can maintain intense concentration for extended periods."[241]

In the classroom, the maximum time of most children's productive attention span may often be closer to 30 or 45 minutes than to 60.

Even when recess is available to American children, schools often get the timing wrong. In 2001, a national study found that fewer than 5 percent of elementary schools had recess before lunch,[242] which is the best timing for recess, not recess after lunch. Recess before lunch is associated with less food waste, more consumption of fruits and vegetables, and better behavior in both the lunchroom and classroom.[243] A study by the Cornell Center for Behavioral Economics in Child Nutrition Programs showed a 54 percent increase in the amount of fruit and vegetables eaten when recess was before lunch, and a 45 percent rise in the number of children eating at least one serving of fruit or vegetable.[244] "Kids come to lunch ready to eat" after recess, explained school wellness center coordinator Shawn Grunwald of Windham, Connecticut, which has recess before lunch at one grade school. "They've worked up an appetite, satisfied some of their socialization needs so the focus then at lunch is to eat." She added, "They may also be better behaved because they have gotten some of their energy out."[245] This is not really "rocket science"—most parents know that playing or being otherwise active outdoors raises appetite. As one pediatrician stated, "Children's hunger for recess is greater than their hunger for lunch."[246]

Recently, recess has experienced a minor revival in the United States, as parents and teachers have fought back on behalf of children's right to move. In September 2015, the Seattle public schools and teachers' union agreed to a guaranteed 30 minutes or more of daily recess for students in elementary school, and school districts in the state of Rhode Island, Louisiana, Texas, and Florida have required daily recess. Pro-recess advocates have recently achieved at least partial victories in Virginia, Florida, Rhode Island, Arizona, Arkansas, and New Jersey.

But according to the 2016 Shape of the Nation report, only 16 percent of states require elementary schools to give children daily recess.[247] That still leaves millions of American children with little or no recess, which is, in terms of childhood health and academic preparation, a national emergency.

* * *

One day in 2017, co-author William Doyle passed by a New York City public elementary schoolyard that was jam-packed with 7- to 11-year-old children playing outdoor sports.

When he looked closer, he saw six adults in sports uniforms labeled "Coach" who were positioned around the asphalt, keeping a close watch on the children at different stations playing various ball sports. It looked like an intensive, structured outdoor gym class.

"Do you always do gym class outdoors?" William asked of one of the coaches.

"This isn't gym," the coach replied, "it's recess."

"Really?" William said, quite confused. "Isn't recess when children play with each other and do their own thing?"

"A lot of children don't know how to play anymore," came the reply. "So we help them get together, form teams, follow rules, share the ball, and keep score properly. This way, nobody is left out and nobody is bullied. The children can choose which activity to do."

Nearby, at each different sports station, the adults were periodically intervening, correcting, instructing, and encouraging the children in sports techniques, just a few feet away from the children. It seemed like the school equivalent of "helicopter parents" incessantly hovering around children in the playground.

Then William realized he was witnessing a new concept in American education—"recess coaches"—and he soon learned that this was part of a national non-profit group that provided such services to public schools, with the costs covered by the schools, parent fundraising, and outside funders. Some school leaders, apparently, loved the program. But this didn't look at all like recess. It looked like gym class. In fact, the promotional website for the group boasted of the power of its "rock star coaches" to "enhance and transform recess and play by orchestrating play and physical activity."

In other words, some American schools have decided to pay extra to outsource recess and hire teams of "recess coaches" and are then taking recess away from children by turning it into a quasi-structured gym class. The children at this school and other schools like it no longer had recesses of child-driven, outdoor play, with real freedom and choice, and the ability to separate from direct adult interference, create their own adventures of pure imagination, or just sit in a play yard corner and relax. They were denied one of the most beautiful and rewarding school experiences of childhood—the freedom to independently negotiate and collaborate with other children to create their own rules and games, and the freedom to have a simple, relaxing cognitive break. The children apparently couldn't be safely trusted to handle any of this.

Instead, every day these children had 20 minutes of outdoor de facto gym class instead of recess. The good news was that the children were moving around for much of 20 minutes, and that was more physical movement than many other American schoolchildren get. But it seemed to William that they should also have a safe period of actual free-play recess every day, without direct adult interference other than safety supervision—plus a daily period of high-quality physical education.[248]

One weekend day, at the beginning of the summer school holiday, William was sitting on a bench in New York's Central Park. He was watching his then 9-year-old son enjoy one of his favorite activities—free play in the playground, hanging off the jungle gym, digging up dirt with a stick, teaming up with buddies and new friends, playing tag, hide and seek, and cops and robbers, making up games and chasing each other around, and getting dirty and happy.

All afternoon, some other parents were cheerleading and correcting their children with constant shouts of "Careful!" and

"Good job—good job!" and "Watch out!" and "Don't go up the slide!"

William, by contrast, having spent some time in Finland, where he developed a fondness for the often strikingly laid-back, hands-off approach of parents there, tried to refrain from this, telling himself, "Quiet, Bill. Be Nordic. Let the children play."

William's family was going to Finland in August, where the boy would be spending weekdays split between school (Finland starts school in August) and an afternoon community play-and-sports club for children. But July in New York was pretty much free, since William and his wife had flexible schedules and would take turns taking their son to playgrounds and museums.

Soon, William joined a group conversation among parents about summer schedules. The subject was their children's summer schedules and how hectic and crammed they were. One father, let's call him Jeff, whipped out his phone and started tapping the screen, revealing an hour-by-hour, week-by-week spreadsheet of his son's entire summer schedule.

The level of detail on the spreadsheet was incredible. Nearly every single day was wall-to-wall activities, transportation logistics, and timetables timed out to the minute.

"Look at this," Jeff announced, "Mandarin class, coding camp, filmmaking school, robotics, chess, tae-kwon-do, STEM camp, writing camp, gourmet cooking class. English and math enrichment. Fencing lessons. French lessons. Next Monday he's got hockey and baseball practice."

Depending on your point of view, it was either a brilliant master plan for getting a 9-year-old on the fast track to be a Master of the Universe, or a rather bleak example of overscheduling.

Many New York children had schedules like this, yet at the same time, their parents often seemed locked in a competitive race of complaining about how overscheduled their children were.

For Jeff's son, every moment of his summer was scripted, every move was supervised and choreographed, every second was accounted for. No time at all was budgeted for one of the most important experiences of childhood—being bored. His childhood summer was a data wall.

Pondering Jeff's summer spreadsheet, William thought to himself, "Maybe I should sign my boy up for some activities. Maybe he would benefit from more enrichment and structure in the summer."

"But let's not go overboard," he thought. "You're only a child once."

7

The Global War on Play

Play in all its rich variety is one of the highest achievements of the human species, alongside language, culture and technology.[249]
—Professor David Whitebread, University of Cambridge

Play deprivation isn't just an American problem—it is affecting children in nations around the world. Unfortunately, a number of "GERM-related" trends, including play deprivation, excessive high-stakes standardized testing, and academic overpressure of younger children, are spreading in other countries.

In several Asian nations, the traditionally high cultural expectations of children's school performance has intensified in recent years, reaching high-stress levels that some parents and students consider to be unproductive and even unbearable.

Professor Yong Zhao of the University of Kansas, an American education professor who was raised in China and studies comparisons between the U.S. and Chinese school systems, notes that a widespread name for Chinese graduates is *gaofen dineng*, which means "high scores but low ability." Zhao told us,

> Play is certainly essential in childhood education because play, especially self-initiated play, is a natural and essential way for children to explore and experiment with the world around them. It is a powerful way for children to formulate and test their hypotheses about the world, about social norms, about laws of nature. It is also a much more impactful approach for children to understand their own agency, the consequences of their actions on others and the environment than direct instruction. And, of course, play brings happiness, which is an important outcome of education for children.

Unfortunately, he noted,

> Play, I mean self-determined or self-initiated play, has not been a big part of formal education in China. Traditionally, Chinese formal education pays much more attention to academic learning than play. Even when play happens in schools, it is typically organized by teachers for some

academic purpose. Children rarely get to just play, for no immediate utilitarian purpose.[250]

For many Chinese children, school has become a cauldron of childhood stress, competitive pressure, and overwork. A survey by the China Youth and Children Research Center found that fully four-fifths of school children in China did 2 hours and 50 minutes of homework every day—on weekends.[251] By promising high test scores, chains of private tutoring service providers for children are booming throughout China. According to the *China Daily*, teachers at Xiaogang No 1 High School in central Hubei province rigged their students up to intravenous drip injections of amino acid inside the classroom, supposedly to give them energy while studying late at night for the National College Entrance Exam.[252] A *New York Times* reporter described visiting student dormitories in Maotanchang, a remote town in Anhui province, and seeing wire mesh barriers installed over the windows to protect students from jumping out the window to their deaths.[253]

In December 2016 the *South China Morning Post* reported that fearful parents were disregarding government warnings and overloading their children with academics and extracurricular activities in hopes that it would give them a competitive edge. "On a typical weekend in Shanghai, eight-year-old Amy is busy shuttling from class to class," the paper reported. "On Saturday afternoons, she learns piano. Sunday mornings are spent attending English lessons and in the afternoons, she goes to Chinese class. Besides these weekend tutorials, the grade three pupil at a public primary school in Shanghai's Xuhui district also attends three-hour mathematics Olympiad classes after school every Tuesday and Friday evening, one of which is designed for grade four pupils." The girl's mother, who takes her to all these private classes, explained the logic: "I don't want my daughter to have to study so hard, but I have no other choice," she said. "Our target is that she can be admitted into a prestigious junior high school. Not studying in a key junior high school means being unable to be admitted by good high schools. Not studying in good high schools means not being able to go to top universities, and a degree from a top university, no doubt, translates into a decent job." The girl attends two types of math classes each week, she said. "To my knowledge, some of her peers attend five or six types of math classes a week." The mother confessed, "I won't let her relax for a single moment. When it's sunny, she can't go outside to run and play." Another Chinese mother explained, "All of my friends and relatives have sent their kids to extracurricular classes," she said. "I can't be the exception, otherwise my boy will be left behind in his studies."[254]

According to Peking University sociologist Zheng Yefu, a "conspiracy" exists between parents and teaching institutions in China to "bully kids" by giving them extra academic classes, tutoring sessions, and crushing levels of homework from very young ages. "It's silly for parents to let their kids study so much and for so long at a young age," he declared. "When the kids grow older, it's quite likely that they will lose interest in their studies and lose momentum in competition."[255] In his 2013 book, *The Pathology of Chinese Education,* Zheng Yefu pointed to China's shortage of Nobel Prize winners as evidence that the education system is "destroying creativity in China."[256]

In a December 2010 *Wall Street Journal* article titled "The Test Chinese Schools Still Fail," Chinese educator Jiang Xueqin, director of the International Division of Peking University High School, wrote of the perils of such a system, which are widely recognized in China: "The failings of a rote-memorization system are well known: lack of social and practical skills, absence of self-discipline and imagination, loss of curiosity and passion for learning." He added, "One way we'll know we're succeeding in changing China's schools is when those scores [on standardized tests] come down." Noting the irony of the world appreciating the strengths of China's education system while Chinese are realizing its weaknesses, Jiang explained, "Chinese schools are very good at preparing their students for standardized tests. For that reason, they fail to prepare them for higher education and the knowledge economy. According to research on education, using tests to structure schooling is a mistake. Students lose their innate inquisitiveness and imagination, and become insecure and amoral in the pursuit of high scores."[257]

Play advocate Professor Peter Gray, a research professor of psychology at Boston College, observed that since many Chinese students spend almost all their waking hours studying, "they have little opportunity to be creative, take initiative, or develop physical and social skills: in short, they have little opportunity to play." Some Western politicians like to glorify the high test scores of Asian schools, but as Gray noted, "unfortunately, as we move increasingly toward standardized curricula, and as we occupy ever more of our children's time with schoolwork, our educational results indeed are becoming more like those of the Asian countries."[258] Private tutoring is booming in China. Technavio, a London-based market research company, forecasted[259] that the private tutoring market in China would grow at an annual rate of 11 percent during the period of 2017–2021.

In 2015, one Hong Kong tutoring center ran an advertising campaign featuring a little girl crying, with the taunting headline, "You don't like competition? But competition will find you!" The product being advertised was an interview training class for children as young as 18 months.[260]

Children in Hong Kong "are becoming increasingly stressed out, overworked and unhappy, and the situation is taking its toll on overburdened psychiatric services," reported the *South China Morning Post* on April 22, 2017. The number of children who are mental health patients is increasing by as much as 5 percent every year, according to a Hong Kong government report issued in 2017, with rising school and family academic pressures considered likely contributing factors. "The crisis suggests Hong Kong's young minds are struggling to cope in the city's emotional pressure cooker," concluded the article. Like children in the U.S. and UK, Hong Kong's schoolchildren are given less time for outdoor exercise than prisoners, according to a 2016 University of Hong Kong study.[261]

In Singapore, leading childhood educator Christine Chen told us that play is threatened by both logistic and cultural barriers that are also common in other teeming urban centers in Asia and elsewhere:

Since about 80 percent of families live in high-rise buildings, outdoor play is limited. Even in preschool, the schedule allows only twice a week of outdoor play. As for indoor play, the preschool curriculum focuses on "purposeful" play. Educators in preschool design task cards for children to engage in to make play purposeful. After the school day, preschoolers engage in enrichment classes, leaving very little time for play. My concern is the sheer lack of outdoor play, and a life devoid of nature.[262]

In South Korea, school life for children can be an intensely stressful existence, with crushing levels of pressure and overwork and a culture of test preparation. Kwon Hee Sun, a 39-year-old public relations consultant and mother of a 6-year-old, explained, "Homework is stressful for parents too. It is a huge burden, especially for working mums," she said. "The education system is so competitive and students have to learn things that are not even proper for their age, like coding and PowerPoint in elementary school."[263]

Academic stress, overwork, sleep deprivation, and ferocious competition for South Korean school children has reached alarming proportions, and play is a rare commodity in the education system. Over 80 percent of South Korean 5-year-olds attend kindergarten classes during the day and then put in a second shift after school at a private academic training *hagwon* facility, or cram school, for up to 4 hours.[264] When four of their fellow students committed suicide in a year, the student council of the Korea Advanced Institute of Science and Technology issued a statement: "Day after day we are cornered into an unrelenting competition that smothers and suffocates us. We couldn't even spare 30 minutes for our troubled classmates because of all our homework." The students lamented, "We no longer have the ability to laugh freely."[265]

One South Korean high school student described a typical day's schedule: about 10 hours of school, a brief break for dinner, then study sessions that last until 10 P.M. Some students then continue after that, by studying at home or at a *hagwon* cram school, which one *hagwon* worker described as "soulless facilities, with room after room divided by thin walls, lit by long fluorescent bulbs, and stuffed with students memorizing English vocabulary, Korean grammar rules and math formulas."[266]

The relentless, 12-year-long academic pressure culminates in a single, make-or-break, 8-hour-long national standardized test called the *Suneung*, or the College Scholastic Ability Test. The prize is admission to an elite university, like Seoul National University, Yonsei University, or Korea University. "Most teachers emphasize that if we failed *Suneung*, the rest of our lives would be failure, because the test is the first (and last) step to our successful lives," said 25-year-old Sina Kim. She described the test as "the final goal and final determinant of our lives. We thought that if we successfully finish the test, then the bright future would automatically follow."[267]

According to the National Youth Policy Institute in South Korea, one in four students considers committing suicide. In fact, South Korea has the second highest youth suicide rate among developed nations. For several years, the South Korean school system has scored high in the OECD's PISA tests, which measure 15-year-old students' reading, math, and scientific literacies. However, the system is often criticized for its emphasis on memorization and test prep with little real-life application. In fact, 75 percent of South Korean children attend "cram schools" where they do little else than prepare for standardized assessments.

Educators in East Asia are increasingly alarmed at the massive failures of their test-obsessed, high-stress school systems. Because students spend nearly all of their time studying, they have little opportunity to be creative, discover or pursue their own passions, or develop physical and social skills. A recent large-scale study found that Chinese schoolchildren suffer from extraordinarily high levels of anxiety, depression, and psychosomatic stress disorders, which appear to be linked to academic pressures. The report's authors wrote, "The competitive and punitive educational environment leads to high levels of stress and psychosomatic symptoms in Chinese primary schoolchildren. Measures to reduce unnecessary stress on children in schools should be introduced urgently."[268]

In India, home to 350 million children under the age of 15, play can be a rare commodity in schools, in a highly fragmented, widely underfunded, and often rudimentary educational system. According to Associate Professor Smita Mathur of the College of Education of James Madison University, teacher preparation "is in its infancy" in the world's most populous nation. "Play is considered child's work in preschool but very quickly Indian families adopt a traditional view of play where play is disconnected with learning, especially in schools," she told us. "Play is seen as mere recreation, and a way to discharge surplus energy. It is often seen as a distraction from education or a relief from schoolwork. Playtime is used as a reward for hard work in school. From elementary school onward, play, art, music, and other activities are very limited."[269]

In England these days, if you're a child and you're caught playing outdoors alone, you could be the target of a criminal investigation. In 2015, in the town of Belper in central England, uniformed police officers were alerted to investigate when a 4-year-old boy and his 6-year-old sister were the target of neighbor complaints that their scooter and go-cart street play was too loud. Their mother, who was stunned that police launched a 45-minute on-scene investigation, exclaimed, "What sort of a world are we living in when children cannot play in the street on a sunny day without the police being called?"[270] In nearby Nottinghamshire, police officers issued notices to the parents of children playing football on Ena Avenue, Sneiton, gravely raising the potential of property damage from a stray kicked ball. Any such "anti-social behavior" or "insubordinate persistence" could incur either a £100 Fixed Penalty Notice or an injunction under chapter 12 of the 2014 Anti-Social Behaviour Crime and Policing Act, the police warned. A newspaper reported of the incident that "an Enforcement Officer from Nottinghamshire Police further emphasized that any breach of such an order is a criminal offence carrying a prison sentence."[271]

Across England, as in the United States, risk is being eliminated from the lives of children for fear of traffic accidents and stranger abductions, sedentary screen time at home is replacing outdoor play, and play is vanishing from school—and being replaced by standardized testing, stress, and anxiety among children. According to a 2015 report by the UK's Parliamentary Group on a Fit and Healthy Childhood,

Over the last 10–15 years, there has also been a shift from the predominantly play-based curriculum traditionally associated with the first year of primary schooling in England to more formal teacher-led instruction. Children in

England are being required, from even age 4, to increasingly learn via formal instruction. However, mounting opinion suggests that 4- and 5-year-olds might not be ready for the formal teaching methodologies that they encounter in primary schools and that being compelled to participate in such approaches at an early age may result in stress and developmental harm to young children."[272]

In 2012, a National Trust report revealed the growing gap between children in the UK and nature.[273] Less than 1 in 10 children regularly played in wild places, it said, compared to half of children a generation ago. The area where children were allowed to range unsupervised around their homes had collapsed by 90 percent since the 1970s.[274] According to the United Nations Standard Minimum Rules for the Treatment of Prisoners, "every prisoner who is not employed in outdoor work shall have at least one hour of suitable exercise in the open air daily if the weather permits." But by one estimate, nearly three-quarters of 5- to 12-year-old youngsters in the UK are spending less time outdoors than prison inmates.[275] An analysis by the Institute of Education at the University of London found that lunchtimes have been shortened and afternoon breaks virtually abolished for 7- to 11-year-old schoolchildren in England and Wales.[276]

In the UK, a national teachers and parent backlash has developed against what some consider the widespread overuse of the universal standardized testing of children in schools and a shift away from play in school and toward excessive stress and pressure. In May 2016, over 44,000 parents across the country signed a petition in support of a boycott of the government-imposed tests. A mother named Ulrike Sherratt joined the strike, explaining, "The reason I'm keeping my children off school today is because I love education. I love seeing my children excited about learning to read and write. Yet I think and see that SATs [government-imposed Standard Attainment Tests] and top-down tests are putting pressure on teachers to teach towards these tests rather than topic and play based teaching." She added, "There is such strong evidence that children learn through play, not abstract lessons that have no connection to their life," and concluded, "Primary school children do not need a national, government-led test and are losing their joy of learning."[277] Another striking mother, Nicola Jackson, kept her children at home and announced, "I disagree with the government's idea that they need to make the curriculum harder to raise standards. Learning happens when children are motivated and interested, not when they are forced to regurgitate facts."[278]

In 2017, teachers at the National Union of Teachers annual conference considered a boycott of the SATs planned for children at ages 7 and 11, which the teachers condemned as harmful to the mental health and educational futures of children and increasing the dangers of narrowing curricula and "teaching to the test." One teacher compared the SATs to a "monster stalking our schools," and another delegate said they should be "decapitated." Yet another teacher declared that educators should "bring down the whole stinking edifice" of the computer-delivered standardized assessment system.[279]

When Chris Ayton, a teacher from Manchester, declared that teachers should be "liberating" children's minds instead of preparing for tests they can't understand, she got a standing ovation. Kevin Courtney, a teachers' union official, noted, "Primary education should be a time in children's lives when they develop a love of learning, not a fear and dread of failure." He added, "Drilling within a narrow set of disciplines and expectations is taking the joy out of learning and much of it is of questionable educational value."[280]

"In my darkest mood, the word abuse comes to mind," said Kathryn Solly, the head teacher of the renowned Chelsea Open Air Nursery School in London in an interview with the publication *Nursery World*. "The right to childhood is evaporating. There will be some children who will not succeed in the reading test. They will be deemed failures. Failing at six? The paranoia among parents will be rife and children will be stressed and traumatized." She reported,

> We see children coming here who know their alphabet and can count but cannot wipe their noses, cannot wipe their bottoms and cannot play socially together. We have lost a generation of children who are being brought up by well-meaning parents who are only doing their best, but they have been guided down a pathway and we don't know where it is going to end. It is dangerous.[281]

"From the moment children in England enter the reception class, the pressure is on for them to learn to read, write and do formal written math," notes David Whitebread at the University of Cambridge. "In many schools, children are identified as 'behind' with reading before they would even have started school in many other countries. Now the government is introducing tests for four-year-olds soon after starting school. There is no research evidence to support claims from government that 'earlier is better' "[282] In 2018, a UK panel of experts issued a report denouncing a government proposal to administer "baseline tests" to 4-year-olds. One of the report's authors, childhood educator Nancy Stewart, pointed out, "The proposal to test 99 percent of four-year-olds in 2020 is based on the false premise that the knowledge and skills of a four-year-old can be accurately measured. But few statisticians believe this, and no research has demonstrated a strong link between attainment measured at four and later progress."[283]

"If you incarcerate kids for eight hours a day, if you give teachers no creative freedom, if you treat them like data points or points on an assembly line, don't be surprised if they don't enjoy it very much. You wouldn't either," notes Sir Ken Robinson, the globally renowned education researcher and play advocate. "If we start to treat students as human beings and schools as living centers of imagination and creativity, then you get a completely different result."[284]

In earlier decades, play was appreciated as a foundation of childhood and schooling in the UK. In 1926, British statesman David Lloyd George pronounced, "The right to play is the child's first claim on the community. Play is nature's training for life. No community can infringe that right without doing enduring harm to the minds and bodies of its citizens."[285] The landmark 1967 Plowden Committee report on education declared, "Play is the principal means of learning in early childhood. It is the way through which children reconcile their inner lives with external reality. In play, children gradually develop concepts of casual relationships, the power to discriminate, to make judgments, to analyze and synthesize, to imagine and to formulate. Children become absorbed in their play, and the satisfaction of bringing it to a satisfactory conclusion fixes habits of concentration which can be transferred to other learning."[286] And the 2009 report of the Cambridge Primary Review, the largest research examination of primary school education in England in 40 years, cited the advantages of play-based early education.[287]

Yet, the forces of GERM—increased between-school "survival of the fittest" competition, standardization of teaching and learning, punitive standardized test-based accountability, and privatization of public education—are rolling over childhood education not only in the United States but also in the Middle East, Sub-Saharan Africa, the UK, and its former colony of Australia. In many Australian schools, play has been sharply curtailed in the wake of a national push for more and more emphasis on basic knowledge and skills at the expense of arts, music, play, and other critical educational foundations.

Throughout Australian schools, play is being increasingly squeezed out of childhood education as more stringent academic demands are placed on younger and younger children. The policy goal is to raise children's scores in the Australian national high-stakes tests called the National Assessment Program—Literacy and Numeracy, or NAPLAN, a AUD100 million (US$75 million) per year standardized testing regime that assesses all students in years 3, 5, 7, and 9 in in reading, writing, conventions of language (spelling, grammar and punctuation) and numeracy.

But with the new waves of time-consuming NAPLAN testing that have occurred since its introduction in 2008, much the opposite has happened—numeracy and literacy scores have flattened or declined.[288] Recently, some states under their education leaders, for example, New South Wales, have called for thorough review and reconsideration of NAPLAN because of its unintended consequences to children and schools.

According to a 2012 study conducted by researchers at the University of Melbourne, 90 percent of Australian teachers reported children are experiencing stress-related crying, vomiting, and sleeplessness over the high-stakes battery of standardized NAPLAN tests.[289] The study raised major concerns about the "unintended side effects" of NAPLAN, including teaching to the test, less time devoted to other subjects, and a negative impact on staff morale and student health. "We are narrowing the curriculum in order to test children," said lead researcher Nicky Dulfer. "There are ways we can support numeracy and literacy learning without limiting children's access to other subjects like music, languages and art."[290]

Beginning in the 2017–2018 school year, children in Scotland as young as 4 years old were subjected to computer-administered online literacy and math tests called the Scottish National Standardised Assessments (SNSAs). One teacher reported, "I have been teaching for 15 years and never seen such cruel nonsense in all of my life!" Teachers called the standardized tests "a shambles" and "completely useless," while children were reported as "bursting into tears, shaking and crying, soiling themselves due to extreme distress," and exclaiming, "I'm no good," "I can't do this," and "Why are you making me do this?"[291] The

SNSAs are not punitive standardized assessments like those in England or the United States but rather are intended to provide teachers with diagnostic information and immediate feedback to help children progress through their learning.[292] But many Scottish teachers and parents are concerned that the tests are too stressful for small children in early primary education and are urging that they be scrapped.

In Ireland, reports childhood education specialist Judith Butler of the Cork Institute of Technology, undertrained teachers don't understand the importance of play. "It is something teachers offer after the lessons are done, not realizing that the most effective 'lessons' can be achieved through play," she told us. "The prevalence of worksheets and workbooks are all too common in schools. One could argue that this 'product' approach does nothing to promote development."[293]

Even in some historically play-friendly Nordic nations, play in school is threatened. In Norway, early childhood education professor Ellen Beate Hansen Sandseter reports that "there is a political push towards more academic and formal teaching in Norwegian *barnehage*, or childcare centers." The push, she told us, started in the early 2000s, when OECD's PISA test showed Norwegian 15-year-olds scoring in the middle of the pack. Early childhood researchers and teachers in Norway are fighting back against this pressure, Sandseter reports, staging a pro-play "insurrection" against calls by politicians for widespread testing.[294] In Iceland, researcher Kolbrún Pálsdóttir at the University of Iceland's School of Education reports that play is emphasized in the Icelandic preschool (1- to 5-year olds), but "less so in the compulsory school (6- to 16-year-olds)."

And in Denmark, reports Stig Broström, childhood researcher and professor emeritus at Aarhus University (Campus Emdrup), where play-based early education in day care, pre-K, and kindergarten still prevails, play had a very minor role in grades 1–9 until a 2015 school reform called for more play and physical activity.[295]

* * *

AND NOW, THE GOOD NEWS!

It's time for some very good news.

In the face of all this darkness, there are glimmers of hope that play in school may in fact be poised for a global renaissance. We have found amazing play-inspired practices being pioneered in schools and classrooms around the world to cultivate children's natural curiosity, imagination, creativity, and learning.

We have witnessed these "play champions" in action all around the world—in Texas and New York, in Scotland, Singapore, Japan, China, New Zealand, and Australia.

Sometimes courageous teachers and parents are fighting for play in a single school alone, and sometimes they working to deliver the right to play to all children.

We call these efforts the Great Play Experiments.

8

The Finland-Style
Play Experiments

School should be a child's favorite place.[296]
—Heikki Happonen, Principal
University of Eastern Finland teacher
training school

WILLIAM DOYLE'S STORY

In the summer of 2015, I moved to Finland to begin a family experiment in the Finnish education system.

I enrolled my 7-year-old son in the second grade of a neighborhood public school in Joensuu, Finland, a remote, bucolic university city in the lush forest and lake district of North Karelia, which is as far northeast as you can go in the European Union before you hit the Russian border. Through a Fulbright Scholar grant supported by the U.S. State Department and awarded on the basis of my experience in the TV and publishing businesses, I joined the faculty of the University of Eastern Finland to teach graduate courses in media and education. Part-way through our stay, my son switched to attend the teacher-training "lab" school at the university, since it was closer to home.

I soon felt like I'd landed on another education planet.

In New York City, I was used to playground discussions with other parents about the brutal competition to get into elite and "gifted and talented" preschools, kindergartens and elementary schools, both public and private. Some parents hired tutors and coaches to prep their 4-year-old children to perform well in high-pressure pre-K admissions tests and interviews. Parents were crushed when they couldn't maneuver their children into a coveted spot.

Many 5- and 6-year-old American kindergarteners are loaded up with hours of homework, driving some of them and their parents to despair and triggering painful family squabbles over how to manage the process. Many children lead sheltered, cocooned, and heavily programmed indoor lives devoted to academics and heavily structured "enrichment" activities, their every waking minute choreographed by adults. In high-poverty areas of American inner cities, schools are often racially segregated, under-resourced and neglected by generations of political bosses. Some alternative "charter" school chains have boot-camp, quasi-prison atmospheres where academic pressure, stress, and overwork are considered critical for children to achieve good scores on standardized tests. Incredibly, some charter schools (alternative publicly funded schools, sometimes privately managed and/or run to make a profit) hire recent college undergraduates with only 7 weeks of training and call them "teachers."

But in Finland, I encountered a nation where most children attend neighborhood public schools that were equitably funded and widely considered to be very good to excellent, where teachers were trained and respected like scientists, and where play was commonly understood to be both the whole point of childhood and the bedrock foundation of effective childhood education. School hours were short and homework was relatively light. Teachers were required to have research-based masters degrees, and extensive, supervised clinical training experience in teaching children, and were given high levels of public respect and professional autonomy. When I told Finnish people about the stress and pressure many American schoolchildren and teachers were being subjected to in school, they reacted with such horror and sadness that I quickly abandoned the subject.

Instead, I heard several mantras over and over from Finnish parents and teachers: "Let children be children," and "The children must play," and "The work of a child is to play." A Finnish mother told me, "Here, you're not considered a good parent unless you give your child lots of outdoor play." For many children in Finland, risky play is tolerated and even encouraged. One day, on a forest path near the university, I came upon a delighted

Finnish father applauding his 6-year-old daughter as she scrambled far up a very tall tree, to a height that many parents around the world would be horrified by. "If she falls and breaks her arm," the father noted nonchalantly, "it will be in a good cause—she will have learned something."

Following the local tradition, my own child learned, at age 7, how to safely walk to school completely on his own, a journey that included navigating eight street crossings and two busy main streets. He did it at an age about 5 or 6 years earlier than would be allowed in most parts of the United States. In Finland, where vehicles automatically stop dead in the road to let pedestrians, especially children, cross streets, it was a perfectly normal routine. When I asked why he enjoyed walking to school so much, he proudly explained, "It makes me feel old." In New York City, allowing a 7-year old child to walk to school and cross streets alone might land the parents in jail by sundown, and probably rightly so, given the city's traffic dangers.

When I was a child I enjoyed long childhood summers immersed in outdoor free play in my mother's hometown, a largely Finnish-American community in the forest of Michigan's Upper Peninsula not far from where Ernest Hemingway frolicked as a boy, but I'd rarely thought about Finland in the decades since. I spent the rest of my childhood in the playgrounds and cement-and-concrete forest of Manhattan, where my parents co-founded the Caedmon School, the city's first modern Montessori elementary school. I could vaguely remember the feeling of my first day in the school's kindergarten, settling in proudly to my own desk and embarking on an early childhood education rich in discovery, exploration, hands-on experiences, and child-initiated, creative play.

How did I wind up in Finland, of all places? In 2012, while helping American civil rights hero James Meredith write his memoir, we interviewed a panel of America's leading education experts and asked them for their ideas on improving America's public schools, a special passion of Meredith's. One of the experts, the renowned Professor Howard Gardner of the Harvard Graduate School of Education, said, "Learn from Finland, which has the most effective schools and which does just about the opposite of what we are doing in the United States."[297] Gardner also recommended that Americans read Pasi Sahlberg's book *Finnish Lessons*,[298] which I soon did. I found the book so fascinating and provocative that I tracked down Pasi during one of his visits to New York.

"If you come to Finland," Pasi told me, "you'll see how great American schools could be if they make better use of their own educators and scholars." The secret, Pasi explained, was a simple one. Finland built its school system on concepts that were largely pioneered in the United States—like teacher professionalism, education research and innovation, cooperative learning, educating the whole child, and learning through play—and then stuck with them. It was, Pasi explained, a nation where educators, not politicians or other non-educators, ran the schools. Finnish teachers are among the best-trained teachers in the world, and partly because of this, there is no need for a national system of universal standardized tests—extremely high quality and high standards were "built-in" at the very front end of the system, in the teacher force. Parents and politicians in Finland trust teachers' collective professional wisdom and judgment in determining how well children learn, not testing companies. Indeed,

Finnish children don't sit for any high-stakes standardized test until the end of high school at the age of about 18 years old. Finnish schoolchildren are being assessed all day, every day—by highly professional educators.

The result: Finland's childhood education system is widely considered to be among the best in the world, achieving the #1 spot in the most recent qualitative rankings by the World Economic Forum Global Competitiveness Report, UNICEF's Sustainable Development Goals Report Card, and the Organization for Economic Cooperation and Development's (OECD's) Better Life Index. Finland has also recently topped the global rankings for the most efficient education system, most sustainable economic development in education, most stable nation, most literate nation, greenest country, happiest nation, cleanest air, strongest political empowerment of women, most freedom of the press, least corrupt state, most innovative economy, strongest government institutions, best human capital, and the best country to live in. Not bad for a century-old nation of 5.6 million people whose economy at the dawn of the 1970s was among the least developed in the OECD.

Perhaps the most surprising part of the Finnish educational philosophy is the central role of play in children's lives, both in and out of school. In the early years, children learn to read and do math through various forms of play, physical activity, music, and drama. Formal learning doesn't start before the first grade, when children are 7 years old and they go to primary school. Before that, children spend their time in play, both free play and play guided by the teachers, to develop a sense of independence and responsibility, and to learn about themselves and others.

Finnish teachers believe that quality learning occurs when you infuse curiosity and active engagement into the learning environment, all of which are enhanced by the concept of play. In short, quality learning happens when students actively build links between their existing knowledge and what is to be learned, links that can be activated and nurtured through play. As the famed Swiss psychiatrist and philosopher Carl Jung argued, "The creation of something new is not accomplished by the intellect but by the play instinct acting from inner instinct. The creative mind plays with the object it loves."[299]

In Finland, I entered a system of childhood education that was built around highly focused, often playful intellectual discovery in the classroom, seasoned with constant bursts of outdoor play. Walking through my son's school one day, I saw a fourth-grade class engrossed in building robots from kits. Small teams of children gathered around instruction charts on desktop screens, then got on the floor on their hands and knees to collaborate in the complex task of assembling wheeled micro-robots that can talk, move, and play music. Their teacher, Jussi Hietava, explained that the children were learning not only critical science and technology (or STEM) skills, they were building skills needed in teamwork, leadership, negotiation, and managing trial-and-error.

In stark contrast to some "no excuses" schools in American inner cities, where low-income students are subjected to prison-style behavioral control and forbidden to talk without permission, to walk in uneven lines, or even to unlock the gaze of their eyes from the teacher's face, these children were expected to giggle, wiggle, and squirm from time to time, since that's what children (especially boys) are biologically engineered to do, in Finland and everywhere else. These children were laughing and having a wonderful time and appeared totally immersed in a state of "flow," or creative and productive absorption.

"They are having fun while they learn," said teacher Hietava. "Why not? They are children!"[300]

The emotional climate of the classroom was warm, safe, respectful, and highly supportive. One Chinese trainee-teacher studying at the university marveled to me, "In Chinese schools, you feel like you're in the military. Here, you feel like you're part of a really nice family."[301] She was trying to figure out how she could stay in Finland permanently.

Standing off to the side of the science class, teacher Hietava said this was one of his best moments as a teacher, because the children were largely on their own, fulfilling the main purpose of education: "They are learning how to learn. By themselves. Right now, they don't need me!"[302]

At the end of the robot-building session, which was, in effect, a period of "guided, playful discovery," with the teacher gently overseeing the process while the students worked largely on their own, the children were turned loose into the freezing ice and snow of the schoolyard for their mandatory hourly 15 minutes of outdoor free play, a physical activity break that Finnish educators believe boosts children's learning, concentration, executive function, and behavior, as well as their mental and physical well-being. Unlike in the United States, where many schools were slashing recess, schoolchildren in Finland have a 15-minute outdoor free-play break every single hour of every school day, no matter how cold or wet the weather is. The children go outside to play even when it's as cold as 5 degrees Fahrenheit (or −15 in Celsius scale). Below that, they still play, but it may be moved indoors.

After the outdoor free-play break, the children raced back into the school building energized and in a state of joy, refreshed and ready for their next activity. Like few other countries on Earth, Finland understands that constant exposure to physical activity, and nature, and fresh-air play, and an emotionally warm, collaborative teacher–student relationship are among the most basic foundations of childhood learning and well-being.

Just as Harvard's Howard Gardner had predicted to me, this was the land of education opposites, a bizzaro-land that achieved excellent results at greater efficiency (and probably much happier and healthier children) than most other school systems, by doing the reverse of what many other nations were doing. Here, fresh air, nature, and regular physical activity breaks were considered engines of learning that improve almost all the "metrics" that matter most for children in school—including cognitive focus, behavior, well-being, attendance, and physical health. According to one Finnish maxim, "There is no bad weather. Only inadequate clothing." One night, I asked my son what he did for gym that day. "They sent us into the woods with a map and compass," he replied matter-of-factly, "and we had to find our way out." A teacher in a bright safety smock was in the woods with them to observe at a distance and keep things safe, but they were learning the science and sport of "orienteering" on their own, at ages 7 and 8.

The atmosphere of play and joy extended to the school's regular daily lunch period (a nutritious hot lunch is provided to all Finnish children free of charge) when I witnessed children racing to the cafeteria in their stocking feet, laughing, hugging, practicing dance steps and cavorting. One girl did a full handstand in the hallway. A distinguished-looking professor beamed at the procession and doled out high-fives to the children. He was Heikki Happonen, principal of the school and a career childhood educator. As chief of Finland's association of eight national university teacher training schools, he was, in effect, the Master Teacher of Finland.

As the children raced by, a beaming Happonen explained to me that the hallway scene revealed one of the secrets of Finland's historic success in childhood education. "To play is very important for adults and children. There are many reasons children must play in school. When they are moving their brains work better. Then they concentrate more in class. It's very important in social ways too. They are negotiating, socializing, building teams and friendships together."

"School should be a child's favorite place," said Happonen. "Children must feel like their school is a home for them, it belongs to them. They are very clever, they feel and appreciate an atmosphere of trust. We offer them an environment where they understand, 'This is a place where I am highly respected. I feel safe and comfortable here. I am a very important person.' My job is to protect that environment for children. That's why I come to work every day."

Happonen designed much of the Nordic-modern school building himself, a network of traditional classrooms linked by spacious hallways, cinematic soft lighting and warm colors, a palatial (by American standards) teachers' lounge for coffee and collaboration (complete with a nearby sauna for teachers), and comfortable scattered nooks, crannies, and couches for children to relax and curl up in with a buddy or a book. Connecting all the pieces, flanked by the high-tech science lab, a fireplace, and plush sofas, was a modular, wide-open library of books and magazines for children to enjoy. It was the focal point of the school. On a recent visit, a teacher from Spain was speechless, on the verge of tears after a few minutes inside the school. "It's so beautiful," she said. "In Spain, our schools feel like prisons. But this—this is like a dream." Upon hearing of this story, one Finnish teacher quipped, "Maybe our motto should be 'come to Finland and cry.'"

In his principal's office, Happonen pointed to a colorful assortment of hand-carved wooden boats mounted on his office wall, featuring different shapes, sizes, and types of vessels. "I saw those boats in a shop," he recalled. "They were so beautiful. I decided I had to buy them, but I didn't know why. I put them up on my office wall so I could see them all day."

"Then I realized what they are," he continued. "They are children. They represent the fact that all children are different, they start from different destinations and travel on different journeys. Our job as teachers is to help children navigate their journeys through storms and adventures, so they move safely and successfully into society and the world. My job is to protect that environment for children. That's why I come to work every day."[303]

I learned that in Finland, as in other Nordic nations, play is "baked in" to children's education from the very start, as it is throughout the culture. Preschools and kindergartens are strongly play-based, and children learn through games, songs, outdoor play, conversation, and hands-on exploration. Formal academic teaching in math and languages is not introduced until children are 7 years old, when most children are ready to smoothly "decode" language and math and begin exploring and mastering various subjects.

Unlike in many other countries, Finnish parents favor a full, enjoyable period of childhood rather than an earlier start of formal learning. Childhood is, they say, the time when children discover the world within them while learning how to be with other children.[304]

Finland's new National Core Curriculum for Early Childhood Education and Care and National Core Curriculum for Basic Education, launched nationwide in August 2016, emphasized each child's individuality, and declared that "children have the right to learn by playing and experience joy related to learning." It said that children should be encouraged to express their opinions, trust themselves, be open to new solutions, learn to handle unclear and conflicting information, consider things from different viewpoints, seek new information, and review the way they think. Teachers were directed to give students daily feedback and measure them against their starting points, not versus other students. These new national core curricula were broad frameworks to guide local planning and teaching, were based on research and evidence, and were developed by educators, with lots of input from parents and children.

Finland's education vision could hardly be less like the one that politicians were imposing on public schools in the United States, England, and elsewhere. In fact, in a startling departure from the prevailing wisdom in other school systems, Finnish teachers were expressly forbidden to measure students' academic performance versus that of other children—the teacher's job is to assess each child's individual growth. Under the new guidelines, in grades 1 through 7, schools were now given the option of reducing the reliance on "data" even more, by dropping numerical or symbolic grades in favor of narrative feedback and formative assessments. Failing students still receive a "fail" grade and can be held back as a last resort.

Living inside the Finnish education system as a public school father and university lecturer, and after talking to scores of my own Finnish graduate students who grew up in that system, it became increasingly clear to me that while having a relatively homogeneous culture helps, the main reason for the success of Finland's schools is not mainly because they are ethnically or culturally Finnish, but because they are correctly organized and supported by society. A whole-child-centered, evidence-informed, and values-based school system, run by highly professionalized teachers and school principals committed to child and teacher well-being, and energized by play, are global education best practices, not cultural quirks applicable only to Finland.

Critically, average class size in Finnish elementary schools is close to 20, versus, for example, a typical class size of 30 or more in New York City public schools. Classes involving lab equipment or machinery, like metal shop, wood shop, sewing and cooking (mandatory for all seventh-graders), must be no larger than 16. With such small class sizes, and with especially strong and early special education interventions, academic "tracking" is considered unnecessary until the tenth grade in Finland.

Finland has a truly inspiring education system, and relative to other nations, Finland arguably has the highest quality and most effective childhood education system in the world, but its schools are far from perfect, and they face major problems and challenges, including budget cutbacks, increasing immigration and diversity, a rapid decline in boy's reading skills in recent years, social pressures, student disengagement from school, and coping with the rapid digitalization of society.[305] Some of Finland's educational strengths may in fact be culture-specific and hard to replicate quickly in other nations. However, Finland's size and demographics are roughly similar to some two-thirds of American states, and education policy in the United States is largely managed at the state and local levels. Finland's schools are the product of a unique culture. But so are the public schools of any other nation.

When my son's surprisingly short school day was over at 1:30 or 2:00 P.M., he made his way across town to a community after-school club, as many Finnish children do. At the club, the children have a snack, catch up with homework, play sports, or go to the library together, but much of the afternoon was devoted to outdoor free play in the backyard. One dark winter afternoon, they spent the whole time bundled up outside playing together in freezing rain, making mud-pies and snowpeople and digging up dirt with sticks. By the end of the day when I came to pick him up, my delighted son was covered in a thick coating of freezing mud. In New York City, I thought, many children this age were sitting at desks all morning and afternoon, or involved in frenetic schedules of multiple high-pressure after-school activities like Mandarin lessons, coding class, hockey practice, and violin lessons. But for an 8-year-old child, I thought, freezing-mud-play might be just as good as any "enrichment class." And maybe a bit more fun.

When I visited Finnish kindergartens, I was surprised that I did not see any teachers or caregivers focusing on formal academic material, as is done in early education in the United States and many other nations. Instead, I saw children learning to become independent in their daily routines, getting along with each other, valuing one another's company, enjoying arts and music, and playing. Children were learning language and basic math concepts, not through drilling and worksheets, but through singing, games, conversations with loving teachers, and hands-on play. The Finnish Law on Early Childhood Education stipulates that the aim of early education, among other things, is to "carry out diverse pedagogical activities based on play, physical activity, artistic and cultural heritage, and enable positive learning experiences." In other words, play is an essential child's right in Finland. Authorities are responsible to make sure that this right is respected in kindergartens and schools around the country.

How did Finland become such a child- and family-friendly nation? When they were recently asked that same question by a delegation of American visitors, two female members of the Finnish Parliament looked at each other and said simultaneously, "Because of us!"[306] They explained how strong representation of women in politics had led to better overall solutions, especially for families, children, and mothers. They explained how many of the key pieces of legislation since the late 1980s have been initiated by legislators who are women, such as the 1986 Finnish

Law on Gender Equality, which requires that in committees, councils, task forces, and other public sector bodies representation of both women and men must be at least 40 percent. All Nordic countries have similar gender equality regulations, universal parental leave and child care systems, public policies that guarantee equal access to high-quality early childhood education, and completely state-funded public education systems, including higher education. In the 2017 UNICEF Report Card[307] on how developed nations meet the needs of their children, the Nordic nations dominated each of the top five national rankings, while the United States ranked 37th of 41 participating countries. New Zealand was 33rd, Canada 25th, Australia 21st, and the United Kingdom 13th.

In another international survey, the World Economic Forum's Global Gender Gap Report (2018),[308] comparing women's economic participation and opportunity, educational attainment, health, and political empowerment, the Nordics (except Denmark at 13th) again dominated the top five ranks in 149 countries of the world, while the United States was 51st, Australia 39th, Canada 16th, United Kingdom 15th, and New Zealand 7th. And in the 2015 Save the Children's annual "State of the World's Mothers" report on women's health, children's health, educational attainment, economic well-being, and well-being, Finland and the Nordics again dominated the top slots in the "Mothers' Index." Of 179 countries, the United States was 33rd, United Kingdom 24th, Canada 20th, New Zealand 17th, and Australia 9th. These rankings suggest that the countries that give a priority to families and children's well-being and education seem to have a smaller gender gap.

The best nations in the world to be a mother and child— Finland, Norway, Sweden, Iceland, the Netherlands, and Denmark—have at least two things in common: they have passed the 40 percent threshold of women in political power in the national parliament or legislature, and their education systems have shared values, including a traditional foundation of learning through play (Figure 5). It might be that the more women a nation has in political power, the more it understands the need for children to play. Interestingly, 10 percent of the members of the 2018 Finnish Parliament have backgrounds in the teaching profession.

As a nation, Finland has also achieved one of the world's highest levels of educational equity, meaning that students' socioeconomic status has little impact on how well they learn in school. Equity is high on the agenda in all successful school systems. A focus on equity means to give high priority to universal early childhood programs, comprehensive health and special education services in all schools, and a balanced curriculum that has equal weight in arts, music, and physical activity, and academic subjects. Fairness in resource allocation is the key to educational equity because schools that cater to larger numbers of children with diverse educational needs also require more funds per student to help all students succeed.

Of all the developed nations, Finland, building on its childhood education foundations of learning through play and teacher professionalism, has achieved one of the best combinations of both educational equity and high achievement scores on the OECD's international benchmark tests, which are admittedly an imperfect, but informative measurement (Figure 6). The progression to

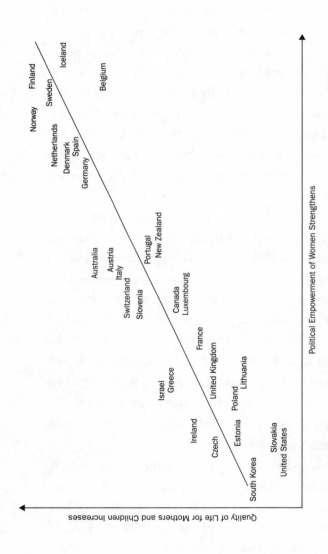

Figure 5. Mother and Child Quality of Life Rises with Women's Political Empowerment. Finland, like other Nordic nations, scores at the top of best places to be a mother and child, and nations with the most politically empowered women. More than many other nations, these countries also understand the power of play in childhood and school.

Data from Save the Children (2016) and World Economic Forum (2016).

Source: Authors.

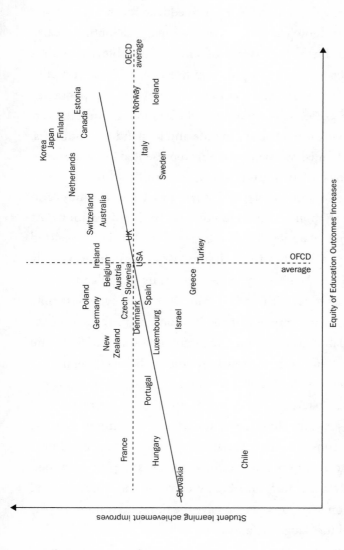

Figure 6. Educational Equity and Quality of Learning Outcomes in OECD Countries. Finland, together with Canada, Estonia and Japan are education systems considered to be high-performing both in terms of academic learning and in the system-wide equity of these outcomes.

Source: OECD, authors.

the highest levels of world leadership in equity and excellence can be viewed as a theoretical "stairway to educational heaven," along with peers including Canada, Japan, Estonia, and South Korea.[309]

From its birth, the nation of Finland was blessed with a striking advantage—the rights and needs of women and children were "baked in" to the culture ever since its independence a century ago. Finnish women were the first in the world to exercise full political rights both to vote and to stand as candidates, and today, Finnish women are highly represented in a wide range of professions. Women are, in effect, nearly full partners in power in many sectors of society, and this translates into family- and child-friendly policies that are common in Nordic nations. At the dawn of the modern Finland Experiment, the nation realized that giving a good start to all children would benefit everybody later on. Since 1949 every expectant family in Finland has received a maternity visit and a "Baby Box" package containing all the basic baby care essentials. Responding to the success of Finland's Baby Box program, some states in the United States are now offering similar boxes free to mothers who need them.

After a child's birth, Finnish families benefit from strong parental leave policies. A child home care allowance is paid until the child is 3 years old if one of the parents is at home with the child. One consequence of these policies is that many of a child's early memories are of long periods of time, and play, with their parents—relaxed, safe, and happy exploration, discovery, and conversation with parents who have the time and support to play with their little daughters and sons.

What happens to children and their families before day one of primary school has a significant impact on children's education later on, and as American economist and Nobel Prize laureate James Heckman declared in 2011, "It is imperative to change the way we look at education. We should invest in the foundation of school readiness from birth to age 5."[310] In a 2012 report by the *Economist* magazine, Finland was awarded the #1 national ranking for preschool education.[311] One American visitor, early childhood educator Erika Christakis, explained when she visited Finland, "I've found it impossible to remain unmoved by the example of preschools where the learning environment is assessed, rather than the children in it. Having rejected many of the pseudo-academic benchmarks that can, and do, fit on a scorecard, preschool teachers in Finland are free to focus on what's really essential: their relationship with the growing child."[312]

In a cultural tradition widely shared in Nordic countries, many Finnish parents agree that age 7 is about the right time for children to go to formal primary school.[313] Before that, children should attend day care and kindergarten, learn to enjoy life, learn to be with one another, learn about themselves, and learn to play, indoors and outdoors, in all but the most severe kinds of weather. In the process, they learn the basics of reading, speaking, and math concepts, in a relaxed, natural, and effective way.

Finland's rankings in PISA tests have slipped in recent years. In many other countries, politicians and bureaucrats would have pushed the panic button and declared a state of emergency. Common remedies would most likely have included teachers being penalized more for inferior standardized test data, and more academic pressure on children. But Finland didn't do this. Instead, educators and government officials did something almost unheard of in the world of education reform. They talked to children. They then realized that one of the big overall problems was a lack of student engagement in schools and the fact that children feel their voices are not heard when it comes to their own learning and lives in school.

Finnish authorities, together with teachers and parents, decided to improve elementary schools with more outdoor play and physical activity, more interdisciplinary learning, more interesting lessons, and more real-life classroom exercises, all with the goal of making school more engaging and interesting to students. In Finland's new national core curriculum for early childhood education and care, there is a sharper focus on teaching children practical life skills and developing habits of mind that will help them to become successful lifelong learners, not on early literacy and numeracy as other nations would have done. For decades, Finland has been conducting what is in effect a national experiment in the power of play, and it's working so well that they're doubling down on it.

In late November, when the first snow of winter came to my part of Finland, I heard a loud commotion outside my faculty office window, which was close to the teacher training school's outdoor play area, with the view blocked by trees. It was the sound of children screaming. Thinking something terrible must be happening, I rushed over to investigate.

It was at the 45 minutes-past-the-hour mark, when all school children in the entire nation of Finland enjoy their guaranteed hourly 15 minutes recess of outdoor free play, which translates to three or four "mini-recesses" per day. The field was filled with young children savoring the first taste of winter amid the pine and spruce trees. They were screaming in delight as the snow piled up. My own son was out there somewhere, but the children were so buried in winter clothes and moving so fast that I couldn't spot him.

The racket of children laughing, shouting, and singing as they slipped and tumbled in the fresh ice and snow was close to deafening.

Looking on was the recess monitor, a special education teacher wearing a yellow safety smock. Like all primary school teachers in Finland, she was trained as a clinical specialist in education, with a master's degree focusing on childhood education research and classroom practice. She was, in effect, a clinically trained educational researcher and practitioner, as all Finnish teachers are, and probably every teacher in the world should be.

"Do you hear that?" she asked through the noise.

"That," she noted proudly, "is the voice of happiness."

A few days later, I joined my son on his morning walk through the dark, freezing woods to the school. When the lights of the school came into view, he said, "Every child should have a school like this."

"You know," I said, "maybe you're right."

THE NORTH TEXAS TRIPLE-RECESS EXPERIMENT

Five thousand miles away from Finland, a woman named Debbie Rhea was launching her own experiment in outdoor play in Fort Worth, Texas.

Rhea is a professor and associate dean of research in the Harris College of Nursing and Health Sciences at Texas Christian

University. Her academic focus is kinesiology, the study of human movement. For years, she had been fascinated by the wide body of research suggesting that physical activity can enhance academic performance in children.

One day, Professor Rhea read about the strong educational results that Finland achieved, while guaranteeing a 15-minute recess break to every school child, every single hour of the school day, all the way to high school. Intrigued, she made a 6-week sabbatical pilgrimage in 2012 to Helsinki and Jyväskylä, where she visited schools and playgrounds and witnessed the strange, beautiful national symphony of thousands of children bursting out of their classrooms at the 45-minute mark every hour, racing around or relaxing in the outdoor play areas, then racing back inside to plunge into their next lesson. After the recess breaks, the children seemed happy, refreshed, and energized, not only through the morning but well into the afternoon, when it can be notoriously difficult for children to absorb academic concepts and stay focused and energized.

The typical Texan schoolchild might get a single 15- to 20-minute recess per day, plus some brief in-classroom stretches, or "brain breaks." "That's not enough for kids. They're not built that way," Rhea thought. Recess, she believed, "reboots the system so that when they go back in [to class], they're ready to learn, they're focused." Children in Finland, with four or five 15-minute recesses spread through the school day, were getting at least triple the recess many American children were getting.[314] On top of regular recess, every child in Finland is offered 1 hour of physical activity during the school day. Finnish Schools on the Move[315] is a national action program aiming to strengthen the physical-activity culture of Finnish elementary schools. Since its inauguration in 2010, now more than 90 percent of municipalities and 80 percent of basic schools ranging from grades 1 to 9 in over 2,000 schools are involved in the program.

When she returned to the United States, Professor Rhea decided to launch an experiment modeled on the Finnish approach to recess. Her reasoning was straightforward: American children have experienced little improvement in reading, math, and science scores over the past two decades, and as a result, a troubling shift toward increased classroom time had occurred at the expense of both unstructured play and recess, and physical education. As the Association for Childhood Education International has put it, "The sad irony of the testing era is that our zeal to improve children's academic performance has led to a decline in children's health, and childhood obesity rates have risen to dangerously high rates. Paradoxically, some of the school policies adopted to help improve test scores may reduce children's chances of performing well by contributing to their ill health."[316]

In a 2016 report published in the *British Journal of Sports Medicine*, a global panel of 24 researchers pointed out the academic benefits of activities that get children moving, like recess: "Physical activity before, during and after school promotes scholastic performance in children and youth," the specialists asserted. "Even a single break for moderate-intensity exercise can boost "brain function, cognition and scholastic performance," they added. "Time taken away from academic lessons in favor of physical activity has been shown to not come at the cost of scholastic performance."[317]

Despite this clear consensus among many researchers and health authorities, Rhea knew that recess was being routinely eliminated or reduced for millions of children in America and around the world, children who were being forcibly confined all day in desolate indoor school environments and denied some of the most essential ingredients of childhood—regular doses of fresh air, open sky, the joy of movement, and unstructured, outdoor free play and socialization with other children—without interference from adults.

As Rhea and her colleagues wrote in a research paper, "when students are required to remain seated for much of the seven hours they are in school, many negative behaviors occur, which teachers then attribute to bad children instead of lack of physical activity and cognitive breaks."[318] These negative behaviors trigger more of the same in a vicious cycle—punishment in the form of withholding recess and more sitting in a chair. Recess based on free play, Rhea believed, was a critical right for developing children, because it provides cognitive, social, and emotional health benefits and gives them a chance to recharge, imagine, think, move, and socialize.

As Rhea thought about how to adapt the Finnish recess model to American schools, she saw a problem. Finnish primary schools do something that is difficult for American public schools to do—they teach religious or ethics lessons to all children in public schools. Finnish children are given lessons in empathy, compassion, and morality, and these are things that might, in combination with physical activity, also contribute to good recess behavior, good classroom behavior, and academic achievement. Her solution was to incorporate a well-respected character development program for children called "Positive Action" as part of her experiment. The Positive Action component consisted of four brief lessons per week that avoided specific religious instruction but stressed compassion, respect, empathy, the "Golden Rule," conflict resolution, and cooperation.

Rhea made her provocative, seemingly counterintuitive pitch—more recess equals better learning—to several Texas school principals and district superintendents, arguing that in a time when many schools were cutting back or eliminating recess to make room for more academics, they should do the opposite. To improve achievement, she contended, they should triple recess from 20 minutes each day to 15 minutes per hour four times a day like Finland does, spread the recesses through the school day, assure that the recesses consist of unstructured, outdoor free play (not structured sports and gym classes, which are given separately), and enhance the effect with the Finland-style ethics and character development lessons.

"I started the program because I was tired of seeing students burn out by third grade, teachers burn out in 5 years, and schools that focused primarily on testing from the time children entered in pre-K or K all the way through high school," Rhea explains. "We're at the point today where we are concentrated on the outcomes of a test score and not as much about the health and well-being of our kids," she said. "We've got to change this pattern." Rhea explained, "We keep thinking as adults that we need to control the way they [children] do things. I wish we'd get out of that. They know how to play, they know how to structure their own play, and they need that time to grow responsibly. That builds their confidence. That builds self-esteem. That builds resilience." Regular bursts of recess, Rhea believed, would meet the typical child's need for movement, reset the child's attention-span "clock," and provide the mental rest needed for a young child to then focus and actively participate in learning.[319]

After seeing Rhea's presentation, an initial two Texas private school principals signed up enthusiastically. The LiiNK Project (for "Let's Inspire Innovation in Kids") started as a pilot in the 2013–2014 school year with four schools in Texas—with half using the program and half not, to serve as "control" schools for comparison.

The initial results of the program were so promising that by the fall of 2017, the experiment had expanded to encompass 20 public and private schools in six independent school districts (ISDs) in Texas and Oklahoma. In the 2017–2018 school year, some 8,000 primary school children were part of the LiiNK program, and another 8,000 were in comparison schools that did not feature the LiiNK intervention. Over time, schools have been gradually expanding the program upward through the grades to reach kindergarteners through eighth-graders. The LiiNK schools serve both poor children and more affluent children of a variety of ethnicities, in urban, rural, and suburban settings in areas like Fort Worth, Irving, and Arlington, Texas. Today, thousands of students from middle- and low-income backgrounds in these ethnically diverse schools are being given more recess than almost any other group of schoolchildren in the United States, a nation where recess has been widely slashed and even eliminated.

So far, the early results of Professor Rhea's LiiNK experiment are so impressive, and so rapid, that the project may have the potential to trigger something close to a miracle in American education—more recess for children. In just the few years the program has been in effect, participating educators are reporting a striking series of effects after these constant doses of unstructured, outdoor free play.

According to Rhea, across all of the "LiiNKed" schools, students "on-task behaviors" improved by 30 percent or more. Writing skills have advanced by at least 6 months in a single year. Empathy and social behaviors (like demonstrating the ability to think before acting) improved dramatically. Classroom misbehavior is dropping. Students' listening, decision-making, and problem-solving abilities are improving. Teachers report that students are more productive, less fidgety, and more focused; they listen more attentively, follow directions, and try to solve problems on their own instead of coming to the teacher to fix everything. There are fewer discipline and bullying issues. Classroom behaviors and attentional focus have seen double-digit improvements. Teachers estimate that the intervention has speeded up learning by months.

In an academic article Rhea and her colleagues published about the experience of one private school with a pilot study of the LiiNK intervention implemented over a 4-month period (using 45 total minutes of daily recess rather than 60), the researchers reported that children were more disciplined and focused in the classroom, they were better behaved, and "academic performance on reading and math significantly increased."

The bottom-line conclusion is something that any child in the world could tell you: More recess equals happier, healthier, and better-learning children. This is recess defined as unstructured, outdoor free play, organized and enjoyed strictly by children, with adults on the sidelines to provide safety when necessary—not structured physical education or organized gym classes, which often reward just the most athletic children and can involve a lot of standing-around time for the rest of the children.

You might think that sharply boosting children's outdoor, free-play recess time would create a series of bloody schoolyard accidents and parental lawsuits. However, the opposite is happening. In these lucky Texas and Oklahoma schools, elementary school children of all races, ages, and income groups are running around their school play areas more—but injuries, scrapes and bruises are actually going down. The children are simply getting more skilled at safely managing their own movements. "What I've noticed about my boys and girls this year," reported a kindergarten teacher at a LiiNK school with a high proportion of lower-income students and ethnic diversity, "is they are just so much stronger than my previous years. I've taught kindergarten for 18 years. You know how you see boys and girls just trip and fall over their own feet? I don't see that anymore. They have a lot more flexibility and a lot more stamina. Another thing: When I start teaching a subject, it's funny, in years past they go, 'Oh no, I don't want to write now' or, 'it's time to read?' I don't have that now. They love to write."

At Saginaw Elementary School, a Title 1 (lower-income) school near Fort Worth, Texas, in a school district called Eagle Mountain-Saginaw, Principal Amber Beene signed her school on to the LiiNK experiment for the 2016–2017 school year because she said her administration was "constantly looking at research-based practices that can assist in closing the academic achievement gap for our students." She explained to us, "I was intrigued by the academic and behavioral benefits, but the psychological benefits—improving emotional resiliency, increasing imagination and creativity, and promoting the development of self-confidence—were the most compelling. Many of our students have family, social, or economic circumstances that hinder their ability to learn at school. If there was a program that could assist our students in closing the achievement gap, while also building social and emotional skills, increasing creativity, and reducing off-task behavior, we needed to provide this opportunity for our students." Principal Beene had a special interest in the program because her daughter was in kindergarten during the 2016–2017 school year and participated in the school's first year of LiiNK implementation.

In her Texas public school, the effects of the program were rapid and significant. Principal Beene reported:

Prior to the 2016–2017 school year, my kindergarten and first grade teachers had to frequently stop instruction for "brain breaks." The number of students off-task was so high that the teachers needed to provide a quick break to refocus them. By the afternoon, the "brain breaks" were not enough to re-engage the students. It appeared as though the majority of the class had difficulty focusing, paying attention, or attending to a task for a set period of time. With the LiiNK Project, no matter what time of the school day I visit the classroom, the number of students off-task [exhibiting behavior not connected to the classroom assignment] is now minimal and limited to the students with true attention, behavioral, or emotional difficulties.

The story of one first-grade girl illustrates the powerful package of benefits. Beene explained:

One of my first-grade teachers met with a parent at the beginning of the school year. The parent was extremely concerned about her daughter. The little girl had major issues with her behavior in kindergarten and this behavior led to academic difficulties as well. When the parent and teacher met again in November, the parent remarked, "It's like she is a different child." The off-task behavior was eliminated. The acting out was eliminated. The student was able to focus and actively participate in the learning opportunities provided her. By the end of the year, the student was on grade level academically as well. By providing the student with age-appropriate, unstructured breaks throughout the day, the problematic behavior was reduced and the behaviors interfering with her academics were mitigated.

At first, the principal was concerned about her school's shortage of playground equipment, and by the fact that some of the breaks had to take place on an empty field.

With no sporting equipment available, what would the students do? I was delighted to see the creativity emerge in our students. To my amazement, I watched students create new games, chase butterflies, dig in the dirt, hollow out a dead tree, and search for rocks, bugs, and leaves. The field has sparked a curiosity about the outdoors and fostered new, or one might say old, kinds of natural play. While Dr. Rhea had mentioned an increase in creativity and play with unstructured recess, it was remarkable to see it unfold in real time with our students.

Principal Beene saw dramatic effects with her own kindergarten-age daughter, effects that she credits to the LiiNK program of multiple recesses combined with character development. Through regular outdoor play, her daughter has fallen in love with the outdoors and developed curiosity and creativity. "Every evening I have to empty my daughter's pockets because they are full of leaves, rocks, acorns, and feathers she has gathered," Beene marveled.

Each day the collection grows. We finally had to put a box in the garage to store all of the "treasures" found at recess. Second, my daughter has developed a fearlessness that was not there before. Due to the unstructured nature of recess, the students witness one another taking risks—navigating monkey bars, climbing poles, jumping off structures. This leads to a willingness to try these challenges for themselves. On a recent family trip to Colorado, my daughter leapt at the opportunity to try a ropes course and zip lining. I do not believe she would have had the confidence to try these activities without her experience in the LiiNK Project. I have also observed a significant improvement in her physical stamina and strength outside of school in recreational soccer, gymnastics, and swimming. When other children seem to tire towards the end of a game, she is noticeably more active and successful than she had been in previous seasons.

At another lower-income, ethnically diverse public school, Elkins Elementary School in nearby Saginaw, Texas, first-grade teacher Kendra Niven reported an unexpected benefit of LiiNK Project—the disappearance of the "helicopter teacher." She explained, "Prior to LiiNK, recess duty included solving disputes among students, preventing students from jumping out of swings or off equipment and reminding them repeatedly that, they might get hurt if they did this or that. We were helicopter teachers, often warning of what might happen and stopping children from self-discovery. Students are now taking chances and discovering what they truly can do! Teachers are no longer solving these little problems, running to the rescue to make sure they are comfortable. Students are learning to take care of their needs." She added, "What I love most about LiiNK is that kids are able to be KIDS!"

The benefits to children, according to Niven, flow through recess directly into the classroom and academics.

During recess, I have observed children exploring with soil, sticks, bugs, grass, shadows, and rocks. They have invented new games with these items as well. Some children have built habitats for insects, practiced the weathering process, and discovered shadows, all while sharing their findings with peers. I have witnessed children teaching peers about the weathering process, shadows, habitats, force and motion, and measurement during their breaks. In turn, I have noticed a tremendous change in my students' writing. They are now able to write stories that are more creative. They are using their imagination to take characters they have invented on wonderful adventures. Many kiddos return to class sweaty, wearing flowers in their hair, sporting a little dirt under their nails, or even a little mud on their shoes. It is okay for our room, students, and even us, the teachers, to be a little untidy during the school day. My kids are overall happier and more creative in the classroom. They are now interacting with students in other classes and able to return to class, after a short break, more focused and alert. They really start to crave that downtime in order to reboot their bodies and brains, for optimal learning. One of the most impressive outcomes from LiiNK is that children take what they are learning academically and apply it during recess. Classroom life has also changed since LiiNK. I spend less time redirecting students and managing behavior, which means more time to teach. When children return to class, they are more focused, alert and ready to jump back into the activity they were working on, prior to the break.

Also near Fort Worth, at the Eagle Mountain Elementary School, Principal Bryan McLain thought that the idea of giving more recess made a lot of sense, since "kids aren't hard-wired to sit still all day." The results are in his words, "impressive." By giving the proper, higher doses of recess, he said, "we are giving children back their childhood." One result of allowing children more time for recess, reports McLain, has been higher-quality instructional time, "because the kids come back in and settle down and get to work because they know they will receive another recess before long." He added, "Our teachers and parents have completely embraced it, and I haven't had a single parent complaint about it," he said. He added, "I can't say enough about how pleased we are with the results we are seeing."

For Debbie Clark, principal of public Oak Point Elementary School in Little Elm, the LiiNK Project is the "glue" that links all the school's learning strategies together to successfully educate the whole child—and maximize their academic success. "Allowing students to have frequent breaks provides time for their brains to 'refocus,' so that when they return to the classroom, they can access meaningful learning that endures," Principal Clark asserted. "The physical activity is linked to longer attention spans, which maximizes the teacher's ability to engage her students. Recess is not just a break but an opportunity for learning. During the unstructured recess, students are thinking, creating, and problem-solving. It improves their social skills and self-confidence. They become more resilient to stress. Overall, our students are more on task throughout the day and less fidgety. They are performing better academically and are more physically fit." She concluded, "Besides the obvious health benefits of additional recess, I believe frequent unstructured recesses promote positive socialization and peer interactions. This in turn improves our school's climate. Students are improving their communication and problem-solving skills. These are critical life skills needed on a daily basis for home, school and future workplace."

It is, at first glance, a paradox: Less time in class means higher-quality learning, if you pump up the recess. Principal Doug Sevier of Little Elm ISD's school Chavez Elementary said some teachers were originally worried about the shift. "To say we're actually going to get more out of kids with less time in the classroom is something that just doesn't make sense," Sevier said. "But the teachers started to realize that the kids actually come back more engaged. Instead of losing time, they're actually gaining instructional time just because of the increased focus of the kids coming back in."

The "North Texas Experiment" is in its early stages, but its founder, Debbie Rhea, has grand ambitions for it. "I truly believe with all my heart that this is the wave of the future," she predicted, and in 30 years, she believes, four recesses a day will be the norm in schools across the United States. "We won't know anything different. Our kids will be happy again. They will be thriving. They won't be anxious. And our teachers will be happy, too; they won't be having breakdowns because they aren't getting to do what they thought they were going to be doing when they went into education."

Debbie Rhea reminds us that "although these changes are wonderful, they don't come easy. Due to test scores still being at the top of the requirements, teachers feel really stressed in the first year of this change. This project doesn't happen without sufficient training on new policies and procedures needed to implement this project prior to launching the changes." Just adding the recesses daily is not enough. "Schools don't stay with the recess and positive action additions without our support and guidance over time," Rhea concludes.

This is play in its most powerful form—a virtually no-cost, low-tech intervention that can sharply boost children's learning and healthy development.

"It's a huge change in the kids, they're happy, they're focused and they're more active,"[320] said Jessica Cassel, a sixth-grade teacher at a LiiNK school in rural Chattanooga, Oklahoma.

"It all sounds too good to be true, doesn't it?" asked the teacher. "It's not. It's wonderful."

THE LONG ISLAND PLAY REVOLUTION

In 2015, a school district in New York State declared an educational revolution.

Teachers and parents decided to rise up and liberate their schools and their children—by giving them more play.

The revolution erupted at the Patchogue-Medford district on Long Island, which serves 8,700 K–12 students, over half of whom are economically disadvantaged, and it is being led by Michael Hynes, the athletic, passionate young district superintendent. He realized that federal education schemes based on the compulsory mass standardized testing of children, schemes like No Child Left Behind and Race to the Top were proven failures, and he figured it was time to try something new, even radical.

Hynes started following his students around through their typical day and was increasingly alarmed to realize how little recess, play, and self-directed time they got. "We have done a great job of stripping away childhood from our children," he thought. "We tell kids what to do from the moment they wake up in the morning until they go to bed. They don't have the ability to take time for themselves, just be kids, to make decisions for themselves."

He remembered his own childhood, and how different things were when he started as an elementary school teacher in the 1990s. "My students were free to play often," Hynes recalled. "I loved watching them benefit physically, emotionally and socially. We would go outside three times a day." A single idea began to dominate his thinking: "Kids must be free to play in school. Childhood itself is at stake. I am sworn to protect children, and I must give this to them."

For years, Hynes had read about the striking successes of Finland's school system, and its strong foundation of play in childhood education. It gave him an inspiring idea, and he presented it to his community. And with the strong support of his school board and local parents, Hynes and his team took a series of steps almost unheard of in American public education today, steps that for some politicians and bureaucrats would be shocking, even downright dangerous, and nothing less than pure blasphemy. They doubled daily recess from 20 minutes to 40 minutes and encouraged children to go outside even in the rain and snow. They brought building blocks, Lincoln logs, toys, and kitchen sets back into the classrooms. They gave each child a 40-minute lunch. They added optional periods of yoga and mindfulness training for K–8 children. They launched an unstructured Play Club for kindergarten through fifth-grade children, every Friday morning from 8:00 A.M. to 9:15 A.M.

They opened "Divergent Thinking Rooms" filled with big foam blocks, where children can negotiate, plan, innovate, collaborate, and construct new worlds of design and architecture together, free from adult interference. A free breakfast program in classrooms was started so children and teachers could eat together every morning. The amount of homework was sharply reduced. Hynes calls the program "PEAS": *P*hysical growth, *E*motional growth, *A*cademic growth, and *S*ocial growth. It has nothing to do with technology. During the play periods there isn't a tablet, laptop, or desktop in use.

In 2018, Hynes sent a letter to his district, informing teachers and students that they were more than a score on a government-imposed standardized test, and they should feel free to toss such test scores in the trash. "We must abandon one-size-fits-all lesson plans and stop drilling to create high scores on year-end standardized tests," he argued. "Instead, children should be involved in play, project-based learning, cooperation, collaboration, and open-ended inquiry."

Based on the available research, Hynes was also no fan of making younger students do schoolwork at home at night. "There is zero evidence, and I mean zero, that there is any correlation between academic achievement and homework for elementary school kids,"[321] Hynes told one journalist. Now, the recommended evening activity for children in his district is to play outside, spend time with friends and family, and read books for a half-hour before going to bed.

When he first proposed that recess time be doubled, Hynes told us, some of his elementary school principals were very concerned, even scared. "They wondered if I'd lost my mind," he recalled. Some teachers wondered, "How will we make up for the lost instructional time? How are we supposed to teach with less time?" and "Now we'll never be able to cover all our material. Plus, with all this recess, the children will come back to class all sweaty and jacked up, and all over the place!" and

"Oh, my God, this is not even going to be controlled chaos, just chaos!"

But the opposite happened. Just as in the Texas, Finland, and other great play experiments, the students thrived. They managed themselves beautifully once the adults quickly learned to back off and let them play. After recess, the children were more focused and more ready to learn in class. And the students did learn more in class. Discipline problems in the district were cut by more than 50 percent. Student attendance went up, and reports of student stress and anxiety went down, both in and out of school. Classrooms became places of joy and extra-productive learning. "I have never seen so many happy and well-adjusted children in my 20 years as an educator," reported Hynes. He thought some parents might object to the radical new play program, but he received zero complaints.

The weekly 75-minute Play Clubs at each of the district's seven elementary schools are a vivid illustration of the revolution-in-progress. The school playgrounds are open for the period, as are several designated free-play rooms indoors. Children decide what they want to do. Balls and sporting equipment are laid outside, and inside there are plenty of materials and activities for the children to select from. At first, Hynes thought perhaps 20 children per school would show up, maybe 25 if they were lucky, and probably mostly the youngest children, those in kindergarten. He was way off. Soon after opening the clubs, they had an average of 100 children per school from all age groups show up every Friday morning to enjoy self-directed, child-led play, the maximum number they could accommodate, and long waiting lists formed.

There are four adults at each Play Club to make sure nobody gets hurt accidentally, but otherwise they are under strict orders to not intervene with the children. "They're there," Hynes confided, "mainly so we can tell parents we had someone there." These days, you can see children doing all sorts of things at the Play Clubs—producing plays, building forts, building and deconstructing block skyscrapers, playing tag and kickball, making up new games and generally running around. It's all self-directed. The children are in charge. "Pretty much everything they used to not be allowed to do, they're now doing," explained Hynes.

The most emotional moment for many of the adults watching the spectacle of the Play Clubs was the sudden realization that children of much different age groups were playing together— a small miracle that educators rarely get to see, since children are usually separated by strict, narrow age groupings. But at the Play Clubs, kindergarteners and first-graders were playing and collaborating with fourth- and fifth-graders, and vice versa. Older children were mentoring the younger ones. Special-needs students felt welcomed by others to play with them.

"This may have been one of the most amazing experiences in my 28 years in education," marveled Lori Koerner, principal of Tremont Elementary School in the district. "To watch children across all ages and grade levels come together to play was fascinating to observe! This club is self-directed with minimal interference from the adult advisors. Children were communicating, collaborating, cooperating and learning together." Barton Elementary principal Judith Soltner agreed, saying, "What was completely unexpected was how the older children took it upon themselves to include and guide the little ones. It was amazing and awesome to watch. Canaan school principal Robert Epstein added, "It is a wonderful opportunity for children to be creative and participate in self-directed play. Students are encouraged to utilize their own conflict resolution skills when the need arises. The ability to resolve conflicts without adult intervention is a crucial component to becoming socially competent. The play club provides the opportunity for students to practice interacting and communicating with one another with minimal adult intervention."[322]

These days, reports Superintendent Hynes, many groups of parents and teachers from other school districts are coming to this beachhead of play-liberated territory in New York State to see the miracle with their own eyes. Then they go home and tell politicians and school administrators that they want the same for their children. The inevitable response: "No way." Hynes told us, "There are lots of communities who would like to do something like this, but for some God-forsaken reason they're not allowed to." He figures the only explanation is bureaucratic inertia, an ingrained, irrational adherence to the status quo. "The cost of additional adult supervision is minimal," he noted. "The return on investment is so significant that it's almost like you're going to invest $100 and you know automatically you're going to get $10,000 in return. Why wouldn't you do it? Money is not an excuse. It makes no sense. You have nothing to lose by trying this."

The play revolution on Long Island is just getting started, and it looks like there's no turning back. The district is opening seven new state-of-the-art school playgrounds so students will have better and deeper play experiences. Things are working so well for his students, Hynes reported, "that if I were to try to take this away, I would be bound, chained and committed by the local population."

What do the parents of this New York school district think of this great play experiment? The comments Hynes hears most often are: "Thank you for doing this!" "My child loves coming to school now, and doesn't feel stressed out at all." "My child can't wait to come to school!"

"If it were up to me," Superintendent Hynes told us, "these kids would have over an hour of recess every day."

"The most important 'data point' that I care about is happy kids."[323]

9

The Great Global Play Experiments

Only by truly taking the stance of the child, can you truly appreciate the meaning of play.

—Dr. Yu Yongping
President, China National Society of
Early Childhood Education[324]

THE CHINA TRUE PLAY EXPERIMENT

In another part of the world, more than 14,000 young children in a revolutionary public school program were learning through play, largely on their own.

They were 3- to 6-year old children in 130 early childhood schools in rural China, and they were being turned loose in wide open play yards to climb trees, swing on tires, pile up pieces of lumber and bamboo, dig ditches, bang nails with a hammer, run fast, make a lot of noise, and fall down—all during school hours.

They spent much of their school days in the fresh air, even when it rained, and they spent every day learning, not at indoor desks, but through open-ended, messy and risky play, much of it outdoors. They learned through construction projects, team-work, and individual effort. They learned by running around, by climbing and jumping from heights. They learned by collaborating to grow their own food in the school garden, and by serving each other hot lunches. Teachers provided safety and overall guidance in the use of materials, but they mostly backed off and let the children play and take charge of their own learning.

Like children in Finland, these Chinese children were learning in an atmosphere of love, warmth, encouragement, and freedom, rather than fear, coercion, and forced physical restraint, with adults hectoring them to "Sit still!" Instead of being measured by standardized tests, children in these schools reviewed their own projects, and each other's projects, in classroom presentations they made to each other at the end of the day. Before the after-noon school pick-up, amazed parents and grandparents gazed through the classroom window at the sight of their 5-year-olds standing at a smart-board and confidently explaining a gardening project, science experiment, or math-block design to their riv-eted little colleagues.

The results being achieved by the school network were stellar. Thousands of children, many of them from lower-income families, have passed through the system so far, and administrators report that they are significantly more creative, confident, expressive, collaborative, better behaved and diligent than other children. Parents love the effect the program has had on their children, and despite some initial skepticism, they are backing it 100 percent. Politicians are so impressed at the results that not only are they starting to convert all the preschools and kindergartens in the county to the new approach, they are urgently recommending that the approach be adopted across the nation.

A striking aspect of the program is that it is happening, in all places, deep in the rural heartland of the People's Republic of China, in a mountainous, bamboo-forested area that is a 3-hour drive from Shanghai. It is happening in China, in the midst of an educational culture that is often criticized by its own authorities and experts as overly structured, test-driven, and averse to creativity and innovation. As Chinese education expert Professor Yong Zhao said, "Self-initiated play has not been a visible part of formal education in China."[325] But here, amid the world's largest national school system, an experiment in play is quickly becoming a national standard of excellence for early childhood education and preparing children for the future.

The program is called "Anji Play," after Anji County in China's Zhejiang Province, where it is based. The Anji Play approach was developed over a period of 15 years, and by 2018 it was the full-time curriculum of 130 schools in China, with plans to expand to many more. The founder and director of the Anji Play network of public Chinese preschools is Cheng Xueqin, the director of the office of Pre-Primary Education for the Anji County Department of Education. She got the idea for Anji Play gradually, after she took on her current job in 1999 and saw teachers trying to tightly control students' play in school, which resulted in a sea of sad faces. Play shouldn't make you sad, she thought. The Chinese government, to its credit, was trying to promote play in early education as "foundational" and "to be included in every type of educational activity," but teachers weren't getting much guidance on how to do it.

Over several years of experimentation, Cheng designed a minimally structured, open-ended early childhood learning environment and provided simple local materials to allow children to play, discover, explore, imagine, and create. The foundations of the program were love, risk-taking, joy, engagement and reflection, and what Cheng calls "true play," or self-determined play. Journalist Chang Jing described the scene at one Anji Play school: "Who would have imagined that when 9:00 A.M. arrived children would fly out of the school building to the materials that they wanted to play with, ladders big and small, wood boards and blocks, tires, cubes and a multitude of other playthings, no teacher explaining the rules of play, no activities organized by the teacher, children independently forming into groups and entering into a variety of play contexts. In the play, no teacher directed children to do or not do anything."[326]

A young American father named Jesse Coffino became so fascinated by Anji Play that he journeyed to China to witness it firsthand, and he now devotes much of his time promoting the program globally. "On any given day in Anji County, children build bridges with ladders and planks," he wrote. "They run across oil drums and construct environments out of bricks and lumber and rope. Their teachers observe this risky, self-initiated play and use their smartphones to film the action. After lunch the kids gather to watch videos of their play and talk about what they were doing. Later in the afternoon they draw what they did that day, often as complex storyboards, schematics and invented symbolic writing systems because that's how they have chosen to describe their experience." According to Coffino, "The deceptively simple ideas behind the Anji Play curriculum are the result of 15 years of development and experimentation at the grassroots level. And it comes at a time when parents like me in America, and around the world, are taking part in a heated debate about education and parenting. We want our kids to be prepared for the 21st century, but we remain tied to ideas from the turn of the last one."[327]

In a wide-ranging interview for this book, Anji Play founder Cheng Xueqin recalled her own childhood memories of play, and how the ideas of love, joy, risk-taking and freedom shaped the philosophy of the new school model she created. She told us the following:

> When I was little I loved to play, and much of it remains fresh in my memory to this day. There were lots of kids in our neighborhood back then. The average family had between five and eight kids. In China in the 1960s mothers were honored for having lots of children. When kids of the same age in our immediate neighborhood got together, we would have a group of as little as five to six kids or as many as ten or more. But my family didn't have many children. Before I was 10 years old, I only had a little brother 3 years younger than me. My mother and father really loved us and

gave us space and opportunities for freedom and play. My memories of play include bringing my little brother along with me to play as part of big groups of local kids, and play alone, by myself. I remember playing hide-and-seek with the neighbors. Our hiding places would grow and shift from one house to another. It was thrilling. In order to make ourselves harder to find, our hiding places grew more and more creative. Once I even used a coffin stored by elderly neighbors in their attic.

The joys we took in seeking and changing hiding places and achieving the goal of finding our object brought a thrill that made play endlessly engaging. We also loved hunting for treasure. Seven or eight of us would imitate scenes from the folktales told by our grandfathers. We would climb the mountains near our house in search of buried treasure. Each of us would play the role of a uniquely equipped treasure hunter. Some of us would carry poles, others would take hooks or shovels, and we would specifically seek out places with ditches and holes and other mysterious characteristics. We were very meticulous in our exploration of the hillsides. I remember very clearly discovering a sooty black earthen jar, and with joyous surprise announcing to everyone that I had found a treasure trove. All of my friends gathered around. With great care I used a shovel to explore the interior of the jar. I sensed that I had hit on something and couldn't wait to dig it out and investigate it. The result was that everyone fled in fear (I had dug up a bone), but today I can still feel that sense of wonder and eager nervousness.

My most heart-warming memory of play was an instance of some of the older boys and girls bringing us to a riverbank to play. We used stones and willow branches to build and play house. The older boys would climb the willow trees to collect branches, some of us would move stones and others built the walls. We moved so many rocks and built such high stone walls, and then the older boys thatched a roof across the stone walls with willow branches, and in that way it became a home. We were all so happy, and we all piled in together to experience the warmth of a home. Then we found flat rocks for bowls and made grass and wildflowers into food. We spent the time immersed in the happiness of home life. It was a kind of joy that to this day is impossible to forget.

As I think back, my memories of personal, solitary play are also rich and meaningful. I remember my mother often used flour and a grass called tufted knotweed to make distiller's yeast that she would then use to make liquor. I thought the whole process was fascinating and funny, and would, by myself, secretly imitate her. I plucked the sesame flowers my mother had planted and used yellow mud for flour. I mashed and mixed the two together and then made them into little balls. I dug little holes in the ground, covered them with leaves, neatly placed the little balls in their respective holes, covered them again with leaves and then sealed them up with mud. I would go back every day to check on them. After a few days I discovered that the little balls had actually begun to ferment and that they gave off a very fragrant, heady aroma. That sense of accomplishment and joy, even remembering it now, fills me with a sense of pride, even though half of my mother's sesame flowers were sacrificed in the process. But I was very fortunate because my mother and father never blamed me or my brother for what we did when we were playing.

Memories of childhood play have provided significant inspiration as I developed the Anji Play approach. These deep memories of play have allowed us to understand what "true play" is, what kinds of materials and environments are best suited to the child's true play, and they guide us in how we get adults to understand and support the true play of the child.

Play is deeply meaningful in terms of the holistic growth and development of the child. If you were to ask me the greatest single benefit of play, I would say that play sparks the formation of knowledge from thought and lays the earliest foundation for development of the individual.

Childhood is a period of preparation for life, it is a period of preparation for the future of humanity. The child of today has to create and confront a future of global knowledge, big data, artificial intelligence, virtual reality, and a continuously emerging stream of new technologies and realities. True play allows the child, through the experience of joy, to imagine and create and test hypotheses. When the knowledge that comes from that kind of thinking is incited, the mind becomes agile, versatile, and creative, and gains the capabilities that will be necessary to adapt to the rapid changes of the future.

As an important form of expression and representation for the child, play reflects the spiritual and cultural world of the child. In the child's self-initiated, self-determined play, and in the child's interaction with other children, there is a continuous and uninterrupted experience of failure and success, rules and freedom, methods and results, and the realization of self-initiated learning. In relationship to others, the child continuously affirms the self. In their interactions with their play partners they seek confirmation of their own existence. This is not only the natural need of the child in the process of physical and emotional development, but also provides the basis for that development to take place. It enriches and perfects the meaning of self for the child.

Contemporary civilization has advanced the cause of human progress, while making significant strides toward meeting the material needs of the world's people, but it has also undermined spiritual consciousness, and negatively affected human development. We often hear about declining psychological health, about problems of behavior, and learning, words like *hyperactivity* and *sensory integration dysfunction* are ever-present in our contemporary discourse. These phenomena have already impacted the healthy development of the child's identity. Growing urbanization has shrunken the child's space for natural play. An increasing interference of technology in the life of the child has simplified the child's process of creation, and a reliance on "smart" technologies has weakened the child's experience of physical activity. These realities should serve as a warning to us and make clear the incredible importance of "true play" in the life and growth of the child today.

Love is the foundation for all relationships. Only in an environment that supports freedom and self-expression can the child engage in physical, emotional, social and intellectual risk, continuously discover and pose questions and challenge oneself to the furthest limit. In Anji Play schools, not only do teachers love children as if they were their own, but the relationships between children, between teachers, between the school and the family, and between the school and the community are characterized by love. Love plays a critical role in establishing the Anji Play ecology and influences Anji Play schools and the life of the community.

Without risk, there is no ability to solve problems. Without problem solving, there is no learning. Children select challenges according to their own ability, time and place. In the exploration of the limits of their own abilities, children discover difficulty and solve difficulty. The teacher is present to observe, document and support, but not to interfere, intervene, or direct (unless there is specific danger to the child or the child has truly exhausted all approaches within their grasp), and, to the greatest degree possible, guarantee the child's access to and enjoyment of physical, social and intellectual risk.

Without joy, play cannot possibly be true play. Joy is the outcome of self-determined participation in play, self-adjustment of the difficulty of play and continuous reflection. A standard that Anji Play educators use to assess the content of each day is whether the child has achieved a state of joy in their activities. In their experience of joy, the child can be quiet or focused, they can be raucous or expressive. Joy is the state of mind that nourishes the life of the child.

True engagement arises from the process of a child's passionate exploration and discovery of the physical and social worlds. Anji Play confers the greatest degree of freedom to the child, allowing the child opportunities to move within an open-ended space, to fully explore and experience the surrounding environment and therefore fully engage body and mind.

Reflection is the crucial process that transforms the child's experience into knowledge. In Anji Play, the child reflects and expresses their daily experiences through a range of means and continuously adjusts their own knowledge of the world on the foundation of their pre-existing experience. The teacher and parent, both through materials and environments, support the self-determined reflection of the child on the child's own experience, and through their observation of the child and exploration of their own memories of play, participate in the child's reflection.[328]

At first, when Cheng began her new program, some Chinese parents in Anji County hated the idea of play in their schools. They were dead-set against the idea of their children getting dirty, taking risks, and, it seemed, wasting time when "they should be studying." They boycotted the schools, wrote protest letters, and reported Cheng to government officials.

In response, Cheng sent copies of the Chinese government's pro-play education guidelines to each household in the county and asked families to come to school to watch their children as they played. "The discovery that their 4-year-olds were possessed of such high levels of bravery, compassion, and intelligence brought many of the parents to tears," reported Anji Play advocate Jesse Coffino. "Overnight, once resistant parents had become adamant supporters and took on the role of training incoming parents on the skills of observation and documentation."

Today, educators from across China and around the world are flocking to the Anji Play schools for inspiration. A 2017 conference on the subject drew a standing-room crowd of over 850 global educators. In 2018, the number of children served by Anji Play schools was expanded to 80,000 children. The Chinese Ministry of Education is showcasing Anji Play as a model for its new national guidelines for kindergarten play materials, and five Anji Play pilot programs have been launched in the United States, in California and Wisconsin.

In a strikingly positive development affecting the lives of tens of millions of school children, China's national Office of the Ministry of Education in 2017 announced a nationwide early education initiative with the theme "Play—Sparking the Joy of Childhood," focusing on 3- to 6-year-olds. The program was aimed at broadly communicating "the important value of play in the lives of children" and guiding both parents and early educators "to a full understanding that play is a unique way in which the child encounters the world and learns." The program was also meant "to create sufficient opportunities and conditions, encouragement and support for children to engage in self-determined, joyous play, reverse a contemporary emphasis on knowledge and skills learning, the neglect and interruption of play, adult 'direction' of play, the substitution of electronic games for play materials and other factors that rob the child of the right to play, and reverse a trend toward 'primary-school-ification' and 'adult-orientation' in early education that impacts the physical and emotional health of the child."[329]

In a major expansion launched in July 2018, Chinese education authorities announced that Anji Play is being adopted as the public early childhood curriculum for all of Zhejiang Province, a district in eastern China that is home to nearly 60 million people. More than 2.5 million children will soon be in Anji Play schools.

Not long ago, Cheng Xueqin, the founder of Anji Play and a champion for the right of children to learn through free play, received her nation's highest honor for early childhood education.

She received the award from the president of the People's Republic of China.

THE NEW ZEALAND RISKY PLAY EXPERIMENT

One day in 2014, an angry-looking father named Roy Waite marched into the office of Bruce McLachlan, principal of the Swanson School in Auckland, New Zealand, an elementary school serving 500 children ages 5 to 13. The parent came through the door with "a face like thunder," recalled McLachlan.

The principal braced himself. He had recently launched a schoolwide experiment of encouraging children to engage in "risky play" with no rules during multiple daily recesses, playing with trees, tires, junk piles, wooden planks, a fire pit, scooters, skateboards, fence climbing and no helmets. This man's son, Curtis, had fallen off a scooter and broken his arm in the school playground. The principal prepared himself to be berated by a furious father and fully expected to be publicly condemned for exposing the boy to such danger. The experiment seemed about to collapse.

But instead, the opposite happened. Rather than chewing the principal out, the father said, "I'm happy that he's fallen off and broken his arm, as bad as it sounds as a parent. I'm happy that he's learned his lesson and hurt himself."[330] The purpose of the father's visit was to make sure the principal continued with the school's "no rules" risky play policy. The father explained, "I just wanted to make sure you don't change this play environment, because kids break their arms." For his part, young Curtis, his son, was very happy that the accident didn't derail the policy. Before the risky play policy, he explained, "I used to hate going to school. Now, I just love it."[331]

Months earlier, after McLachlan took away the rules and gave the children lots of space to play during their outdoor recesses—twice per day for 40 minutes each—misbehavior among students dropped. Serious injuries actually went down. Children displayed more independence, concentration, problem-solving, improved creativity, healthy risk-taking, less falling, less bullying, better coordination, and improved attention in the classroom.[332]

Simply stated, Principal McLachlan reasoned that children should be in charge of their own play during recess. "What children do in their own time, away from the control of adults, is what they have always done: play," he explained. "With the increasing sanitization of the play experience by well-meaning adults, the opportunities for children to learn through play have been reduced. Play is how a child learns about risk, problem-solving, consequences and getting along with others. These learning experiences are arguably just as important as the traditional learning experiences that schools provide children."[333]

The Swanson School isn't the only place where free play is celebrated in New Zealand, a nation that has a long history of offering children opportunities for outdoor play. Since the 1940s, a national nonprofit network of "Playcentres" has served parents and children throughout the country, offering opportunities to raise children in play-rich and creative environments. Playcentres are built around the ideas of child-initiated play and parents as a child's first and best educators. There are currently over 400 Playcentres where parents run 2.5- to 4-hour play sessions and learn themselves how play is important part of learning and growing up. And today, learning through play continues to be a foundation of kindergarten education in New Zealand.

Also in New Zealand, a team of researchers led by Rachael W. Taylor of the Department of Medicine at the University of Otago conducted a fascinating 2-year study of risky recess play at school.[334] The randomized controlled trial involved 8 control schools that were asked to not change their play environment, and 8 intervention schools that offered children at recess increased opportunities for risk and challenge, like rough-and-tumble play, fewer rules, and more loose parts to play with, like tires. The study measured results among 840 primary school children. The results: While children in the intervention schools unsurprisingly reported more pushing and shoving, they simultaneously reported being happier in school. Their parents agreed—their children were enjoying school more. And their teachers reported significantly less bullying complaints.

How did the teachers explain this?

The children, they realized, were becoming more resilient!

SCOTLAND'S ACTIVE PLAY EXPERIMENT

In Scotland, education officials share much the same philosophy as play champions like Cheng Xueqin, Debbie Rhea, and Bruce McLachlan. Unlike in next-door England, where politicians and government officials have largely abandoned play advocacy in recent years, Scottish leaders have become forceful play advocates. They've become so alarmed at the poor health and inactivity of Scottish children that they are launching a series of major educational campaigns to get them to play outdoors, in and out of school.

Maureen McKenna, the Director of Education for the city of Glasgow, Scotland, for example, is one such advocate. Glasgow is Scotland's biggest population center and suffers from chronic bad health and inequality. In partnership with schools, university researchers, and Inspiring Scotland, a venture philanthropy charity, she has spearheaded an ambitious "Active Play" outdoor play-based learning program to support the physical health and well-being of Scottish schoolchildren. Active Play has two strands: delivering Active Play outdoor play sessions for 8- and

9-year-old children in primary schools and providing "Play Champion" aides to select groups of 10- and 11-year old children in primary schools. The program started in 2016 in 30 Glasgow primary schools and is proving so successful that another 100 are scheduled to come on board soon.

One Scottish primary school teacher reported that the Active Play sessions had a very positive effect on her class, helping them to "be more active, gain confidence, build relationships and friendships, and work better in the classroom." She noticed that her pupils were better able to focus on work right after the outdoor play sessions than they had been before. "Pupils were also more confident about what they could do and things they could try in the classroom because they had tried so many new things during Active Play." Another teacher reported "a real improvement in pupil confidence," which she attributed to the creativity that the Active Play sessions encouraged. Interestingly, her students saw the sessions as resilience-building opportunities, as "a safe place to fail where trying news ideas is encouraged."

Another school that took part in the Active Play program in the 2017 spring term is Miller Primary School in Glasgow's Castlemilk area, a school for children aged 5 to 12. The program included weekly Active Play sessions in school, separate from physical education and break time. Teacher Jacqui Church immediately saw great value in Active Play for pupils, particularly in their ability to solve interpersonal problems. Taking their experience from the games and free play of child-led Active Play sessions, pupils began dealing with behavioral conflicts in the playground among themselves rather than running to an adult. Church also noted a real improvement in pupil confidence that was attributed to the creativity that the Active Play sessions encouraged, with children designing and playing their own games free from the prescription typical of physical education and classroom lessons. Active Play sessions were seen as a safe place to fail, where trying news ideas was encouraged.

"They are much more willing to try new things without worrying about failure; now they are saying, 'I can do this'. There was little resilience before," Church reported. This has transferred to the classroom, too, with children having the confidence to engage more in lessons without the fear of getting things wrong. Pupils have also developed their social skills when children play in larger social circles and interact more across classes and year groups during playtime. "Active Play is really bringing the children together," said Church.

Class teachers throughout the school have also observed how pupils engaged with Active Play and have brought techniques from the Active Play program into the classroom and woven literacy and numeracy into outdoor games.

Parents reported children playing outside more after school since the Active Play program began, with one parent saying her child enjoyed it so much she would wake the parents up for school on days when they had Active Play.

The Scottish government has pledged to increase the number of free childcare hours available in Scotland to nearly double the current amount. This creates an opportunity to extend the benefits of outdoor play and learning for young children.

Inspiring Scotland, a national project to deliver strategic, targeted, long-term funding to the Scottish voluntary sector, has developed a solution by linking Scotland's natural assets and green spaces to existing nurseries and developing outdoor nurseries. Research has shown that natural outside play increases health and well-being outcomes for children, but children in low-income urban families tend to have less access to the natural environment and large physical spaces. The model of outdoor pre-K and "forest kindergartens" is well established in several other countries. However, focusing on lower socioeconomic areas and linking education programs with the natural surroundings is a new direction in Scotland.

Inspiring Scotland is working with government policy teams, local authorities, and funders to review access to natural outside play in the early years. In partnership with the Glasgow City Council, an experiment with nurseries in three low-income locations began in August 2017. Inspiring Scotland plans to take this further and expand it throughout the country if it proves to have the impact that existing evidence suggests it will.

Inspiring Scotland's play fund is now developing a vision for Scotland where its children will be the healthiest in the world, both physical and mentally. Through innovation in play delivery and collaborative partnerships both at home and abroad, it focuses on the health, well-being, and learning of children and helps them become future custodians of the environment.

It is the Scottish way to let the children play.[335]

THE SINGAPORE EXPERIMENT: LESS STRESS, MORE PLAY WITH A PURPOSE

In a shift away from decades of stress-based schooling, the high-performing Asian education superstar nation Singapore is launching a bold, top-to-bottom overhaul of its pressure-cooker childhood education system to better prepare its children for the future, in part through "purposeful play" for children in school.

The island nation often tops the world in educational rankings, but it has been considered an underperformer when it comes to the well-being of its children or the entrepreneurial skills of its workforce. A survey of over 100 U.S. businesses in Singapore by the U.S. Chamber of Commerce saw the local workforce score high on technical skills, but lowest among the Southeast Asian nations on innovation and creativity.[336]

Right now, in Singapore's schools, outdoor learning and "purposeful play" for young learners are increasingly emphasized, and children are being encouraged to develop their interests, talents, and life skills. The new approach doesn't stop at kindergarten. The revamp is part of Singapore's bigger shift away from domination by periodic national assessments toward a deeper, more holistic system built on a foundation of curiosity and a love for learning.

According to one of the leaders responsible for leading Singapore's youth into the 21st century, "purposeful play" in school is a critical foundation of the reform. Chee Meng Ng is a former fighter pilot, a retired Singapore Air Force Lieutenant-General, and, until 2015, Singapore's Chief of Defense Force. Now a Minister in the Prime Minister's Office and Deputy Secretary-General of the National Trades Union Congress, he served from 2015 to 2018 as the Minister overseeing the nation's primary and secondary schools, junior colleges, and preschools. He is concerned that Singapore's schools have not been fostering student innovation, well-being, and creativity, and instead have been overly focused on doing well for national assessments.

In 2016, Minister Ng and the Singapore Ministry of Education announced the start of a series of major structural reforms, including changes to the grading of the national PSLE exams [Primary School Leaving Exams] in science, languages, and math. Beginning in 2021, to reduce the extreme levels of ranking and competition between students, the exams will be marked on a set of criteria instead of students being ranked against each other. Schools plan to emphasize outdoor play in physical education classes, reduce the "streaming" of children in primary school, and reduce the volume of homework. "We need to free up time and space to nurture other dimensions that are just as important for our children's development," Minister Ng said when he announced the changes. "Let them not just study the flowers but also stop to smell the flowers."[337]

In an interview for this book, Minister Ng told us of his vision of play in his world-leading education system:

> In Singapore, we recognize the importance of "play" in education, and it's a deliberate, purposeful word. Our educators are constantly encouraged to help students discover their interests, grow their passions, and develop a love for learning by connecting with their interests, daily experiences, our community and technology. This is in line with our belief that through education, students should not only develop strong academic foundations, sound values and critical life skills; they must also find learning enjoyable and develop a lifelong passion for learning. Only

with the intrinsic motivation to learn would our children embrace the lifelong journey of learning, unlearning and relearning. This is also exactly why we are moving away from an overemphasis on grades, so that our children will find passion and purpose beyond the A's and B's.

A Chinese proverb says "it takes 10 years to grow trees, but a hundred to nurture people." While education is a far more complex and arduous task than growing trees, we can extract useful insights. As gardeners, we must tend our seedlings with great skill, care and love: by ensuring the plant has sufficient, but not overly harsh sunlight, and watering the plant based on how much the soil can take. Most importantly, as the seedlings grow and take root, we should hold back and give them enough space and freedom to flourish. We must not over-shelter them or suffocate them with much watering and over-fertilizing, but allow them to grow upright, strong and sturdy, and resilient to any storms. I fear we are overcrowding our young ones with a narrow focus on academics.

I'm not much of a gardener, but I did plant some green beans for a school project when I was a small boy. I remember waking up each morning, impatiently monitoring my glass jar day after day, waiting for the first shoot to sprout. I soon realized that over-watering my seedlings did not make them grow any faster. In fact, it stifled them. I believe our children, like young seedlings, ought to have time and space to breathe, learn and dream.

It is easy to get fixated on what is measurable. We put a score on something and that makes it easy for us to compare with one another. But what is measurable sometimes may not be what is most important in the long run. Chasing after that last point in an exam could come at a cost to other aspects of our children's overall development, especially at such a young age. Too many anxious nights, too much tuition [private cram schooling], and too little quality time for family and friends, for play and for exploration.

We must nurture the joy of learning in our children. This intrinsic motivation will drive them forward to explore and discover their interests and passions. School should not just be about doing well in exams. It should be an exciting place to acquire knowledge and skills, where learning is fun and with the necessary rigor.

This is why we are doing our best to develop the love for learning within our children right from preschool, where our children learn and play so that they can grow their imagination, creativity and social-emotional skills. At the Ministry of Education's kindergartens, children are exposed to a variety of experiences for them to take an interest in the world that they live in, and to interact and build relationships with others. For example, using props and various set pieces, we would simulate scenes in a supermarket or on a public road, so that while our children develop numeracy and literacy through fun role-playing, they also learn important life skills through these interactive activities!

The Ministry of Education's kindergarten teachers make use of two core pedagogies to engage children—purposeful play and quality interactions. Through purposeful play, children participate in planned activities, which are fun and allow them to actively explore, develop and apply their knowledge and skills. Quality interactions happen when the teachers and children engage in shared and sustained conversations, as they work together to investigate a topic, solve a problem, clarify a concept or tell a story. The children do not have spelling lists or memorize multiplication tables; instead their learning progress is charted in portfolios that are shared with their parents. Time is also set aside for the children to delve further into projects that capture their imagination and interest!

Naturally, the notion of "play" also extends to our primary and secondary schools and junior colleges, where educators create environments which inspire students to explore, showcase their creativity, build confidence, and own their learning. Besides using student-centered pedagogies in the classroom so that students construct their own learning, our students are also regularly exposed to learning outside the classroom through learning journeys, camps, and community service projects. For example, they could be camping outdoors for one week, or using a maker space to design a prototype to help the elderly. Our students also look out for needs in the community, and design and implement solutions to meet them.

In fact, our curricula and school programs also utilize applied learning approaches in a myriad of fields, ranging from robotics and food science to media communications, the arts, and music. Through hands-on lessons and experiential programs, we want our students to see their learning come alive, as their knowledge and skills take on real-world meaning and relevance. This is "purposeful play" that suits their learning needs—they laugh, learn, and make a positive impact on themselves and others.

Through all these efforts, we are determined to help all our students develop a lifelong passion to learn. This intrinsic motivation to learn will be the internal engine within each of them, driving them to meet their personal aspirations and contribute meaningfully to Singapore and indeed, the world.[338]

In July 2018, in an address to the business leaders of Singapore, the nation's new Minister for Education Ye Kung Ong declared that the traditional and deeply ingrained test-driven Singapore school culture could be exacting "too high a price in terms of stress and killing the joy of learning." He contended, "there must be joy in learning and sustained curiosity. Without it, we cannot be motivated to learn, keep up or stay ahead of changes." The minister added, "Our society needs to have a greater appetite for calculated risks, and tolerance for setbacks and failures." He also argued that schools and society should enable children to have fun, to play with friends, and discover their strengths and passions. He said that rigor in education is a good thing, but he expressed sympathy for the view that "students have their whole life to learn, so there is no need to frontload so much at a young age."

The minister told the story of how one day, during a meeting with Singaporean parents and children, he was asked by a parent how he would make sure that every school is a "good school."

He turned to the parent's child and asked, "Do you like your school?"

"Yes" said the boy.

"Are the teachers good and helping you learn?"

"Yes."

The minister asked if the child enjoyed his friends and his extracurricular activities. The boy reported that he did.

Then the minister asked the one key question that perhaps every teacher, parent, and policymaker around the world should ask a child, before any other piece of data is collected.

He asked the child, "In the morning, when you go to school, are you happy?"

"Yes."

The minister concluded, "Then you are in a good school." He explained, "We must define a good school from the perspective of the child. If a school meets the needs of the child, it is a good school—never mind if it is not popular or branded."[339]

Also in July 2018, Indranee Rajah, Singapore's 2nd Minister of Education, said, "We don't want the children's years in school to be only about homework, tests, assessments, grades and exam scores. It must also be an enjoyable educational experience, built around a love of learning, of exploration, and of play.[340] Another Singapore education leader thoroughly agreed with the emerging new philosophy. "Education is moving beyond the transactional approach of sitting and clearing exams, to imbuing that love for learning," said secondary school principal Madam Sharma Poonam Kumari. "The future we are preparing children for is going to be very complex, and textbook knowledge will not always get them through."[341] May Wong, principal of a primary school in Singapore, noted that potential employers "are not going to look for the person with the highest aggregate score."[342] Instead, they will seek skills and talents like empathy, resilience, creativity and teamwork. Pak Tee Ng, an Associate Professor at Singapore's National Institute of Education, Nanyang Technological University told us, "We are putting in more efforts to emphasize values inculcation, lifelong learning, holistic education and 21st century skills. We hope to encourage joyful learning and help our students develop resilience and an entrepreneurial spirit."[343]

In late 2018 the Ministry of Education announced that standardized tests for first- and second-grade students, as well as class rankings in primary and secondary school, will be scrapped. Singapore's Minister for Education, Ye Kung Ong, stressed that children should learn from an early age that "learning is not a competition, but a self-discipline they need to master for life."[344]

The jury is out on whether Singapore's famously high-expectations culture will allow these reforms to flourish—one member of the nation's parliament noted that "more and deeper work will have to be done on transforming the mindset of parents, and even some educators and students themselves"[345]—but they are off to a promising start.

Singapore isn't the only Asian nation where play is gaining ground. In 2013 and 2014, a team of reporters from Singapore's *TODAY* magazine traveled to five Asian mega-cities—Hong Kong, Shanghai, Seoul, Taipei, and Tokyo—and made a surprising discovery. The stereotype of Asian toddlers and preschoolers being required to master advanced academics was beginning to change, and it was being replaced with a highly powerful concept—play, at least in the early years of education.

Each of these cities, the journalists reported, had created "a pervasive all-play environment in their preschools despite the pressure-cooker education systems that children subsequently enter."

The cities had launched a common effort to boost public awareness of the benefits of play for a child in the early years. In South Korean preschools, 5 hours were set aside each day for children to play freely. Math, reading, and writing lessons were banned. Chung-Ang University's early childhood academic Cho Hyung-Sook said there was a growing acceptance of learning through play among South Korean parents, thanks to the government's major investments in early childhood research, including launching the Korea Institute of Child Care and Education. For Japanese kindergarteners, the emphasis was not on drilling and academics, like many of their counterparts in the United States were enduring in public schools. Instead, for 4 hours in the morning, teachers played with children on swings and slides and helped them build improvised toys with household materials. Children were having "a ball of a time" at Ochanomizu University Kindergarten, reported *TODAY*. "Some were playing with autumn leaves in the outdoor compound while others jumped up and down trying to pluck oranges from trees." Inside, children danced in groups, listened to stories, and ran through the hallways.

The higher grades in Japanese education may often have a pressure-cooker atmosphere for students, but here in preschool, it was all about play and socialization in a welcoming atmosphere that featured large, boisterous groups of children. "It is the Japanese culture," explained researcher Kyoko

Iwatate of Tokyo Gakugei University. "Parents believe that in pre-schools, children play and should be part of a large community." One Japanese mother said, "As long as my child is exposed to interacting and playing with others, I am not too worried about the rest."[346]

THE SCHOOL OF DREAMS IN TOKYO

Let's go back in time—and forward in time.

Let's be children again.

Let's choose a kindergarten together, for ourselves.

Let's get into our private jet and fly around the world and look at all the kindergarten classrooms and buildings the planet has to offer.

You may not believe it, but there is one kindergarten in particular that is so astonishing, so child-friendly, and so filled with warmth and beauty that we would claim it for ourselves and never want to leave.

That school really exists, in the Tachikawa district of western Tokyo. It's called Fuji Kindergarten, and over 600 children aged 3 to 6 are lucky enough to go to school there. In 2011, the OECD named it the world's most outstanding learning environment. You could call it the "kindergarten of dreams."

This masterpiece of a school is the brainchild of Tokyo-based architects Takaharu and Yui Tezuka, a husband-and-wife team who are also business partners, and the parents of two children. They created Fuji Kindergarten in collaboration with the school's principal Sekiichi Kato, and designer and art director Kashiwa Sato. Together, they created a Montessori-style kindergarten that's not just a building but a love song, a poetic rhapsody to the learning power and joy of childhood—and hands-on play.

How do you create the world's greatest kindergarten, a place that is perfectly built to develop social interaction, joyful learning, and physical exploration? These designers came up with an elegantly simple formula—design a school from the perspective of children and break every rule you can think of.

Most schools are shaped like boxes, in square and rectangular combinations. But Fuji Kindergarten is shaped like an oval, with a circular courtyard at the center. Most school roofs are empty and unused. The team came up with a radical, astonishing idea—turn the roof into a play deck where children could race around in the open air and sunshine.

Most schools are set off from nature. At the Fuji Kindergarten, three 25-meter tall Zelkova trees, or Japanese elms, actually grow inside the one-story school itself, poking holes through the roof, complete with netting to help children climb them, as many as 100 children at a time. "If you make buildings too safe, children lose the opportunity to learn about danger," declared architect Takaharu Tezuka. "I think it's important to leave some amount of danger."[347] He also noted, "Children are strong and capable enough to stay outdoors. Of course they need protection in extreme weather, though not all the time."[348] Play flourishes when children have all the protection they need, but not all the protection that is possible.

There are no walls between class spaces, and side doors to the courtyard are left wide open for much of the year. Skylights connect to the roof, so children can peer down and check out what their buddies are doing in class below.

No play equipment is needed—the building is one gigantic playground, built within a school. Children are encouraged to roam around freely, fall down, tumble around, and get wet on occasion. The theory of action—don't overprotect or over-control children. They need to move a lot, and sometimes get wet and dirty.

What happens if the children get wet? The school principal Sekiichi Kato gets this question a lot from foreign visitors. His answer is simple. "In Japan, children change their clothes if they get wet, they have human skin and are waterproof. Unlike a mobile phone, children do not break when wet."[349]

The school's oval layout encourages both collaboration and independence, without forcing children to be quiet and still for extended periods. Some schools go to great lengths to suppress every possible source of noise, but at Fuji Kindergarten, moderate levels of noise from multiple sources are thought to have a calming effect that enhances children's play and learning. The school is suffused with soothing levels of ambient, natural "white noise"—the sounds of a distant piano, of running water, of children playing, running, chatting, and laughing. "We consider noise very important," declared Takaharu. "When you put children in a quiet box, some of them get really nervous."[350] He argued, "Just as a fish cannot live in purified water, children cannot live in a clean, quiet and controlled environment."[351] Water-well stations are scattered through the school, so children can gather, collaborate, and talk with each other while rinsing objects or drawing water to play with. "These days Japanese kids only talk to computers," explained Takaharu. "I hate it. I thought, if we put a well in each classroom, they'll be forced to talk to each other. There's a phrase in Japanese, *ido bata kaigi*, which means, 'conference around the well.' Women used to meet and exchange information when they went to get water. I wanted the children to do the same."[352]

Takaharu explained that the design for the structure was based on what he calls a "nostalgic future," a vision of the way children would naturally choose to play without gadgets and screens, the way they played and learned not long ago, and may again some day in the not-too-distant future.

Some people see the future of education as being a profusion of computer screens and clean, safe, antibacterial classroom surfaces. "If you look at many of the latest school designs, the modern school building is getting bigger and bigger and looking more like an IT company's headquarters," observed Takaharu. "In these buildings, children never go outside." He stated, "Many people believe that this is the future but I am always against these choices for children. These artificial controlled environments are not the vision of the future anymore; they are slowly killing the children." His theory: "It is quite possible that the children who have access to the latest technology are not receiving a better education than the children with little access to the technology but learn in a natural environment."[353]

The formula for the Kindergarten of Dreams is so inspiring and so successful that Takaharu predicts that 50 years from now, Fuji Kindergarten will be unchanged and exactly the way it is today.

The most striking aspect of Fuji Kindergarten is its circular play deck roof. The idea came from Takaharu and Yui Tezuka's own children, who were small at the time and kept running around a table in their house. "We thought, that is a way to make architecture," recalled Takaharu. "We made a circle, so children could keep running."[354] On paper, the idea made sense, but the design team hoped that their theory would hold up once the school was filled with children.

On the day that Fuji Kindergarten opened in 2007 and several hundred Japanese children experienced their new architecturally utopian play school for the first time as students, everyone's dreams came true. The children ran to the roof in a state of rapture. "It was simple, they just started running," reported Takaharu. "It was beyond our expectations. I was sitting with the principal and everyone had tears. It was amazing, an instant reaction."[355]

Ever since that day, year after year, the children of Fuji Kindergarten have kept on running, for an average of about 5 kilometers a day, and there is no sign that they'll ever stop.

THE PLAYGROUND BY THE SEA: THE CROATIA EXPERIMENT

One day in 2017, a playground appeared on an island in the Adriatic Sea.

The island is Hvar, located between the islands of Brac and Korcula, some 12 miles off the Dalmatian Coast of Croatia. It is home to the largest fertile plain in the country, mountains and rolling hills that slope to the ocean blanketed with vineyards, groves, and gardens, and some of the most stunning scenery in Europe.

"Hvar is arguably one of the most beautiful islands in the world," wrote Lenore Zann, a visitor from Australia. "The only way to get there is by sea, and when you step upon the land it feels like you have stepped into a world where time stands still. The air seems different—alive and magical—due to the stimulating mixture of lavender, rosemary, olive and pine."[356]

On the north side of Hvar, at the edge of a long, protected harbor, is a town of some 3,000 people called Stari Grad—the Old Town. Amid all this beauty, the young people of the town were missing something critical to their health and happiness. They didn't have a proper playground.

The playground is one of childhood's miracles, a place of joy, friendship, and learning, a "school of life" and a direct extension of both the school and the home where children practice a multitude of skills they will enjoy as adolescents and adults. But the children of Stari Grad didn't have one.

At the edge of town next to the busy farmers market and the primary school was an old site that housed the broken-down remnants of something that used to be a playground, but it was ugly and downright dangerous. In fact, in the previous several years, seven children playing there had been badly injured by broken equipment. It was a dilapidated, abandoned space that had never had any maintenance and was therefore not safe anymore for children to play.

Something had to be done, and fast. So a group of mothers in the town formed a committee, called in architects and contractors, raised funds, and started building a brand new playground. The women made a blueprint for a modern, child-friendly and safe playground and started to look for potential partners to finance their project. In less than a month they had what was needed for a down payment. Suddenly one private donor and the local mayor decided to top up their budget. Pasi's wife, who grew up nearby, joined the campaign. The plan was a modest one, but it would be a beautiful little spot for families to meet and children to frolic, designed so children with special needs could enjoy it, too, with fun, inclusive equipment like swings, a slide, seesaw, sandbox, and swing net. There would be benches for the adults, and a ban on cell phones, so parents and grandparents could make friends, disconnect from the grid, and enjoy watching their children together.

News spread through the community, and the children of Stari Grad were gripped with excitement. Each day, pockets of children appeared on the edge of the building site, their eyes popping as the construction workers fashioned their special new meeting place. Kindergarten students created signs about safe and correct behavior in the playground. The new playground was ready to be up and running in less than a month.

Before long, boys and girls formed a neighborhood watch group, so no one would sneak in before the official opening day. Day and night, the children took turns standing guard.

When the grand opening day came, there was the kind of pomp and circumstance you'd expect for such a historic occasion. There were singers and music groups, and the town mayor made a speech while flanked by the entire city administration and representatives from all political groups.

When the mayor cut the ceremonial ribbon at the entrance, a clown was supposed to lead a march of children for one loop around the playground. But all order broke down as the children, including Pasi's sons Otto and Noah, swarmed into the play-ground in a stampede of little feet, waving hands and crying cheers of delight.

Today, the playground is a center of the community's life, a place where families gather and enjoy childhood together. "I have never seen our children so happy," one mother said. "I've watched that old playground for years and thought this would never be possible," she said.

A few months after the grand opening, we visited the play-ground of Stari Grad and spoke to parents and children there and in playgrounds, schools and play groups in nearby towns about what play means to them.

We held interviews and conversations with over 50 children and 20 adults on the subjects of child's play, playgrounds, and childhood in general. We were pretty amazed by how strong and well expressed their opinions were, and how they echoed things we've heard from other children, parents, and teachers all over the world. Even the 4-year-olds had highly developed opinions on play!

Here's what the mothers and fathers told us about play while their children were having fun in the new playground:

—Playing means spending time pleasantly, especially for a small child, where they learn very important physical things that they will need throughout their lifetime, such as agility, skillfulness and resourcefulness. Basically, playing is one of life's biggest lessons.

—My son learns the most through playing and can be reached best through play.

—Play is how a child develops their feeling and imagination. Playing is the most important thing for children to develop in the right direction.

—Playgrounds are important so children can socialize and play, and spend as little time as possible in front of the TV or tablet!

—Outside play is best. Because nature is the more normal environment for any human, to be outside rather than inside. Even though our house is big, it was made to sleep in and to go outside in the morning, and go back in at night.

—I think socializing with children is much more useful for my child. Playing outside in fresh air, with other children. It is much healthier than sitting around and playing inside.

—I play with my son every day, several times, several different games. We play what he wants to play, we have a large selection of games so we play whatever we feel like doing that day. Since he's a preschooler, I always try to sneak in some learning.

—Play is important, but not on the cellphone, because it's a waste of time.

—I think adults should play too because we are all children at heart, and children like it when their parents give them the leisure of playing with them.

—Through play, I think my child has learned, at least I hope he did, that things can't always be the way he wants them to, that he needs to listen to someone, that he has to be a team player.

—By playing, my child learns to communicate, cooperate with others, learns to respect others, learns rules, adopts new knowledge about things, and expands his vocabulary.

—It helps children to learn to lose, which they find very difficult, and to learn something about someone they are playing with. They can be playing with someone they don't know, and playing helps them get to know them. It's also fun, after all!

—I think that in playing with others a child learns most important things: how to share, how to fight and make up and respect one another.

—Children are nicer after playing, they have a bigger smile on their faces. I think people have somehow forgotten how to play, which makes everyone so grumpy and grumbly.

—Playing is happiness, through which he learns to socialize, and he also goes to bed tired but peaceful—so the whole combination does him very well.

—I also love playing with my child, because I think there's nothing better than seeing your child happy. It's normal to sometimes be tired from it all, but then he comes over with the ball, and as soon as you start playing—you need to remember this—the tiredness not only disappears, but a new energy comes along.

— At the moment when I feel tired, when I would mostly just like to be in front of TV or computer, my child pulls me out from that tiredness and takes me out to fresh air. And in that one moment you just start to shoot the ball, run, have fun—what an amazing change! In only one moment! Can you imagine now if we would do that all the time—how our lives would change?

—Childhood is the most beautiful time that one experiences in a lifetime. It is the best time of life. The longer you play, the more beautiful your life is.

The boys and girls we spoke to ranged in age between 4 and 10 years old, and this is what they told us.

—My name is Prosper. I'm 10. Play is when my whole body is happy. I like to play with my friends, my father, sister and brother, and other people. Play is fun and pleasure. I love to play on the playground. Play is important so we can grow and enjoy and be happy, and to spread love and all those nice things.

—I am Ivan. I am 7. I like playing tag and hide-and seek. Play is important so we can be in good shape and good condition. The essence of the play is to entertain. I think all adults should play with their kids. Kids should play every day, because it is good for their fitness. Play helps me. I put myself in order and solve my problems with my friends. Through play we can forget about all the problems we have. That's the greatest thing.

—My name is Paula. I'm 4 years old. Play is to have fun, pleasure and enjoying with your friends or yourself your favorite toys, dolls and babies. It is extremely important to children so they will not be bored.

—The playground? I love it! It's the best! It's my favorite! I play there a lot. Adults do not play, because they have their own business. They have to work, they have to work, and it is a lot for them. Sometimes it's too much, so they need to rest.

— My name is Lucija. Play is important so I can develop and grow up. My mother and father are playing with me. Everyone can play. Even grandmothers and grandfathers can play. Play helps me to run and jump as much as I want to. It is very much important for children.

—I could play with small Lego blocks the whole day long.

—My name is Marcela. I'm 6 and a half. Play is entertainment and pleasure. To play means to enjoy. My favorite games are hide-and-seek and tag.

— Playgrounds are important so that kids can enjoy and get entertained. Do you need anything more than that?

—I learn a lot in the playground. I watch others and I learn from them. Now I know how to climb the play house and spin on the swing. Those things I didn't know before. Now I can even run faster than before. I know now also I have to wait my turn for the swing and that I should behave nicely toward others.

—I am 5. Play is helping me a lot. If you hurt yourself somewhere and then you start to play immediately after that, you stop thinking about it, and stops hurting you. Isn't that magic?

—On the playground I learn how to behave nicely and how to enjoy and play with other kids and friends.

—On the playground I learn that I should not be angry, I should accept something like losing, and fail.

—Adults should play so they can finally laugh!

Finally, we posed a controversial idea to the children about play—why do we even need it, and what would the world be like without it? "If adults were to tell you that play is not important for children," we asked, "what would you tell them?"

This provocative question triggered a chorus of indignation— and firm opinions:

I would tell them "shame on you, to play is extremely important and you should know that."

—6-year-old girl

I would tell them that this is simply a big lie.

—10-year-old boy

I would say, "OK." Of course, we have to listen to adults. I would tell them "OK" and then continue playing.

—5-year-old boy

I would tell them: "Just check it out—let your children check out this statement." I think it is extremely important to play.

—7-year-old boy

I would tell them they are not funny at all.

—8-year-old boy

I would simply tell them that play is extremely enlightening.

—7-year-old boy

I would tell them that's not true, because it is extremely important for everyone to play with friends and to be outside on the fresh air.

—10-year-old boy

Oooh, I would tell them that play is important. Play is important for both—for you as well as for us!

—8-year-old girl

Oooh, I would tell them, Come on—let's play! (followed by hearty laughter)

—4-year-old boy

One of the strongest opinions came from a 9-year-old boy, who declared unequivocally, "I would tell them that they don't have a clue what they are talking about, because they don't know what play means to me and I would not listen to them." He concluded, "I would walk out and continue playing."

Perhaps one lesson of this "playground by the sea" is that you shouldn't wait for somebody else to improve the situation or solve the problem, you should take charge yourself and with your community to give play to children. Also, we can think of these children in Croatia as spokespeople for hundreds of millions of children all around the world, who, we strongly suspect, have similar opinions about play.

And finally, we can see the playground as a sacred place not only for children to play and learn in the "school of life" in a play world where they are largely in charge, but also for parents and grandparents to think and talk about their children's lives, and to witness the unfolding miracle of childhood. For Stari Grad's playground is a symbol of the future, of the life that flows through one community's children as it has done for 3,000 years in a little-known pearl of the Mediterranean Sea.

* * *

Right now, there are real-life "great play experiments" flourishing all around the world, benefitting multitudes of children in both developing and developed nations.

In Bangladesh, Uganda, and Tanzania, thousands of young children are participating in "play centers" organized by BRAC, a leading multinational non-governmental organization. The Bangladesh government is taking a keen interest in incorporating play into its national primary school curriculum and is piloting new play programs in 300 schools.

In 2010, Wales became the first country in the world to guarantee the child's right to play, by passing legislation requiring that local governments "must secure sufficient play opportunities in its area for children." In the Canadian province of Quebec, authorities have announced that in the fall of 2019, elementary school children will be guaranteed two twenty-minute recesses per day. In the United States, some communities and states are beginning to require recess in school again. In 2018 and 2019, officials in a South Carolina school district began giving elementary school students a 15-minute outdoor recess every hour of the school day. Where did the idea come from? From Dr. Danny Merck, the District Superintendent of Pickens County, South Carolina—after he returned from an inspiring trip to observe Finland's schools.

In Aylesbury, in central England, a few years ago, teachers at the Long Crendon School decided to create an outdoor learning space at an unused strip of land on the school grounds. "We have lots of space but not much money,"[357] noted head teacher Sue Stamp. So the school launched a fundraising appeal to the parents, businesses, and the community for landfill material to make little hills, and unused play equipment to build a trail and tunnels for the children to explore. Pretty soon, the site blossomed with children playing in a fully equipped thatched mud kitchen, and a system of pulleys and pipes to transport water around.

In communities around the world, parents and teachers like these are beginning to restore play to schools and to childhood. They deserve our help.

Many of us think that if you seek success in life, you should keep work and play separate. Hard work is commonly seen as a virtue that those who look for good life should pursue. It means spending long hours in work and sacrificing weekends and part of holidays to get unfinished business done. We all know workaholics who come to work before anybody else and leave after all others are gone. They are the same people who often stay away from picnics and parties that are organized by their colleagues to have fun. Fun is not part of their recipe of good work. Play is what you do if there is time left after work. We are sure you know many people like that, as do we.

Some business leaders try to bring better balance to people's work and life through their own example. Sir Richard Branson, the founder of Virgin and one of the most successful entrepreneurs today, advocates the "work hard, play hard" philosophy, showing the world how he likes to play as hard as he works. He claims that it is the best way to give work and family life equal weight. He is also quoted as saying, "If everyone could live with the spirit of the child, the world would be a better place."[358] For Sir Richard and many others, playing is an essential part of good life. Unfortunately, only a few of us adults remember to practice play every day.

Curiosity, creativity, empathy, and learning from failure have become hot currencies in human capital in many organizations and businesses today. Success in the workplace no longer depends on how long, fast, or hard people work, or how many facts you know. The most outstanding academic scholars do not necessarily publish more articles and papers than others. Successful people today are those who are curious to figure out why things are as they are, continuously look for new ways to get the job done, and try to understand what the world looks like from other person's perspective. Therefore, a regular question asked in a job interview is, "What has been your biggest failure and what did you learn from it?" These are human qualities that are difficult to teach without a school atmosphere of play, discovery, exploration, experimentation, and the freedom to learn from failure.

A school district in New England had for a long time been intrigued by what schools in Finland had been able to accomplish. They knew that Finland has one of the most equitable school systems and that children also learn well. Teachers have a lot of professional autonomy and they are trusted and respected by the rest of the society. They also knew that schools don't compete against one another in Finland and that public schools are not targets of standardized tests, external inspections, or harsh criticism by politicians, parents, or corporate leaders. And, moreover, all children in Finland have 15-minute recess after every lesson in addition to the minimum of 1 hour physical activity every day in school.

The district leaders and teachers were particularly interested in finding effective ways to improve their own pre- and primary schools. The last decade had brought along new state and federal education policies that had increased pressure in schools to focus more on test scores and employ standardized pedagogical procedures, or scripts, as teachers call them.

One day in spring 2016 they called Pasi to have a conversation with the chairman of the school board and some influential members in the community.

"So, what advice would you offer us?" the host asked Pasi in the meeting.

"First, I would warn you not to try to copy what Finland or any other education system has done. You need to find your own way, adapt inspirations to your own national culture, build your own Finland. But one thing that would probably improve your schools would be to give students more time to play," Pasi proposed.

"I understand that it might be good for very young kids," said the official, "but we are looking for something that would help us to raise the learning standards for all, to make sure that everybody graduates."

Pasi replied, "The experiences of Finland and Scotland, for instance, are very promising. Children have frequent recess and a certain amount of physical activity every day in school. Students' well-being and health are directly linked to their engagement and achievement in school."

"But our students already have [fewer] school days in their annual schedules than in Finland or Scotland. We can't reduce their learning time in school even more, can we?" asked a member of the local chamber of commerce.

"That is not really so. American schools, on average, have fewer days but they are longer, often much longer than in Finland. So, you should not worry about not having enough time for instruction in schools. Just try rescheduling daily timetables in schools so that students have time to rest and play."

"We appreciate your ideas, but I think what works in Finland doesn't probably work here," said the school board chairman.

"Yes, I understand that Finland and the United States are different in many ways. But I believe that children everywhere will benefit from having enough time to play," Pasi insisted.

"Maybe in Sweden or Finland," said the chairman, "But our culture here in America is different. Taking time away from instruction and learning would be a bad idea here."

"Perhaps you should think of play as part of learning, not a substitute," said Pasi.

"Well, but what about the cultural differences between us and you?" a parent asked.

"I think it's great that these are indeed cultural differences, rather than something that we couldn't change," offered Pasi. "We can change cultures. American culture has changed a lot in recent history, and so has ours. Cultures evolve all the time. I believe you could lead that change in your community by helping people to look at the school and especially what our children should learn there from other perspectives," Pasi replied.

"Yes, but this will be hard," several present in the meeting mused.

"For sure," added Pasi and continued, "fortunately, there are many things that you and your community can do to change the situation. And this is a goal worth fighting for!"

We believe that children should have more opportunities to play in and out of school. When we talk to parents, we often hear about busy family schedules and how parents are afraid to allow their children to play alone outside. We also hear how children's free time after school is filled with homework and other activities that parents believe will help children to do better in school and find successful careers later. Sometimes children are signed up for activities that they have not chosen, or not even interested in in the first place. Children may enjoy these activities, but play, as we understand it, should always be based on a child's own initiative, intrinsic motivation, and non-stressed frame of mind.

Our children don't just need more time to play, they also need "deeper" play.

THE POWER OF DEEPER PLAY

We believe that when children play, everybody wins. This doesn't mean that any kind of play is automatically good for physical health or learning in school. More play is not necessarily better. Sometimes less is more in play. High-quality play that triggers a child's engagement, curiosity, passion, and imagination is more meaningful even in small doses than extended involvement in activity that only marginally includes these critical features of play.

For a child, higher-quality play, or what we call "deeper play," applies to both indoor play and outdoor play, and to intellectual and physical play. We believe that deeper play has five main ingredients:

- Self-direction
- Intrinsic motivation
- Use of the imagination
- A process orientation
- Positive emotions

In deeper play, the child takes the initiative and the responsibility for what happens during play. Teachers and parents provide the child with overall support and guidance when needed, and a safe enough environment and materials and projects to "play with," but then they back off and let the child play largely on their own and at their own pace (Figure 7).

Children should have the opportunity, often, to choose, manage, and reflect on their play activities. *Self-directed play* means that we let children to decide their own play in a safe and rich environment where they are comfortable to explore their

The Classroom Continuum

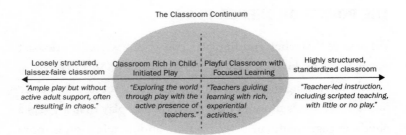

Loosely structured, laissez-faire classroom	Classroom Rich in Child-Initiated Play	Playful Classroom with Focused Learning	Highly structured, standardized classroom
"Ample play but without active adult support, often resulting in chaos."	"Exploring the world through play with the active presence of teachers."	"Teachers guiding learning with rich, experiential activities."	"Teacher-led instruction, including scripted teaching, with little or no play."

Figure 7. The "Sweet Spot" of Play in School. The shaded area represents a theoretical ideal balance for a kindergarten classroom, and the place where "deeper play" can flourish and boost a child's learning outcomes. The logic can be applied to higher grades as well.
Adapted from Miller, E., & Almon, J. (2009). *Crisis in the Kindergarten.* College Park, MD: Alliance for Childhood.

own mind and potential through play. Self-directedness can occur when children are playing alone as well as when they play together. The key condition of self-directed play is that child is free to choose what to do, how to do it, and what are the rules of play. Self-directed play is also self-organizing. It means that it is a spontaneous process where some form of order emerges from interactions of the parts of a disordered system. Spontaneous play means that it doesn't require external control and it is often initiated by random events and then reinforced with internal positive feedback.

Self-directedness is an important ability in play that children should continuously develop. It includes "meta-cognitive" skills such as self-regulation, reflection, and executive control that are fundamental elements of higher order learning. Modern theories of learning maintain that learning is an active construction of knowledge and skills by the learner. Self-directed play can support children's abilities to learn and understand their learning. When self-directedness in play is weak it eventually becomes externally directed. This means that control of actions in play, including initiative, decision-making, and judgment in action, are done by someone other than the child. Externally directed play often occurs at home when parents or siblings tell the child what to do and what not to do. Too rigid rules and clear expectations by other people can be harmful for self-directedness in play.

In *intrinsically motivated play*, children behave or perform an action because they enjoy it and find inspiration in the action itself. Intrinsically motivated children play because they love it. Intrinsic motivation is rooted in three fundamental psychological needs in children's development: autonomy, or having the ability to initiate and direct one's own behaviors and actions; competence, or having the sense of ability to accomplish tasks; and relatedness, or the ability to create stable relationships with other people in play situations. Focusing on these needs is essential for enforcing intrinsic motivation during play. Intrinsic motivation often manifests itself as genuine interest in doing something. It is closely related to curiosity that is often seen as a source of intrinsic motivation.

When children play, curiosity is also triggered. Research has revealed that curious children learn better and remember more than those children who are not curious about what they do. Curiosity that boosts student engagement in school and enhances self-directed learning thereby helps children's higher order learning, and helps them find their talents and passions, which should be central goals of education. When children play because they expect to receive rewards from parents or teachers, they are mostly extrinsically motivated to that activity. It is important to realize that higher quality play requires that we allow children to initiate play and make all major decisions regarding how they play themselves without parents or teachers interference.

Imagination is the great power of our mind. It enables us to form mental images of something that is not present to our senses or never before perceived in reality. We can imagine new ideas that can improve our lives and change the world. Sir Ken Robinson says that "imagination is the source of all human achievement,"[359] and it is therefore an essential condition for creativity and innovation. Play is the best way to learn that you hold this power of imagination and that you can use your mind to make the most of your life.

Creativity, problem-solving, and being able to come up with new ideas that have value are among the most important qualities of well-educated people today. They have become equally as important as the basic skills of reading, writing, and mathematics. We are frequently encouraged to think outside of the box and come up with solutions to real life problems. Creative problem-solving becomes easier when we use our imagination and see beyond reality. Advanced schools that are committed to teach children these skills use play, arts, and physical activity to help students to realize the power of their minds. Imagination is closely attached to learning and can greatly enhance cognitive development. Pretend play and imaginative play are common forms of play that allow children to use their imagination.

Early on in school, children learn that it is better to be realistic and reasonable if you want to succeed. It is true that often reasoning is better than wild thinking. But many important inventions and innovations happened as a result of imagination. Many people have learned only after they have left school or university that imagination can often be more valuable than reality. Imagination sparks passion, stimulates risk-taking, creativity and innovation, and helps to create alternative futures. Play is a natural context for children to use their imagination.

Most schools, at the moment, don't do a very good job of cultivating children's imagination and creative habits of mind. Overemphasis on standardization and testing, narrowing curricula that mathematics and language arts dominate at the expense of arts, music and physical activity, and fear of failure have transformed schools into assembly lines where teachers are expected to teach according to predesigned scripts. Standardization has become the worst enemy of creativity and imagination in teaching and learning in school. The best way to teach children the power of imagination is to have schools where teachers can experience that same power for their own work.

Process-oriented play is enjoyable for the sake of the activity itself, and is not concerned with an end result or product. It is important that adults don't over-direct children in play. The purpose of play is for children to enjoy the process, and not be judged on the outcomes. Process orientation as one of the key elements of play is the glue that binds together all other dimensions of play.

Play should be pleasurable. When children play, they should have a deep sense of enjoyment and fun, and may also feel joy, gratitude, inspiration, hope, love, and a sense of flow, or the full absorption in the process. Play is an important part of children's emotional development. Therefore, parents and teachers should do everything they can to make sure that children's play environment is psychologically, physically, and socially safe enough for positive emotions to flourish.

These five dimensions—self-directedness, intrinsic motivation, imagination, process orientation, and positive emotions—can be used as the framework for indicating the presence of "deeper play" among children (Figure 8). When all five dimensions of play are fully engaged, we call it deep play. Each of the five dimensions can be scaled from weak to strong, or using continuums, such as self-directed—externally directed, intrinsic

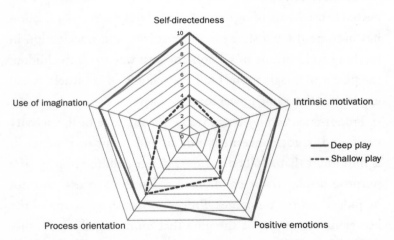

Figure 8. The Five Elements of "Deeper Play." When the values of these dimensions increase, so does the quality of play.
Source: Authors.

motivation—extrinsic motivation, and positive emotions—negative emotions.

When the strength of the five dimensions grows, so does the depth and quality of play. These are the qualities of play we should be supporting in our schools and homes.

10

Play in the Schools of Tomorrow

Children are not the people of tomorrow, but people today. They are entitled to be taken seriously. They have a right to be treated by adults with tenderness and respect, as equals. They should be allowed to grow into whoever they were meant to be—the unknown person inside each of them is the hope for the future.[360]

 —Janusz Korczak, Polish educator who died for his students, 1942

Some day the system will be such that the child and teacher will go to school with ecstatic joy. At home in the evening, the child will talk about the things done during the day and will talk with pride.[361]

 —Ella Flagg Young, Chicago Superintendent of Schools, 1909–1915 n his speech at New York City's Riverside Church in April 1967, the Reverend Martin Luther King Jr. said, "a time comes when silence is betrayal."

All too often we are silent about the declining health and well-being of our youngest citizens. Our politicians can often seem to care little about truly helping children and their families and schools. In the United States, for the first time in history, the next generation of young adults will be less educated and many of them will die younger than their parents. Now a quarter of the world's population is composed of children age 14 or younger. We must put children first. A Brooklyn-based poet and educator, Taylor Mali, asks in one of his poems: "Shouldn't the children of the country that is the wealthiest also be the children of the country that's the healthiest?" The time to break the silence is now.

Our world changes for different reasons. From north Texas to New York's Long Island, from China and Singapore to Scotland and Bangladesh, persistent professional advocacy and research on children's well-being, health, and learning have convinced school officials and parents of the power of play and changed what children do in schools. In Finland and other Nordic countries, children have the right to play, to healthy daily school lunches, to healthcare, daycare, and early childhood education, in part because women's voices have been clearly heard in politics and policymaking.

How many great play experiments do we need to see before we realize that when children play, they learn and thrive? How many courageous play advocates do we need to meet until we understand that we can do better for our children by simply letting them play? When will we wake up and realize that many "education reforms" have failed and put us on the wrong course? When will we see that it is the child's perspective that can change and uplift the world?

The school improvement champion and senior assistant of instruction of the New York City public schools (1977–1980), Ronald Edmonds, one of the first African American school improvement scholars and pioneer of fairer education for all, collected data from hundreds of schools to show that schools *can* make a difference. In 1979, after a decade of research and groundwork, he wrote, "We can, whenever and wherever we choose, successfully teach all children whose schooling is of interest to us. We already know more than we need to do that. Whether or not we do it must finally depend on how we feel about the fact that we haven't so far."[362] We share his optimism, and we hope that the world's teachers and parents will reclaim play and put it back in the lives of all our children, in and out of schools. We believe that, indeed, we can, whenever and wherever we choose, let the children play for the benefit of their joy, well-being, learning, and happiness. And yes, we already know more than we need in order to do so.

We are optimistic about the future. Good things are happening around the world to bring play back into the lives of all children in every school. More parents, teachers, and youth are joining this movement every day.

Someday soon, the parents, teachers, and children of the world will rise up and join together to build a new generation of schools for all children, schools built not on stress and fear but on play, joy, learning, and love. We have everything we need to make the change.

The great cultural anthropologist Margaret Mead wrote, "Never doubt that a small group of thoughtful committed citizens can change the world; indeed, it's the only thing that ever has."[363] Right now, around the world, parents, teachers, and citizens are fighting for children's right to play.

You can be a change-maker, too. Here are some examples of what to do next:

1. Switch off the screens, go to the playground with your child, play with your child every chance you get, and give your child lots of free, unstructured indoor and outdoor unplugged play for as long as they are a child.

   Go to the playground three times a week and make it a habit. If the weather doesn't permit, prepare a magic suitcase that is full of books, blocks, toys, and things kids can use to play with. Adopt a "no excuse" policy with going out to play. Children learn very quickly that you are committed to doing something with them regularly and they begin to expect it. Use the deeper play framework that is explained in this book to gradually enhance the quality of children's play. If you have a choice between playing outside or in the house, go out.

   Have conversations with your children after each play session. Ask them what they did and how they felt about it. Try to understand children's emotions while they were playing. Provide them with a safe environment, but not one without risk. Let children fail. Repeatedly. Let them figure out how to solve problems. Let them be bored. Only intervene when it is absolutely necessary. Help children negotiate when they are in a conflict situation. Talk to other adults about play and what their playtime practices are.

In 2015, Professor Claire Hughes of the Centre for Family Research at the University of Cambridge and her colleagues published the results of their study of 1,500 children between 2.5 and 5.5 years of age. They found that the two strongest predictors of a child's school readiness, language, and cognitive development when starting school were the extent to which a child "talks about fun activities at home" and "reads regularly at home."[364] The lesson: If you want to get your young child ready for school, read to them—and play with them!

The Center on the Developing Child at Harvard University has created an online resource on play and executive functioning, with suggested activities for children and parents: http://developingchild.harvard.edu/wp-content/uploads/2015/05/Enhancing-and-Practicing-Executive-Function-Skills-with-Children-from-Infancy-to-Adolescence-1.pdf.

2. Be a community play activist: Show up at the school board and town council meeting and demand that play and physical activity be included as a regular part of the school schedule, as recommended by the American Academy of Pediatrics, the Centers for Disease Control and Prevention, the National Academy of Medicine and the Association of Childhood Educators International.

If you have school-age children, ask them how much time they have to play during the day. "Little or none," they may answer. If you ask your school board or school principal about reasons for the play deficit, they might say, "We must maximize the instruction time to raise standards," or "Safety is the priority and the school grounds are dangerous and risky for children." You should explain that deeper play during the day can enhance student learning, and yes, we can make school grounds safer with just a little effort.

If your politicians or school officials resist your pro-play suggestions, remember that the evidence, and the expert opinions, are on your side, and have them do their homework—require that they read these essential, easily-googled "top 7" reports, and report back to you:

- *The Importance of Play in Promoting Healthy Child Development and Maintaining Strong Parent-Child Bonds,* American Academy of Pediatrics Clinical Report, 2007
- *The Association Between School-Based Physical Activity, Including Physical Education, and Academic Performance,* Centers for Disease Control and Prevention, 2010
- *Educating the Student Body: Taking Physical Activity and Physical Education to School,* National Academy of Medicine (then called Institute of Medicine), 2013
- *The Crucial Role of Recess in School,* American Academy of Pediatrics Policy Statement, 2013, reaffirmed 2016
- *The Importance of Play in Promoting Healthy Child Development and Maintaining Strong Parent-Child Bonds: Focus on Children in Poverty,* American Academy of Pediatrics Clinical Report, 2012

- *Strategies for Recess in Schools,* Centers for Disease Control, SHAPE America (Society of Health and Physical Educators), 2017
- *The Power of Play: A Pediatric Role in Enhancing Development in Young Children,* American Academy of Pediatrics Clinical Report, 2018

3. Speak out for play: Make a 3-minute speech at your town hall meeting based on what you've read in this book and your own research and post your own version of "The Declaration of Learning and Play: Call to Halt the War on Childhood" (see page 367) far and wide.

4. Ask hard, blunt questions of people who have power over children's lives: Ask local authorities, school board members, and politicians to produce hard evidence and research on how mandatory, universal standardized testing of children helps them learn, ask exactly how much the testing costs, and ask why children are not instead tested and evaluated by their own classroom teachers. Ask other hard questions, like "Why doesn't my child receive sufficient recess time, when students in Texas, Oklahoma, Long Island and in other nations do?" "Why have you cut arts, music, history, home economics, and shop class?" "Why don't disadvantaged and disabled children have as much opportunity to play as any other child? What are you doing specifically to fix this?"

5. Write an op-ed to your local newspaper: Post it to your Facebook and Twitter feeds. Blogs, short essays, and op-eds are powerful platforms today to communicate ideas. Even short letters or commentary published in a newspaper or magazine

can have a huge impact. A good op-ed either outlines the problem or suggests a solution to a problem. Write op-eds to your local newspaper about children's play. Write an opinion piece about how more play in school helps children's health and learning. Use the research cited in this book and other evidence to make your point. There are always teachers, activists, and others who have blogs and websites where your opinions and ideas could be shared with your community.

6. Launch a play experiment in your local school: Suggest an experiment that could be run in your school. Depending on the readiness of the school and the parents, this could be a modest increase in indoor time for free play and passion projects, or more recess time for all children every day. Or it could be a bold, big transformation of the school schedule to give students significantly more indoor and outdoor play. One lesson from the Texas play experiment is to include a good character education program to better children's understanding of their behaviors and those of others.

7. Organize a schoolyard and playground fundraising and improvement campaign to make it more play-friendly. We have visited schools where the costs of standardized tests, investments in technology, and austerity-driven budget cuts have been cited as excuses to not have better outdoor spaces for children to play. A lack of safety in school surroundings is also mentioned as a reason to keep pupils inside all day long.

The quality of play depends on the quality of the schoolyard. The cost of a proper, play-friendly schoolyard is a fraction of what school buildings cost. Although many public schools today operate at the edge of their financial limits, investing in the improvement of school playgrounds is a realistic and smart choice. This is what you could do: Organize a group of parents and community members who think that children should play more outdoors during schooldays. Visit schools where there are nice outdoor playgrounds and where play is part of the educational plan. Partner with teachers and play experts to make a new design for your school. Fund-raising may be an option to supplement the school's own resources to renew the school's playground facilities. Remember that an environment that boosts play doesn't necessarily have to be very expensive.

8. Raise awareness in your community about understanding the effects of over-testing, standardization, and narrowing curriculum. Join pro-play groups on social media and in your community to advocate for more play and join groups to lobby for our public schools. Many people feel passionately about education, especially when it is about their own children. Everybody seems to have an opinion about how to improve education. But we all have a lot to learn from each other and from other families and cultures.

9. Launch a periodic "Failure Academy" at your local school to encourage and celebrate experimentation, failure, and learning from failure as a pathway to success. It could be an interdisciplinary project in school in which students study risk-taking and trial and error in culture and science, experience failure by doing something in a new way, and celebrate failure at school, home, and the workplace, as pathways to success.

The pursuit of academic or educational success often comes with avoidance of failure. In success-obsessed environments, children learn that the opposite of success is failure. They often experience that if you fail, you will be punished or not rewarded. Children will not learn the critical importance of failure. In real life, failure often precedes success, and often serves as the critical predicate for success.

If all children have more time to play in and out of school in the future, we will need to protect our public schools from harmful policies that put stress and overwork before well-being and health. Children need a better education, not necessarily more of it. A better education should include a "whole-child" approach that shifts the focus from narrowly defined academic standards created by politicians and testing companies to teaching that promotes the development and growth of all children.

10. Work with your neighbors to launch a play-safe zone in each other's backyards and communities, with parents and citizens volunteering to provide safety overwatch. You can start by linking two or three blocks together and expand from there.

11. Declare your home an unplugged Free Play Zone for at least part of the week, with plenty of simple, engaging play materials, and an atmosphere of celebrating unstructured free play and experimentation. Allow your children to be bored. For an excellent resource on children, the media, and play, we recommend the website and materials of the non-profit Center on Media and Child Health,[365] created by Harvard Associate Professor of Pediatrics Dr. Michael Rich, otherwise known as "The Mediatrician": http://cmch.tv/moreplaytoday/.

12. Listen to children's voices; they have a lot to say about play. And we adults have a lot to learn from them. We should also listen to teachers' voices. We recently heard from a group of American teachers who said that their opinions are rarely if ever consulted in the day-to-day process of teaching imposed on them by government officials. But parents should feel free to approach teachers and ask them for their ideas—teachers want to share them!

WHAT ABOUT DIGITAL PLAY?

There are obvious benefits to some technology in schools. Technology can be an effective tool in a teacher's "toolbox," especially in STEM classes and long-distance learning and special needs contexts, and there are studies that suggest possible cognitive or physical benefits to children from some video game play, such as improved reaction time and problem-solving skills. Digital platforms can help children learn about a wide range of subjects.

But there is no convincing body of evidence suggesting that "digital play" in or out of school is any better than real-world play. For that reason, we should not automatically accept screens as a play substitute, no matter how many millions of children are immersed in the digital world, no matter how many "digitally native, efficiently multitasking children" adults think there are (which is a myth—both adults and children are equally inefficient "multi-taskers"[366]), and no matter what the latest sales pitch in the booming $60 billion "edu-tech" industry may be, as it rapidly turns classrooms into what one physician calls "a digital playground that includes Chromebooks, iPads, Smart Boards, tablets, smartphones, learning apps and a never-ending variety of 'edu-games.' "[367]

As the American Academy of Pediatrics 2018 clinical report on play stated, "Media (e.g., television, video games, and smartphone and tablet applications) use often encourages passivity and the consumption of others' creativity rather than active learning and socially interactive play. Most importantly, immersion in electronic media takes away time from real play, either outdoors or indoors." The doctors' report stressed, "It is important for parents to understand that media use often does not support their goals of encouraging curiosity and learning for their children," and "it is parents' and caregivers' presence and attention that enrich children, not elaborate electronic gadgets."[368]

There is surprisingly little evidence of learning benefits for the vast majority of technology products in school. As John Vallance, the headmaster of Australia's prestigious Sydney grammar school, has said: "I think when people come to write the history of this period in education, this investment in classroom technology is going to be seen as a huge fraud."[369]

Some of Silicon Valley's leaders, in fact, largely shielded their own children from digital devices until they were in their mid-teens, and some had very low-tech childhoods themselves. Google founders Larry Page and Sergey Brin and Amazon creator Jeff Bezos all attended tech-light or tech-free Montessori schools. Bill Gates confessed in 2017 that he and his wife "didn't give [their] kids cellphones until they were 14 and they complained other kids got them earlier."[370] Steve Jobs, when asked in 2011 about his children using the iPad, declared, "They haven't used it. We limit how much technology our kids use at home."[371] Way back in 1996, Jobs expressed sharp skepticism about technology in the classroom, saying, "I've probably spearheaded giving away more computer equipment to schools than anybody on the planet. But I've come to the conclusion that the problem is not one that technology can hope to solve. What's wrong with education cannot be fixed with technology. No amount of technology will make a dent."[372] A number of other tech executives and engineers feel the same way, as they send their children to tech-free Waldorf schools.[373] President Obama and his wife Michelle wouldn't give their oldest daughter a cell phone until she was 12, and tightly restricted their children's computer and TV time at home.[374] Are these parents onto something?

"In Silicon Valley, the higher up somebody is in the tech world, generally speaking, the more they try to insulate their kid from any of our products," explained Jaron Lanier, Interdisciplinary Scientist at Microsoft Research, and a pioneer in the development of virtual reality. "What I see is executives at the big tech companies putting their kids in [low-tech] Waldorf schools." He added, "They just don't let their kids go online except in very limited and strictly supervised ways and preferably not at all. The people who do this stuff really don't want their kids to be around it."[375]

In October 2018, the *New York Times* published a startling series of articles by its San Francisco–based technology reporter Nellie Bowles about a "dark consensus about screens and kids" and a "fear of screens" that "has reached the level of panic in Silicon Valley," with some parents demanding that screens be banned from classrooms. "Technologists know how phones really work, and many have decided they don't want their own children anywhere near them," wrote Bowles. A consensus was forming in Silicon Valley, she reported, that "the benefits of screens as a learning tool are overblown, and the risks for addiction and stunting development seem high."

"I am convinced the devil lives in our phones and is wreaking havoc on our children," declared Athena Chavarria, who works at the Chan Zuckerberg Initiative, Mark Zuckerberg's philanthropy. "It wasn't long ago that the worry was that rich students would have access to the internet earlier, gaining tech skills and creating a digital divide," wrote journalist Bowles. "But now, as Silicon Valley's parents increasingly panic over the impact screens have on their children and move toward screen-free lifestyles, worries over a new digital divide are rising. It could happen that the children of poorer and middle-class parents will be raised by screens, while the children of Silicon Valley's elite will be going back to wooden toys and the luxury of human interaction."[376]

In the classroom, in fact, technology has so far had little overall positive effect on childhood learning. That's the startling finding of the OECD's 2015 report "Students, Computers and Learning: Making the Connection." The report found that despite billions of dollars of frantic government spending, where ICTs [information and communications technologies] are used, their impact on student performance has been "mixed, at best," in the words of the OECD's Andreas Schleicher. "In most countries, the current use of technology is already past the point of optimal use in schools," said Schleicher. "We're at a point where computers are actually hurting learning."[377]

The report went on to assert that technology is "of little help in bridging the skills divide between advantaged and disadvantaged students." And, "put simply, ensuring that every child attains a baseline level of proficiency in reading and mathematics seems to do more to create equal opportunities in a digital world than can be achieved by expanding or subsidizing access to high-tech devices and services." The study concluded, "Students who use computers very frequently at school do a lot worse in most learning outcomes, even after controlling for social background and student demographics." With some exceptions like distance and special needs learning, there is little evidence that digital tools are inherently superior to analog tools in the hands of qualified teachers in teaching children the fundamentals of learning, especially in the early years.

The OECD report, which was based on data collected in the early 2010s, suggested that teachers need to be better trained in the use of technology in school. But it also found that children may learn best with analog tools first before later adding digital platforms, and that a few hours a week of classroom screen time may be optimal for children, beyond which learning benefits drop off to diminishing, or even negative, returns.[378]

This argues not for the 100 percent screen-based classroom proposed by some enthusiasts, but for a far more strategic and cost- and learning-effective model. Digital tools are quite obviously here to stay, and they offer potential to enhance the childhood learning experience. But screen-based learning products should be rigorously tested and validated by independent research and classroom teachers before precious resources are spent on them. Technology should be a servant of the classroom, not the master. The successful "digital leap" in childhood education is not toward 100 percent screen-based learning or the indiscriminate proliferation of screens in the hands of children. It is toward the careful, measured, evidence-based use of digital tools in the classroom as an effective complement to proven analog tools, without wasting time and money on products with little demonstrated value to authentic learning.

Social media, TV, and digital games occupy a significant proportion of young people's days. In the United States and Finland, for example, teenagers spend approximately half of the time they are awake each day online, connected to social networks and other media in the Internet. When children hang out in social networks and entertainment in the Internet, are they playing? We doubt that much of that time has much to do with high-quality play. According to some studies, one in five teenagers is addicted to social media and smartphones. Addiction is not a feature of authentic play—most descriptions of play include as one of the foundational requirements children's own choice to be engaged in a playful activity.

A barrage of alarming research from around the world has emerged in the last several years highlighting the limitations, risks, and potential dangers of excessive screen time and technology use by children and young adults, including associations with physical and behavioral health problems in children. According to the American Academy of Pediatrics, these include obesity, violent and aggressive behavior, depression, anxiety, earlier sexual behaviors, poor academic performance and self-image, nightmares, and tobacco and substance abuse.[379]

An ongoing research project titled "Growing Up Digital,"[380] in the Canadian province of Alberta, is taking a closer look at this conclusion. Dr. Michael Rich of Harvard Medical School and Dr. Phil McRae of Alberta Teachers Association have collected data that show how teachers see the obvious benefits of technology in classrooms: searching information, analyzing data, and communicating findings. But at the same time, teachers in Alberta report grim observations in their classrooms: 90 percent of teachers say that the number of students with emotional challenges has increased, 86 percent of teachers say that the number of students with social challenges has increased, and 75 percent of teachers say that the number of students with cognitive challenges has increased during the past 5 years. Cause and effect are unclear. But warning signs are ominous over excessive screen time and social media use.

In the United States, reported acts of violence like kicking and punching against parents taking away children's video games number in the thousands.[381] Sometimes, schools make the problem worse. When a Long Island mother found out her 5-year-old son in kindergarten was going to be required to use an iPad in class, she complained and threatened to pull the child out of school. School officials threatened to turn her in to child protective services.[382] According to psychiatrist Dr. Nicholas Kardaras, who treats digital addiction among children at his rehab center in New York State, over 200 peer-reviewed studies correlate excessive screen usage with a host of clinical disorders, including addiction, increased aggression, depression, anxiety, and psychosis. "We are projecting our own infatuation with shiny technology, assuming our little digital natives would rather learn using gadgets," Dr. Kardaras wrote, "while what they crave and need is human contact with flesh-and-blood educators."[383] In Marin County, California, when Barbara McVeigh tried to take her 9-year-old son's digital device away, "he beat the shit out of me," she told Dr. Kardaras, attacking her "with a dazed look on his face—his eyes were not his." Responding police asked if the boy was on drugs. When she pulled her son out of his suburban tech-heavy public school and sent him to a more rural, lower-tech school, his behavior improved markedly. Then she found out that all fourth-graders in the new school would be learning how to create "coding" for video games, and instead of going outside to play at recess, children were being permitted to play violent video games indoors. "I am prepared to go to war with our public education over technology use," declared the mother. "This is wrong." She said, "I feel like there is a war going on against our children," "and it's come so fast that we're not even questioning it."[384]

"Make no mistake," wrote Naomi Schaefer Riley, a visiting fellow at the American Enterprise Institute, in the *New York Times*, "The real digital divide in this country is not between children who have access to the Internet and those who don't. It's between children whose parents know that they have to restrict screen time and those whose parents have been sold a bill of goods by schools and politicians that more screens are a key to success. It's time to let everyone in on the secret."[385]

A paper published in 2016 by the Centre for Economic Performance at the London School of Economics found that grades improved when phones were removed from the classroom. The comprehensive study involved 91 schools with a total of 130,000 students. The researchers found schools' test scores jumped by 6.4 percent after phones were banished. The benefit to underachieving poor and special education students was even bigger—their average test scores increased by 14 percent.[386] Four years earlier, a major meta-analysis, or "study of studies," had found that "technology-based interventions tend to produce just slightly lower levels of improvement when compared with other researched interventions and approaches." The study concluded, "Taken together, the correlational and experimental evidence does not offer a convincing case for the general impact of digital technology on learning outcomes."[387] In a study published in 2013 in the *International Journal of Educational Research*, Professor Anne Mangen of the University of Stavanger in Norway and her colleagues found that students who read text on computers performed worse on comprehension tests than students who read the same text on paper.[388] Students in one 2011 study preferred good old-fashioned human contact, or "ordinary, real-life lessons" over e-learning. These findings surprised the researchers: "It is not the portrait that we expected, whereby students would embrace anything that happens on a more highly technological level. On the contrary—they really seem to like access to human interaction, a smart person at the front of the classroom."[389]

Valerie Carson, Assistant Professor of Physical Education and Recreation at the University of Alberta, reported on results of the "Growing Up Digital" study in December 2015: "We found that the more physical activity children do, the better [their] cognitive development. The more time they spend on screens, like tablets and cell phones, tends to be either detrimentally related to their development or not related at all."[390] Dr. Nicholas Kardaras has concluded, "The key is to prevent your 4-, 5-, or 8-year-old from getting hooked on screens to begin with." This means "books instead of iPads; nature and sports instead of TV." He suggests to parents that if they have to, "demand that your child's school not give them a tablet or Chromebook until they are at least 10 years old (others recommend 12)."[391]

The bottom line: Real-life play has a very wide range of benefits for your child. Digital play has a lot less.[392] The vast majority of educational technology products have little to no rigorous, independent evidence to support their use by children.

THE SCHOOL QUALITY DASHBOARD

43 Questions to Help Save Our Schools and Make Children Thrive—Put Your School to the Test

We test students—why shouldn't we test schools?

We entrust our children to them, we pay for them, we support them, we often vote on the officials who run them—why shouldn't we require schools to answer basic questions about quality and minimum standards?

Let's turn the tables on testing—put your school to the test!

How can you judge the quality of your public school, and the public schools in your community?

One way to look at a school is to ask, "How did it do on the state standardized tests?"

You can look at data from the mass standardized testing of children in a few subjects, such as math and language skills, then compare those scores and trends with those of other schools.

This has become the dominant governing mechanism of school management in the United States and some other nations.

Some politicians and administrators like these scores because they give them a few "quick and dirty" numbers they can try to manage or manipulate. If the numbers can be made to look good, policymakers can publicly congratulate themselves and strike a heroic pose. If the numbers are bad, they can blame teachers and students and dodge their own responsibility for neglecting, underfunding, or mismanaging an education system.

But standardized tests alone don't provide the correct, complete information needed to judge school quality—because they don't fully account for income, family background, learning history, peer effects, access to proper out-of-school nutrition and intellectual enrichment, emotional life, conditions in the home, and a host of other factors that affect a child's learning, development, and growth. Every child begins at a different starting point, and every child learns at their own speed. Plus, standardized tests are not designed to measure school's performance, only that part of students' cognitive ability or domain that the tests are designed to measure. And there is very little evidence that school evaluation systems based primarily on such testing are improving childhood learning or reducing achievement gaps.

Among the many dangers of an overreliance on such measurements is that they miss a host of other critical skills and subjects, many of which can't be reduced to standardized test data. They also tend to push play, breaks, recess, and physical activity out of school, along with many critical non-tested subjects, like hands-on science and lab work, the arts, second languages, history and social studies, life skills, vocational skills, and civics.

They are therefore very incomplete and essentially obsolete measurements.

Analyzing school quality is complicated, and no method of judging it is perfect. But instead of looking only at data from standardized test scores in two or three basic knowledge areas, a more accurate, advanced, and sensitive way to help understand school quality is to ask school administrators—and the elected officials who oversee schools—for a full "dashboard" portfolio of information about a school or a school system, including information on the critical educational foundation of play, to inform your opinion. You can think of it as a "qualitative standardized test" for a school, and give your own grades to the answers they give you. You may have your own questions to add to the list.

Here are some basic questions on school quality and standards that we as parents, taxpayers, and citizens should ask any public school or school system to help inform our discussions and work to improve our schools and help children thrive:

1. What is the school's teaching and learning philosophy?
2. What are the goals of education in school, and how does the school achieve those goals?
3. Does the school understand that, in the words of the American Academy of Pediatrics, "the lifelong success of children is based on their ability to be creative and to apply the lessons learned from playing"? Does the school follow the recommendations of the American Academy of Pediatrics, the National Academy of Medicine and the CDC for play, recess, and physical activity in school? If not, why not?

4. How does the school develop and support a child's social-emotional, academic-cognitive, and physical health and growth?

5. How does the school develop a child's basic literacy, language and math skills, executive function, self-regulation, creativity, compassion, risk-taking, health and well-being, love of learning, management of failure, collaboration, and self-expression?

6. Is each child respected, assessed, and supported as an individual learner?

7. Does each child have access to a fully qualified, certified classroom teacher with a graduate degree and extensive classroom training? If not, why not?

8. How rich are the curriculum offerings in hands-on science and lab work, the arts, second languages, history and social studies, life skills, vocational skills, and civics?

9. How are children supported in times they experience stress, failure, conflict, frustration, or crisis?

10. What is the average class size, and would be the ideal class size? Would children benefit from more teachers per student?

11. How safe is the school?

12. Do all students receive the same degree of access to educational services and advantages as students elsewhere in the community and district? If not, why not?

13. How are students', parents', and teachers' views respected in shaping and improving school policy and practice?

14. Is the school resourced and funded adequately and equitably compared to other schools in the district?

15. Does the school provide healthy meals and free, high quality after-school programs?

16. Are health and social support services available in school if needed?

17. Is the school racially and economically desegregated, and does the school reflect the diversity of the broader community?

18. How is the school making the best use of direct instruction, cooperative learning and other small-group work, free outdoor play, guided play, and self-directed learning?

19. What are the policies and practices in school for children with special educational needs, including both highly advanced and struggling students?

20. How will the school help a child identify and develop her or his strengths and passions?

21. Is the schoolyard open for an optional period of safely supervised free play before school starts?

22. What is the condition of the school infrastructure, building, and play area?

23. How much time for play, recess, physical activity, choice time, and passion projects are provided to children?

24. Are teachers and staff expressly forbidden from using recess as an incentive or punishment for academic or behavior reasons? If not, why not?

25. How often are field trips offered?

26. What are the school's direct and indirect costs of preparing for and administering standardized tests?

27. How are children's learning and development assessed in school?

28. How are students and parents involved in assessing student learning?

29. Do parents have the right, without penalty, to "opt-up," or upgrade, their children's learning evaluations from taking standardized tests to higher-quality assessments designed and supervised by his or her classroom teacher? If not, why not?

30. Does the school have an atmosphere of warmth, collaboration, and support, rather than stress and fear?

31. How will the school help children learn from mistakes and failures?

32. Are parents welcomed into the school to volunteer and to observe classes?

33. Are the school's finances and governance fully transparent?

34. How does the school communicate with parents?

35. Are there opportunities for children to perform community service and volunteer work?

36. What are the data and trends of attendance, graduation, and teacher and student turnover?

37. What is the school's discipline policy and process?

38. Do teachers regularly participate in high-quality professional learning and leadership development?

39. In kindergarten, elementary school, and middle school do parents have the right to upgrade their children's homework from hours of night-time drilling and worksheets to higher-quality homework, such as independent reading, family time, outdoor play, and healthy, early bedtimes? If not, why not?

40. How does the school deal with digital devices in school, especially those brought to school by children?

41. How does the school know how happy parents are with the school?
42. How does the school know how happy teachers are with the school?
43. How does the school know how happy the children are in school?

* * *

The awareness of childhood learning through play is as old as humankind itself. As the biblical force known as Wisdom recalled in Proverbs 8:30–31, "I was with him forming all things: and was delighted every day, playing before him at all times; playing in the world. And my delights were to be with the children of men."

Today, what our children need most in school is not more disruption, "digital learning," apps, screens, "data-driven instruction," "personalized learning" delivered mainly by screens, edufads, and standardized teaching and testing. What our children need is not teacher de-professionalization and constant interference in education by politicians and ideologues who know little to nothing about education. The last thing our children need in school is stress and fear.

What our children need most are schools built upon the strengths, talents, and dreams of childhood—schools that are deeply informed by the perspectives of children, safe and supportive, filled with discovery and exploration, and run by highly skilled, collaborating, professional teachers.

Our world needs schools that welcome and nurture all children, of all backgrounds and talents, of all strengths and challenges.

Our world needs schools for children where experimentation and failure are celebrated as pathways to success—schools that help children experience and understand life in all its beauty, diversity, and richness.

Our world needs schools that teach children basic skills, including how to think for themselves, learn how to learn, learn to love learning, learn how to fail and how to succeed, and learn to work together, help each other, dream of making a better world, and master their own destiny in life.

What our children need most in our schools and homes is a childhood that is built on a foundation of the most mysterious and powerful gift that children can give themselves: play.

It is time we give it to them.

THE GLOBAL PLAY SUMMIT

How can play be integrated into schools, and how should we build the schools of tomorrow?

To begin exploring answers to that question, we interviewed a global "brain trust" panel of experts, individually, both in person and digitally. The panel included some of the world's greatest minds in education from around the world. This is what they told us about play and about creating the schools our children need.

Nancy Carlsson-Paige, Professor Emerita, Child Development, Lesley University; Co-founder, Defending the Early Years:

If I were building the schools of tomorrow, I would want to put play (also known as children's work) at the center of the curriculum for pre-K through third-grade classrooms. There would be activity areas—blocks, building and math materials, sand and water tables, easels and art materials, dramatic play, a reading corner, a science area, a drawing and writing area, and special projects. Each area would be well stocked with a range of open-ended materials that would allow children to bring their own interests and questions to the materials and to use them in ways attuned to their developmental levels. There would be outdoor play every day and natural objects to explore and use in play. Even in urban areas, teachers could encourage children to play outside with natural objects such as leaves, rocks, water, and sand.

The atmosphere of the classroom would be warm, friendly, and playful. There would be a structure to the physical space and the schedule that children could easily understand. This would provide for them the sense of security kids need in order to become deeply engrossed in play. Spaces would be designed for children with materials organized on shelves at their level. The usage patterns of the room would be easy for children to understand and would support them in knowing what is available and what to do. Choice boards listing the activities available each day in words and or pictures would help children make more intentional choices. Children would be encouraged to play with each other, to enjoy creating together, and to naturally learn the many social skills inherent in cooperative play.

Teachers in the schools of tomorrow would be adept at building curriculum from children's interests and needs, and know how to introduce new learning and skills based on children's play and developmental levels. They would have solid backgrounds in child development and be skilled observers of play. They would know how to understand children's learning and needs by what they do in their play. Such teachers would observe the themes coming up in children's play and know how to interpret them. For example, if a child were frequently acting out the role of a scary TV monster, a teacher would know how to explore this theme with the child and perhaps even the child's family.

Teachers would also be skilled at supporting children's social and emotional learning. As they observed play, teachers could notice what conflicts arose. Later in working with the whole group, teachers could find creative ways, such as through storytelling and the use of puppets, to pose to the children similar conflicts to those they had observed, and ask for ideas that might help "solve the problem." If there were conflicts in play that escalated to the point of needing intervention, teachers would know how to step in to help children talk and listen to each other, look for ideas for how to solve their problem, and find solutions that both children could feel good about.

Each day would include a group time when children could share what they had done that day in their play/work. This sharing would create enthusiasm and a sense of community among the children. Children could ask each other questions about their work and share ideas. This kind of group time would stimulate new ideas, strengthen relationships, and inspire children to return to play activities with deepening interest.

Yong Zhao, Foundation Distinguished Professor, School of Education, University of Kansas; Professorial Fellow, Mitchell Institute for Health and Education Policy, Victoria University, Australia; Global Chair, University of Bath, UK: First, we must recognize the value of play in education. Education leaders, policymakers, and parents need to understand that play is not a stupid waste of time but rather an essential and powerful educational experience. The second recommendation is that schools should create space in the curriculum for play and provide facilities, opportunities, and encouragement for play. Third, teachers can model play in their own way by playing with ideas, playing with hypotheses, playing with solutions, playing with colleagues, and playing with students.

Susan Linn, Lecturer on Psychiatry, Harvard Medical School; Research Associate, Boston Children's Hospital: Play is the foundation of learning, creativity, self-expression, and constructive problem-solving. It's how children wrestle with life to make it meaningful. Children are born with an innate capacity to play, but as a society we seem to be doing everything we can to prevent them from playing.

Play is being drummed out of schools, even in pre-K. Opportunities for play are lost when schools opt out of recess, art, and music and when they opt in to scripted and/or rote learning, "teaching to the test," and rigidly structured classrooms.

Schools need to bring back opportunities to play through recess, art, and music. They need to minimize rote learning and provide children with opportunities to explore and to experience initiating rather than merely reacting.

Stephen Siviy, Professor of Psychology, Gettysburg College:
Opportunities for free play should be integrated throughout the school day and should never be used as leverage to foster either good behavior or improved learning. We need to stop thinking of formal education only in terms of cognitive development and begin to take a more holistic view and begin to more tightly integrate cognitive, social, and emotional development. Play may be the glue that helps bind these together.

Gloria Ladson-Billings, President, National Academy of Education; Professor, Department of Curriculum & Instruction, Kellner Family Distinguished Professor in Urban Education, University of Wisconsin–Madison:
Children utilize play to develop their imaginations and their higher-order thinking skills—such as problem-solving and creativity. Play provides freedom from the structures of typical classrooms that often emphasize conformity. Group play also provides an opportunity for developing social skills that are vital to success in life.

Anyone who fully understands child development knows that children's "play" is children's "work." It is through play that children "rehearse" the social and cultural roles of the society in which they find themselves. The child who is playing "house" is rehearsing elements of roles she or he sees at home . . . cooking, cleaning, teaching, storytelling. Some of the more productive meetings I've attended had things for people to play with DURING the meeting at their seat (e.g., Slinky toys, bubbles, coloring pages, yo-yos).

Perhaps the real question is how to integrate SCHOOL into play where we recognize play as the primary function. In the best preschools I have observed, play holds a central role. Children are allowed to explore, imagine, construct, communicate, and cooperate. They are afforded many choices—play on existing structures, play with temporary structures (e.g., sand tables or sand boxes), play with non-specific toys such as blocks and Legos.

Selma Simonstein, President, Chilean National Committee of the World Organization for Early Childhood Education; Professor, Metropolitan University of Education Sciences, Santiago, Chile:

Play is a spontaneous tendency in childhood and must be present always and in every stage of the child's life; also, it is a right of all children established at the Convention on the Rights of the Child. Educators must give them the opportunities to make this happen.

It is necessary to recognize children as unique beings, full citizens able to know and to transform the world through play, facilitating the imagination, communication, and understanding. Play is affected when government policies don't visualize it as an important element, or by over-schooling, by use and abuse of technology, by the demands of families, and, of course, by schooling with a traditional approach to school.

It is also affected when the homogeneity and the control of academic results are valued, giving priority to memorization and homework. Play is devalued as a pedagogical strategy, despite this being a natural and proper way in which children learn and interact with the world, emphasizing the development of mathematics and language. We should consider work in projects where children can find areas of interest outdoors as well as indoors for

their development. We should give children the possibility to choose what to play and what to create, allow children to create new knowledge and not depend solely on the information provided by the educator. We should promote environmental education: recycling, protecting nature, preparing compost, taking care of a garden. We should move in different spaces and facilitate areas where children can decide which space they want to be in and for how long—spaces that favor teamwork and cooperation. **Fraser Brown, Professor of Playwork, Core Member, Institute for Health and Wellbeing, Leeds Beckett University; Co-editor, *International Journal of Play*:**
If I were building the schools of tomorrow I would certainly recommend a radical rethink of our current approach. School should be a playful experience. Another setting where we might consider placing Plato's "play sanctuaries" is the school—after all, that is where children already spend a great deal of their time. Unfortunately, school is too often a deeply unpopular place among the very children that it is supposed to serve. Most schools have interpreted the Every Child Matters agenda (in the UK) and the No Child Left Behind agenda (in the United States) as being a call for more classroom time. Sadly, in that regard they are reflecting what most politicians seem to think—namely, that getting our schools' teaching methods right is the single best thing we can do for our children.

On the contrary, there are numerous studies that suggest it would be far more effective simply to empower children to play. Play researcher Brian Sutton-Smith says that after moments of playing everyone feels better and subsequent events work better. The opposite of play—if redefined in terms that stress its reinforcing optimism and excitement—is not work, it is depression. Players come out of their ludic paradoxes with renewed belief in the worthwhileness of merely living. The logic of this as applied to the school day would be for the curriculum to be designed around children's play opportunities—not in the current half-hearted sense, where play is used as a tool to enable teachers to trick children into learning the things that adults think are important. Instead, if there were as much time given to play in the school day as was given over to adult-directed teaching, there would be a double benefit. Not only would the children have the opportunity genuinely to learn while they are playing, but also when they returned to the classroom, they would be so much more ready to learn because of the energizing nature of free play. What we are proposing here is a school day that is extended to accommodate working parents, but structured around alternate 45-minute periods of free play and classroom learning. It would not be reasonable to expect the teachers to fulfill the dual role implicit in this arrangement, and so this revised approach would involve the employment of play-workers alongside teachers.

There are two more steps our schools can take to make themselves more helpful in addressing all the needs of the children they serve. First, they should be telling the children about the importance of informal play, and encouraging them to engage in free play, rather than concentrating on homework. Second, they should be opening their playgrounds after school. Most school playgrounds are a wasted resource, as they are often the only large open space within a community, and yet the gates are often locked by 6:00 P.M. and all over the weekend. Employing play-workers to work during the school day and at weekends would be a novel and imaginative step toward making the school into the hub of its community.[393]

Helen May, Emeritus Professor of Education, University of Otago, New Zealand:

If I were building the schools of tomorrow, there are lessons from the schools of the past. I believe that play, and more broadly playfulness, should be integral to schooling of all ages. I taught over many years in early childhood education but also the primary school sector (up to age 10). Across settings, play, creativity, project work, and art were how we always started our day—from this came our writing and conversation. With school-age children there were times later in the day for reading and math, but it was my view that where these could be integrated into a playful and creative program they were most successful.

Stig Brostrom, Professor Emeritus, Danish School of Education, Aarhus University:

Play is a fundamental aspect of children's learning and development. In short, play contributes to children's general development and to a number of psychological dimensions: thought, speech and languages, social development, fantasy, and problem-solving.

Important changes take place in the preschool child's psyche through play. They pave the way for the child's transition to a new level of development. The leading function and impact of play activity have a number of causes. Through interaction with peers and adults, the child deals with signs and symbols representing the culture. In accordance with cultural-historical theory, signs have an influence on the development of higher mental functions when these are a part of a human interaction.

Secondly, in play children are able to master ideas and carry out more advanced actions than what is possible for them in non-play situations. In other words, in play, children increase the demand on themselves and with that bring themselves into the zone of proximal development.

However, the optimistic idea that play has a leading and developmental function has been overinterpreted, and the (often misunderstood) phrases "in play a child always behaves beyond his or her average age" and "play always leads to a more advanced level of development" have been discussed and criticized. For example, one argument is that play does not in itself contribute to the child's development—play has a developmental potential only when the play environment has the potential to challenge children to cross their "zone of proximal development." This calls for social interaction in which the teacher or other adult plays an active role, challenges the child, and provokes him or her to create new meanings and understandings. This form of play goes beyond traditional role play and is called "border play."

In addition, play helps children overcome their egocentricity. When a child identifies herself with the role of the mother, she has to take over the motives, feelings, and actions attached to the role. Role play also contributes to the inhibition of spontaneous actions. In order to be able to play, children have to reflect on and arrange some play actions. Play implies that children reflect on and express their thoughts linguistically and finally carry out the play actions. In other words, there is a gradual movement from unconscious and impulsive actions to conscious, strong-willed actions. The order action–speech–thought is changed to the reverse order: thought–speech–action.

Play develops imagination and fantasy. The child can only carry out role play if he or she in fantasy is able to imagine the role and the actions. Children have to ascribe another meaning to the play actions and play accessories. Moreover, play develops children's social capacity and social cognition. The individual role demands particular play actions. Because play is an activity, children want to enter into an agreement with each other. Play helps children in a meaningful way to submit to one another's play wishes, and this play develops skills in problem-solving.

I have argued for the implementation of four forms of play in school:

1. Open holistic activities based on children's own experimental investigations plus child-initiated free play, which also opens up teachers' observations and participation.
2. Play implemented by children and teachers together that is based on a theme. Adults and children make up a shared fiction, a play world, or structure of play where children and adults can play and create dramas around a theme.
3. Academic play-based activities that are goal directed and integrate different school subjects (math, literacy, science, etc.) and in which children appropriate academic competencies through play.
4. Dialogical reading followed by play and aesthetic activities like drawing, dance, and storytelling. The point here is that, based on and inspired by a book of high quality, the children work on and reflect interesting parts of the book via play— and (sometimes) they change the content of the book and make up a new version. They become storytellers themselves.

Ulina Mapp, President, World Organization for Early Childhood Education—Panama; Professor, Director of Research and Postgraduate Studies, ISAE University:

If I want a child to learn, I must let the child play.

Playing is fun, but it is also a strategy to develop skills, and that is a reason for teachers to plan different games in their classes so they can be more interesting.

Children around the world need a place to play: at home, at school, in the park, in the garden, or somewhere else. No matter what people's age is when they play, they have fun and laugh, and that keeps them healthy. When children play they develop skills, habits, and attitudes that will stay with them for years or throughout life. Playing helps children learn to get along with others, manage frustration, and try again if they fail. It also helps them to improve their skills, share with peers and others, and incorporate their fantasies.

Integrating play in the schools of tomorrow will help students develop more values and innovation.

Chika Matsudaira, Associate Professor, Social Welfare, University of Shizuoka, Japan:

There are many discussions in Japan about the need for play, especially in children's early years and in education. Play is the most efficient way to learn and experiment. Imagination and creativity are needed in order for children to lead a fulfilled life, and play has a fundamental role in achieving this. Play is a child's language; therefore, we need to connect through their language. I would like people to think about play from children's eyes, not adults' eyes. This means that if the child says this is play, then it is play, and it does not matter whether it is indoors or outdoors.

Play can happen anywhere as long as children feel the safety they need.

Judith Butler, President of World Organization for Early Childhood—Ireland; Course Coordinator, Early Years Education, Department of Sport, Leisure & Childhood Studies, Cork Institute of Technology:

Play is the process through which children develop in an integrated and holistic manner. It is essential for development. Without play a child is deprived of a childhood. It is the tool we use to extend children's learning and development. There is nothing else that we need!

At the policy level, we must increase and recognize the importance of play. Play can have a low status, usually by those who are untrained, including parents. This can in turn put pressure on teachers to revert back to more traditional and didactic methods of teaching and curriculum implementation. Additionally, I believe that internationally we are overregulated in relation to risky play that is essential to children's holistic development. Evidently, our regulatory frameworks impinge on outdoor play provision.

As a result, our children are experiencing difficulties emotionally (no outlet for pent-up emotion) and physically (obesity is one example). Teacher training colleges need to place emphasis on training teachers to use play as a process. Teachers need to become skilled in facilitating play for learning. Active hands-on learning and heuristic [discovery through trial and error] learning are essential, and these need to be emphasized more in pre-service and in-service education for teachers.

Outdoor play and risky play, the Cinderella sister of play in school, need to be afforded more status. Research indicates that prisoners spend more time outside than our school-going children. We seem to be all about children's rights in terms of protection but not in terms of provision.

My favorite quote of all time is "The days that make us happy make us wise."

Sergio Pellis, Professor and Board of Governors Research Chair, Department of Neuroscience, University of Lethbridge, Alberta, Canada:

Based on my reading of the literature, the opportunity for free play by groups of peers has been greatly curtailed over the past two generations in Western countries. Moreover, where play is encouraged, it is a structured kind (e.g., sports). Yet, it appears that it is the act of negotiating the game to be invented and played, the rules to be followed, and the injunctions meted out for infringement of the rules that provides the training for the prefrontal cortex. Following preordained rules that are enforced by someone else (e.g., teacher, umpire) is not as effective in such training.

Not all children are the same; therefore, in my view there is no one program that would work for all. Rather, I think the approach should be to provide both indoor and outdoor settings that allow for children to select the venue, and types of play afforded by that venue, as they see fit. Associated with that choice would be affiliating with peers with similar interests to engage in those play activities. Initially, less socially mature individuals may elect to play video games indoors with equally sedentary peers, but as their skills in social settings increase, they may take up other opportunities for more expansive playful activities outdoors. The problem has been over 50 years in the making, so rectifying the negative effects of reduced opportunities for play need to be improved gently, in ways that the children self-select as rewarding.

Jeanne Goldhaber, Associate Professor Emeritus, College of Education and Social Services, University of Vermont:
I've always argued in support of the role of play in children's lives and have worked these many years to prepare early childhood educators to look to play as their pedagogical cornerstone. I see play as the vehicle through which children construct an understanding of and relationships with their physical and social worlds. Play is the context that allows children to pursue their own questions and theories; to construct an understanding of self, other, and community; to take risks, face challenges, and redesign intentions.

Now that STEM is receiving so much attention, perhaps we can make a strong case that play is foundational to STEM learning. I would also recommend that we look at the research related to the role of the natural world as an open-ended and play-centered context that supports children's emotional, social, and cognitive development. Finally, I recommend that we pay close attention to the role of the teacher. Her or his role is not a passive one; play is not the time to sit idly by or to do paperwork or chat with colleagues. Rather, it is a time when the teacher is an active observer who is prepared to respond in the moment or over time with changes to the physical or temporal environment. Being a teacher who values play and sees it as the primary pedagogical activity must be prepared to play an active and engaged role in the classroom as observer, documenter, and promoter of the children's meaning-making.

Nel Noddings, Lee L. Jacks Professor of Education, Emerita, Stanford University; Past President of the National Academy of Education, the Philosophy of Education Society, and the John Dewey Society:

I'm interested in helping high school kids develop an affective-receptive mode of attention to intellectual ideas. Instead of concentrating endlessly on "learning objectives," we should encourage kids to let the story or object speak to them and explore "what is there." They may be accused of daydreaming, but some wonderful things come out of such open, receptive, playful exploration. Everything, including play, is too highly structured today.

Jonathan Plucker, Julian C. Stanley Professor of Talent Development, School of Education, Johns Hopkins University:

We often treat learning as though it's an individual activity, but it is almost always social in nature. I worry that we are starting to view learning as solitary, when in fact it involves interactions with other people. And play, more than almost any other type of socializing, is how we learn from each other. Social skills, problem-solving, creativity, concept learning—play facilitates all types of learning.

Play is especially critical for the development of imagination, which is a key input for human creativity. Seeing what "could be" is a common part of play—what are the limits of your imagination, and how can you expand those limits? Pretend play is what we use to explore those questions.

The current state of play in school, and out of school, is dreadful, to the point that I worry about it all the time. When I was in elementary school, we had three recesses per day through third grade and two up until middle school. We played after school and on the weekends in the neighborhood, and all of this recess and play were usually unstructured. We had some organized sports, but they didn't consume our free time. For example, my friends and I played baseball, and although we belonged to a formal team, we also played pick-up games in our backyards—a lot. Contrast that to my children's experiences— one brief recess per day, and every activity is scheduled. Pick-up games are largely extinct. We are quickly driving play out of children's lives, and all for what? Higher test scores and better athletes? Spoiler alert: Ridding play from our children's lives has not resulted in appreciably higher test scores or better athletes!

My recommendations:

1. Schedule deliberately unstructured playtime into each school day.
2. Make learning activities FUN, moving beyond test prep to focus on problem-based learning and design-based activities.
3. Limit children's structured, out-of-school activity time.
4. Realize that some students won't know how to play and will need to be scaffolded into it.

Henry Levin, William H. Kilpatrick Professor of Economics and Education, Teachers College, Columbia University:
Play gives children agency in making decisions about relationships and how to handle them. They have to go into somewhat ambiguous situations and get experience in dealing with them. They have access to new and continuing friendships.

They can enjoy themselves. They learn social rules for interacting with others in both formal play and informal play. They gain experience in physical activities and games.

The schools of tomorrow should focus on the range of cognitive, emotional, and social experiences that make for healthy and productive human development and try to see how these can be combined in school experiences as well as "free" opportunities for students to use elected time.

Marcelo M. Suárez-Orozco, UCLA Wasserman Dean and Distinguished Professor of Education, UCLA Graduate School of Education & Information Studies:
According to the Dutch philosopher J. Huizinga, in his book *Homo Ludens: A Study of the Play-Element in Culture,* play "is older than culture, for culture, however inadequately defined, always presupposes human society, and animals have not waited for man to teach them their playing."

Play is fundamental in early childhood education as it structures cognition and emotion, social relations, and meaning-making in children.

I suspect that children today are hurried, and play, above all spontaneous play, may be a casualty of the increasing regimentation of childhood.

All meaningful, organic, and foundational learning is at heart playful and ludic. A few years ago we reported the findings of a study in which children and youth filled in the sentence "School is ____." Overwhelmingly, the response was "boring." Boredom is the antonym of curiosity.

Playfulness is curiosity's cousin. We must reimagine and engineer its place in education.

Serap Sevimli-Celik, Assistant Professor, Elementary and Early Childhood Education, College of Education, Middle East Technical University, Ankara, Turkey

I think if we truly want to include play in our classrooms, it is important to reconsider how we arrange our learning environments. When we think about the way children explore the environment, it is all about moving and playing. It is vital for them to be able to use movement to explore their environment, practice physical skills, and interact with people and objects around them. Through this opportunity, children develop active and healthy bodies, which may significantly affect their quality of life in later years. To be able to accommodate the play and movement needs of children, we need to rethink classroom designs both indoors and outdoors.

At a time when the potential of the mind is being emphasized over that of the body in a child's early years, the need for play and movement has increased even more. Approaching educational issues mostly from a cognitive perspective heavily influences the learning practices in the long term. How we arrange our classrooms and structure our curricula does not leave much space for young children to explore their surroundings and express themselves in physical ways. In addition, the tendency to recognize the learning potential or predict the future performance of children based on their intellectual ability usually creates a problematic relationship with the emotional and physical needs of young children.

Brief intervals of time for quiet reflection should be provided for even the very young. These are periods of genuine reflection only when they follow times of more overt action and are used to organize what has been gained during periods of activity in which the hands and parts of the body other than the brain are being used. Freedom of movement is also important as a means of maintaining good physical and mental health. We have yet to learn from the example of the Greeks, who saw clearly the relation between a sound body and a sound mind. From my own professional experience as a teacher educator and a practitioner in movement education, it is relatively clear to see the negative attitudes toward the activities that are physically expressive, creative, and playful. Teacher education is one important way to alter such negative attitudes and help restructure the status of play and movement. Providing courses on play, adopting different pedagogical strategies to foster learners' understanding of play, and creating classroom environments where pre-service teachers rehearse and enact play skills could increase their motivation to become a playful teacher.

Gene Glass, Senior Researcher, National Education Policy Center, University of Colorado Boulder, Regents' Professor Emeritus, Arizona State University:

The idea that play is a state of being in which serious cognitive processing is turned off for the duration is simple nonsense. Such an idea harkens back to naïve thinking of 50 years ago about "culturally deprived" [minority] children. Persons who should have known better conceived of urban minority children existing in a state of suspended animation in which their minds were completely unengaged because of a lack of "inputs." This was and is absurd, of course. When a person appears to be unconnected in a cognitive and conative way, it is simply that the observer is ignorant of what is going on in that person's mind. That observers cannot conceive of what is going on in the mind of a child who is "at play" does not mean that that child's mind is not involved in complex and indelible learnings.

We have to teach children how to engage with their creative, playful, and emotional lives. Learning about art and music are goals worthy of human beings freed from the drudgery of work. A liberal education was once said to be education for a person freed—liberated—from work. Every child should leave the education system with a lifelong interest in a sport—not being a spectator, but being a participant. A child should be helped to develop habits of mind and behavior that prevent the abusing of their own bodies. Lifestyle sicknesses (diabetes, heart disease, various addictions) are epidemic and are one of the biggest detriments to the U.S. economy. Perhaps it is no coincidence that this has happened at the very same time that education has turned away from play.

Reesa Sorin, Associate Professor, Coordinator, Early Childhood Education, College of Arts, Society and Education, Division of Tropical Environments and Societies, James Cook University, Queensland, Australia:

Everyone learns best through play. When you are relaxed and having fun you are more likely to remember, experiment, look deeply. I believe that all learning should be fun, engaging, and playful.

I would have a play-based curriculum at all year levels, meaning that learning is engaging, fun, and playful. Here in Australia, we are concerned because Finland is leading the world in educational outcomes while Australia is somewhere down the line. Yet, instead of learning from the Finns—who trust their teachers, follow student interests, and make learning enjoyable and engaging, we develop more and more formal learning experiences, testing and direct instruction, disengaging learning experiences. I have heard of so many children in their first year of formal schooling, and even before then, who are stressed and don't want to go to school anymore and think they are "stupid." It makes me angry.

Another problem for children today is that they are trapped in indoor, tech-based environments and are losing touch with the outdoor environment. They need to reconnect with the outdoors and be playful—both inside and outside.

Eric Contreras, Principal, Stuyvesant High School, New York City:

We have undervalued the role of play in school to our own detriment as educators, and that of our students. In a culture where standardized testing has crowded out inquisitiveness and play, our students don't get an opportunity to tinker and experiment without high stakes judgments. Without play, teachers don't get to learn from watching their students be unbound by their inner creative selves.

When children play, we observe the possibility of their imagination, and retool our structured classroom learning to create activities that model the authentic play and joy of students. It's a missed opportunity to learn from a feedback loop on what comes naturally to children. Play can liberate the power of inquiry in classrooms, that ironically can produce better test scores. Kudos for being so bold with this book!

Smita Mathur, Associate Professor, College of Education, Department of Early, Elementary, and Reading Education, James Madison University:

Play is innate, joyful, child (student) driven and makes learning stick. It can foster physical, social, emotional, cognitive and language development in all children, including children with special needs. I think play has value across grade levels and within all learning objectives. In the schools of tomorrow, play will be and should be center stage.

Jo Boaler, Professor, Mathematics Education, Stanford Graduate School of Education:

Play is a critical opportunity for students to learn to think, explore, and be creative, which is really important for mathematics learning, as well as for all other subjects. In our current U.S. system students are performing at the expense of learning. In mathematics education students rarely learn to think creatively, or to love mathematics, because they are always performing.

Math, unfortunately, is the most tested and most graded of all subjects, but the performance pressure does not stop in school. Math is also the subject with the most homework. This is despite the fact that homework is one of the biggest causes of stress for students. There is no evidence that it increases achievement, unless it is meaningful, and plenty of evidence that it is a large source of inequity.

Finland used to be a low-performing country in international tests, yet over recent years they have moved to being one of the top performing countries in mathematics. What changed? They stopped giving students homework and worked to make students feel more free and to have time to just be children. This could not stand in starker contrast to the United States, where students struggle every night working through meaningless math homework that robs them of important family time and helps them know that in math they are always performing.

My research on math learners suggests that when students think they're in class to learn—to explore ideas and think freely—they understand more and achieve at higher levels than when they think the point is to get questions right.

Anxiety is not limited to low-achieving students. Many of the undergraduates I teach at Stanford University, some of the most successful students in the nation, are math traumatized. In recent interviews, students have told me that learning math in school was like being on a "hamster wheel"—they felt like they were running and running, without reaching any meaningful destination. A seventh-grader told me that math learning was like prison, because his mind felt "locked up."

Our grading and testing practices are largely responsible. It's bad enough when students receive grades at the end of each unit or course that tell them how capable they are, but technological advances like digital grade portals have meant that students can see where their grades stand, and when they change, every minute of every day. This has amplified the performance pressure on students. Research has shown that students only have to think they're being graded for their achievement to go down. Math teachers who replace grading with constructive written comments increase students' learning. I know the most freeing comment I give to my Stanford students is this: "I am not going to give you a grade for this class. Do this for yourself, for your own learning."

The best mathematicians are often deep, slow thinkers— qualities that run contrary to what students are taught to prioritize and perform: speed. Some people thrive under the pressure to answer speedily in the classroom. Typically, it's the fast calculators who've been made to feel superior to others—even though they're doing something that's really not useful or necessary today.

Until we change the way we teach math to emphasize learning and exploration, rather than performance, we'll continue to produce students who describe their math experience as a hamster wheel or, worse, a prison. We'll continue to produce anxious students who experience fear when they see numbers. The performance culture of mathematics has destroyed a vibrant, essential subject for so many people. As schools have worked to encourage a few speedy calculators, they've neglected to teach the kind of creative, quantitative thinking that can open new worlds. If we encourage new generations of students who love learning and love math, we'll raise up kids who are prepared to take their place in society as free, empowered thinkers.

My recommendation for schools is to eliminate homework and give students time to spend with family, to play, to think, and to be children. I also recommend that we eliminate the performance culture in schools and make school about learning. Structured time for students to play should be a part of any school, K–12. This is the time that students learn to be creative and to expand their minds.

Charles Ungerleider, Professor Emeritus, Educational Studies, University of British Columbia:
All human beings require the opportunity for exploration, because exploration is essential to learning. Early childhood environments should encourage children to use their imagination, test and verify hypotheses, investigate new roles, and combine ideas in novel ways, free from serious injury but not from risk. There should

be plenty of material or fabric of varying kinds from which children can manufacture what they conceive, dress themselves in costumes of their design, and enact roles of their choosing. The material need not be expensive, but it should be plentiful.

The people who work with the children must be prepared to make open-ended comments ("Tell me about what you were thinking when –") and ask open-ended questions ("What do you think might happen if —?") without preconceived notions about the form or content of the response the child may make. Their interactions should prompt the children to reach beyond their previous boundaries in knowledge and experience, to be curious, and to be playful. It is important that those who work with children have the capacity for spontaneity and the ability to see things from the point of view of the children.

Sophie Alcock, Senior Lecturer, School of Education, Victoria University of Wellington, New Zealand:
I recommend the "schools of tomorrow" empower students in schools to play by valuing and building on students' social and creative interests and supporting their expression through the medium of play, indoors and outdoors. This includes students playing and expressing ideas and feelings in many ways, with many languages. Mathematics, music, dance, sports, art, gardening, earth sciences, physics, pottery, or bee-keeping; whatever arouses and sustains interests and aliveness between and among students, teachers, and communities may be explored through playing (alongside other styles of learning). The process of play underpins all creative processes and creative solutions to the multitude of issues that pervade this earth, and these are needed now more than ever. So bring on play!

THE DECLARATION OF LEARNING AND PLAY—CALL TO HALT THE WAR ON CHILDHOOD

For children, intellectual and physical play is a critical foundation of learning, healthy development, academic achievement, and life skills.

Play is a fundamental right of the child, in the school, the home, and the community.

A strong scientific and medical consensus confirms that children in school need to play—but politicians and schools are eliminating play in school and replacing it with failing and counterproductive policies of physical restraint, recess reduction and cancellation, overwork, fear, and stress, and school system management based on the compulsory mass standardized testing of children as young as 8 or even younger. These policies do not support learning. They constitute a war on childhood. They must stop.

Therefore, all school children should be given:

1. A school experience rich in discovery and experimentation, encouragement, conversation, intellectual challenge, free play and guided play, playful teaching and learning, and respect of children's voices and individual learning differences; schools that develop a child's social, emotional, and cognitive strengths; schools that are equitably funded and provide social support services when necessary, including healthy meals; manageably small class sizes; safety and security; schools that deliver a full curriculum including the arts and physical activity; regular high-quality assessments by fully

qualified professional teachers instead of standardized tests; schools that follow the American Academy of Pediatrics guidelines on recess and play, including never withholding recess from a child as a punishment; and schools run by teachers and administrators fully trained in educational research, childhood development and classroom practice, including the effective use of play and physical activity to enhance learning.

2. At least 60 minutes per day of unstructured recess, outdoors whenever possible (the minimum time recommended by the United Nations Standard Minimum Rules for the Treatment of Prisoners);[394] and as recommended by the National Academy of Medicine,[395] high-quality physical education of an average of at least 30 minutes per day in elementary school and 45 minutes per day in middle and high school.

3. Regular periods of school time devoted to child-initiated classroom play and hands-on "passion projects" of the child's choice.

4. The freedom to fail and learn from failure as a pathway to success.

5. Schools that encourage an out-of-school childhood rich in play, physical activity, independent reading, mental health and physical well-being, sleep, unplugging, family time, and downtime.

School budgets and schedules should be revised accordingly.

Politicians and administrators should be held directly accountable to deliver these minimum standards.

Add your voice to this declaration at https://www.change.org/p/u-s-house-of-representatives-the-declaration-of-learning-and-play-call-to-halt-the-war-on-childhood.

The Children's Charter

WHITE HOUSE CONFERENCE ON CHILD HEALTH AND PROTECTION, RECOGNIZING THE RIGHTS OF THE CHILD AS THE FIRST RIGHTS OF CITIZENSHIP, PLEDGES ITSELF TO THESE AIMS FOR THE CHILDREN OF AMERICA.

I. FOR every child spiritual and moral training to help him to stand firm under the pressure of life.

II. For every child understanding and the guarding of his personality as its most precious right.

III. For every child a home and that love and security which a home provides; and for that child who must receive foster care, the nearest substitute for his own home.

IV. For every child full preparation for his birth, his mother receiving prenatal, natal, and postnatal care; and the establishment of such protective measures as will make child-bearing safer.

V. For every child health protection from birth through adolescence, including: periodical health examinations and, where needed, care of specialists and hospital treatment; regular dental examinations and care of the teeth; protective and preventive measures against communicable diseases; the insuring of pure food, pure milk, and pure water.

VI. For every child from birth through adolescence, promotion of health, including health instruction, and a health program, wholesome physical and mental recreation, with teachers and leaders adequately trained.

VII. For every child a dwelling-place safe, sanitary, and wholesome, with reasonable provisions for privacy; free from conditions which tend to thwart his development; and a home environment harmonious and enriching.

VIII. For every child a school which is safe from hazards, sanitary, properly equipped, lighted, and ventilated. For younger children nursery schools and kindergartens to supplement home care.

IX. For every child a community which recognizes and plans for his needs, protects him against physical dangers, moral hazards, and disease; provides him with safe and wholesome places to play and recreation; and makes provision for his cultural and social needs.

X. For every child an education which, through the discovery and development of his individual abilities, prepares him for life; and through training and vocational guidance prepares him for a living which will yield him maximum satisfaction.

XI. For every child such teaching and training as will prepare him for successful parenthood, home-making, and the rights of citizenship; and for parents, supplementary training to fit them to deal wisely with the problems of parenthood.

XII. For every child education for safety and protection against accidents to which modern conditions subject him— those to which he is directly exposed and those which, through loss or maiming of his parents, affect him directly.

XIII. For every child who is blind, deaf, crippled, or otherwise physically handicapped, and for the child who is mentally handicapped, such measures as will early discover and diagnose his handicap, provide care and treatment, and so train him that he may become an asset to society rather than a liability. Expenses of these services should be borne publicly where they cannot be privately met.

XIV. For every child who is in conflict with society the right to be dealt with intelligently as society's charge, not society's outcast; with the home, the school, the church, the court and the institution when needed, shaped to return him whenever possible to the normal stream of life.

XV. For every child the right to grow up in a family with an adequate standard of living and the security of a stable income as the surest safeguard against social handicaps.

XVI. For every child protection against labor that stunts growth, either physical or mental, that limits education, that deprives children of the right of comradeship, of play, and of joy.

XVII. For every rural child as satisfactory schooling and health services as for the city child, and an extension to rural families of social, recreational, and cultural facilities.

XVIII. To supplement the home and the school in the training of youth, and to return to them those interests of which modern life tends to cheat children, every stimulation and encouragement should be given to the extension and development of the voluntary youth organizations.

XIX. To make everywhere available these minimum protections of the health and welfare of children, there should be a district, county, or community organization for health, education, and welfare, with full-time officials, coordinating with a statewide program which will be responsive to a nationwide service of general information, statistics, and scientific research. This should include:

a.) Trained, full-time public health officials, with public health nurses, sanitary inspection, and laboratory workers
b.) Available hospital beds
c.) Full-time public welfare service for the relief, aid, and guidance of children in special need due to poverty, misfortune, or behavior difficulties, and for the protection of children from abuse, neglect, exploitation, or moral hazard.

FOR EVERY CHILD THESE RIGHTS, REGARDLESS OF RACE, OR COLOR, OR SITUATION, WHEREVER HE MAY LIVE UNDER THE PROTECTION OF THE AMERICAN FLAG.
The Children's Charter, White House Conference on Child Health and Protection, November 22, 1930 (https://catalog. archives.gov/id/187089).

NOTES

1. Milteer, R. M., Ginsburg, K. R.; Council on Communications and Media, & Committee on Psychosocial Aspects of Child and Family Health, American Academy of Pediatrics (2012). Clinical report. The importance of play in promoting healthy child development and maintaining strong parent-child bonds: Focus on children in poverty. *Pediatrics, 129,* e204–e213. The first quote, in its entirety, is "Pediatricians can advocate for safe play spaces for children who live in communities and attend schools with a high proportion of low-income and poor children by emphasizing that the lifelong success of children is based on their ability to be creative and to apply the lessons learned from playing."
2. Sukhomlinsky, V. (Trans. A. Cockerill). (2016). *The School of Joy: Being Part 1 of My Heart I Give to Children* (p. 111). Graceville, Australia: EJR Language Service.
3. Henley, J., McBride, J., Milligan, J., & Nichols, J. (2007). Robbing elementary students of their childhood: The perils of No Child Left Behind. *Education, 128*(1), 56–63.
4. Bradbury, R. (1990). *Medicine for Melancholy* (p. 102). New York: Bantam.
5. Green, R. (2013). *Mandela: The Life of Nelson Mandela* (p. 13). New York: Macmillan.
6. Remarks to 2012 National Day Rally, quoted in Hartung, R. (2019, August 29). What are kindergartens really for?" *TODAY* (Singapore).
7. The Children's Charter, White House Conference on Child Health and Protection, November 22, 1930. College Park, MD: U.S. Children's Bureau Files, National Archives. The conference was convened by President Herbert Hoover.

8. Ginsburg, K. R.; American Academy of Pediatrics Committee on Communications; American Academy of Pediatrics Committee on Psychosocial Aspects of Child and Family Health. (2007). The importance of play in promoting healthy child development and maintaining strong parent–child bonds. *Pediatrics, 119*(1), 182–191.

9. Centers for Disease Control and Prevention. (2010). The association between school-based physical activity, including physical education, and academic performance. Atlanta, GA; Centers for Disease Control and Prevention, U.S. Department of Health and Human Services. Retrieved from https://www.cdc.gov/healthyyouth/health_and_academics/pdf/pa-pe_paper.pdf.

10. Resolution on Early Years Learning in the European Union, adopted by the European Parliament, May 12, 2011.

11. Milteer, R. M., Ginsburg, K. R.; Council on Communications and Media, & Committee on Psychosocial Aspects or Child and Family Health, American Academy of Pediatrics. (2012). The importance of play in promoting healthy child development and maintaining strong parent–child bonds: Focus on children in poverty. *Pediatrics, 129*(1), e204–e213. This policy statement was reaffirmed by the American Academy of Pediatrics in 2016.

12. Murray, R., Ramstetter, C.; Council on School Health; American Academy of Pediatrics (2013). The crucial role of recess in school. *Pediatrics, 131*(1), 183–188.

13. Institute of Medicine [now called National Academy of Medicine]. (2013). *Educating the student body: Taking physical activity and physical education to school.* Washington, DC: National Academies Press.

14. Shinozaki, K., Nonogi, H., Nagao, K., & Becker, L. B. (2016). Strategies to improve cardiac arrest survival: A time to act. *Acute Medicine & Surgery, 3*(2), 61–64.

15. Centers for Disease Control and Prevention and SHAPE America—Society of Health and Physical Educators. (2017). *Strategies for recess in schools.* Atlanta, GA: Centers for Disease Control and Prevention, U.S. Department of Health and Human Services.

16. *China Education Daily*, May 7, 2017, translation on Anji Play Facebook post of May 9, 2017.

17. World Bank Group. (2017). *World development report 2018: LEARNING to realize education's promise* (p. 69). Washington, DC: World Bank Publications.

18. Yogman, M., Garner, A., Hutchinson, J., Hirsh-Pasek, K., Golinkoff, R. M.; American Academy of Pediatrics Committee on Psychosocial Aspects of Child and Family Health, Council on Communications and Media. (2018). The power of play: A pediatric role in enhancing development in young children. *Pediatrics, 142*(3), e20182058. This landmark clinical report focuses on younger children, but the report's authors confirmed to us that its implications extend to older children as well. In this book, we consider a "child" to be "a human being below the age of 18 years," which is the definition used by the United Nations Convention on the Rights of the Child. When we refer to "childhood education" the same logic applies.

19. These passages are inspired by Dwight D. Eisenhower's "Chance for Peace" speech on military spending, also known as the "Cross of Iron" speech, given to the American Society of Newspaper Editors on April 16, 1953; and George Kennan's May 1981 speech accepting the Einstein Peace Prize.

20. The Editors of Time. (2017). *TIME, The Science of Childhood: Inside the Minds of Our Younger Selves.* New York: Time Inc. Books.

21. Finland has been qualitatively ranked as the #1 education system in the world or the developed world by UNICEF Office of Research (2017), Building the future: Children and the Sustainable Development Goals in rich countries, *Innocenti Report Card 14*, p. 10; by the World Economic Forum Global Competitiveness Index, 2017–2018; and by the OECD Better Life Index, 2017. Additionally, a global team of researchers published an analysis in *The Lancet* online on September 24, 2018, that ranked Finland as the nation with the #1 highest level of expected human capital, a combined measure of education and health that is considered an important determinant of economic growth. See Lim, S. S., Updike, R. L., Kaldjian, A. S., Barber, R. M., Cowling, K., York, H., . . . Murray, C. J. L. (2018). Measuring human capital: A systematic analysis of 195 countries and territories, 1990–2016. *Lancet, 392*(10154), P1217–P1234.

22. Papert, S. (1993). *The Children's Machine.* New York: Basic Books.

23. On publication bias in research, see, for example, Egger, M., & Smith, G. D. (1998). Meta-analysis bias in location and selection of studies. *British Medical Journal, 316*, 61. On research study weakness in general, see the provocative article by John Ioannidis (2005). Why most published research findings are false. *Plos Medicine, 2*(8), e124. On the problems in research of publication bias, outcome reporting

bias, spin, and citation bias, see pediatrician Aaron E. Carroll's article in the September 24, 2018, issue of the *New York Times*, titled "Congratulations. Your Study Went Nowhere."

24. *The Republic* [Section IV], quoted in Panksepp J. (2007). Can PLAY diminish ADHD and facilitate the construction of the social brain? *Journal of the Canadian Academy of Child and Adolescent Psychiatry*, 16(2), 57–66.

25. Stillman, J. (2017, June 22). Here's Einstein's advice to his son on how to accelerate learning. Inc.com.

26. Beatty, B. (1997). *Preschool Education in America: The Culture of Young Children from the Colonial Era to the Present* (p. 3). New Haven, CT: Yale University Press.

27. Hirsh-Pasek, K. (2009). *A Mandate for Playful Learning in Preschool: Applying the Scientific Evidence* (p. 3). New York: Oxford University Press.

28. Ginsburg, K. R.; American Academy of Pediatrics Committee on Communications; American Academy of Pediatrics Committee on Psychosocial Aspects of Child and Family Health. (2007). The importance of play in promoting healthy child development and maintaining strong parent–child bonds. *Pediatrics, 119*(1), 182–191.

29. Ibid.

30. Center on Media and Child Health. (n.d.). *#MorePlayToday*. http://cmch.tv/moreplaytoday/.

31. The Council of the European Union. (2011, June 15). Council conclusions on early childhood and care. *Official Journal of the European Union*, C 175/8.

32. Yogman, M., Garner, A., Hutchinson, J., Hirsh-Pasek, K., & Golinkoff, R, M.; American Academy of Pediatrics Committee on Psychosocial Aspects of Child and Family Health, Council on Communications and Media. (2018). The power of play: A pediatric role in enhancing development in young children. *Pediatrics, 142*(3), e20182058.

33. Author interview.

34. Groos, K. (1898). *The Play of Animals* (E. L. Baldwin, Trans.) New York: Appleton; Groos, K. (1901). The theory of play. In *The Play of Man* (chapter 1, pp. 361–406). (E. L. Baldwin, Trans.). New York: Appleton.

35. Ward, H. (2012, November 2). All work and no play. *Times Educational Supplement*.

36. Chudacoff, H. (2008). *Children at Play: An American History* (p. 126). New York: NYU Press.

37. Brown, C. (2016, April 27). Kindergartners get little time to play. Why does it matter? *The Conversation*.

38. Quoted in White, R. (2013). *The power of play: A research summary on play and learning*. Minneapolis: Minnesota Children's Museum.

39. Ortlieb, E. (2010). The pursuit of play within the curriculum. *Journal of Instructional Psychology*, 37(3), 241–246.

40. Yogman et al. (2018). The power of play.

41. Plato. (1970). *The Laws* (T. J. Saunders, Trans.) (p. 278). Harmondsworth: Penguin.

42. Quoted in All-Party Parliamentary Group on a Fit and Healthy Childhood. (2015). *Play: A report by the All-Parliamentary Group on a Fit and Healthy Childhood*.

43. Froebel, F. (1912). *Froebel's Chief Writings on Education* (p. 50). London: Longmans Green.

44. Gopnik, A. (2016, August 12). In defense of play. *The Atlantic*.

45. See The World Bank. (2016, October 3). *The power of play*. It contains links to the original Jamaica study and follow-up reports: http://www.worldbank.org/en/programs/sief-trust-fund/brief/the-power-of-play.

46. Wolfgang, C. H., Stannard, L. L., & Jones, I. (2001). Block play performance among preschoolers as a predictor of later school achievement in mathematics. *Journal of Research in Childhood Education*, 15(2), 173–180. doi:10.1080/02568540109594958

47. White, R. (2013). *The power of play: A research summary on play and learning*. Minneapolis: Minnesota Children's Museum.

48. Whitebread, D. (2013). *University of Cambridge research: Starting school age: The evidence*. Retrieved from https://www.cam.ac.uk/research/discussion/school-starting-age-the-evidence.

49. Institute of Medicine [now called National Academy of Medicine]. (2013). *Educating the student body: Taking physical activity and physical education to school*. Washington, DC: National Academies Press.

50. Yogman et al. (2018). The power of play. The authors of the report noted that further research is needed to clarify these points.

51. Barker, J. E., Semenov, A. D., Michaelson, L., Provan, L. S., Snyder, H. R., & Munakata, Y. (2014). Less-structured time in children's daily lives predicts self-directed executive functioning. *Frontiers in Psychology*, 5, 593. The researchers noted that their findings indicate

correlation, and not necessarily causation—it could be, for example, that children with strong executive function gravitate toward less-structured activities.

52. "Kids whose time is less structured are better able to meet their own goals, says CU-Boulder study." *CU Boulder Today*, University of Colorado Boulder, June 18, 2014.

53. Yogman et al. (2018) The power of play.

54. A recent review by researchers at the Lego Foundation found that there is evidence, among other things, that: physical play is linked to motor development, and some tentative evidence that it is linked to social development; unstructured breaks from cognitive tasks improve learning and attention, though it is unclear whether play leads to greater improvements in learning than simply taking a break and, for example, talking with friends; block play leads to improvements in spatial processing/mental rotation; construction play relates to language development, and this relationship may be strongest in infancy, with pretend play becoming more important for language as children enter toddlerhood; word-play and word-games relate to language development; pretend play relates to language development, and particularly narrative skills; pretend play—and particularly fantasy-oriented pretense—may relate to learning-to-learn skills such as executive function and self-regulation; board games (particularly those with numbers and linear number sequences) lead to improvements in numeracy/mathematics ability; and physical games with rules help children (and especially boys) adapt to formal schooling." See Whitebread, D., Neale, D., Jensen, H., Liu, C., Solis, S. L., Hopkins, E., Hirsh-Pasek, K., & Zosh, J. (2017). *The role of play in children's development: A review of the evidence (research summary)*. Billund, Denmark: The Lego Foundation.

55. Ginsburg et al. (2007). The importance of play.

56. Sylva, K., Melhuish, E., Sammons, P., Siraj-Blatchford, I., & Taggart, B. (2004). *The Effective Provision of Pre-school Education [EPPE] Project: Findings from pre-school to end of key stage 1*. Nottingham, UK: Department of Education and Skills.

57. Author interview.

58. Brussoni, M., Gibbons, R., Gray, C., Ishikawa, T., Sandseter, E. B. H., Bienenstock, A., . . . & Pickett, W. (2015). What is the relationship between risky outdoor play and health in children? A systematic review.

International Journal of Environmental Research and Public Health, 12(6), 6423–6454.

59. University of British Columbia. (2015, June 10). Risky outdoor play positively impacts children's health, study suggests. *Science Daily.*

60. UNICEF. (2012). *The State of the World's Children 2012: Children in an Urban World.* New York: Author.

61. Tremblay, M., Gray, C., Babcock, S., Barnes, J., Bradstreet, C. C., Carr, D., . . . & Brussoni, M. (2015). Position statement on active outdoor play. *International Journal of Environmental Research and Public Health, 12*(6), 6475–6505.

62. Ulset, V., Vitaro, F., Brendgen, M., Bekkhus, M., & Borge, A. (2017). Time spent outdoors during preschool: Links with children's cognitive and behavioral development. *Journal of Environmental Psychology, 52,* 69–80.

63. He, M., Xiang, F., Zeng, Y., Mai, J., Chen, Q., Zhang, J., . . . & Morgan, I. G. (2015). Effect of time spent outdoors at school on the development of myopia among children in China: A randomized clinical trial. *JAMA, 314*(11), 1142–1148; Rose, K. A., Morgan, I. G., Ip, J., Kifley, A., Huynh, S., Smith, W., & Mitchell, P. (2008). Outdoor activity reduces the prevalence of myopia in children. *Ophthalmology, 115*(8), 1279–1285.

64. Patte, M. (n.d.). *The decline of unstructured play.* Retrieved from http:www.thegeniusofplay.org.

65. Institute of Medicine [now called National Academy of Medicine]. (2013). *Educating the student body: Taking physical activity and physical education to school.* Washington, DC: National Academies Press.

66. Ibid.

67. Yogman et al. (2018). The power of play.

68. National Association of Elementary School Principals. (2010, February 4). Principals link recess to academic achievement in latest Gallup Poll.

69. Hillman, C. H., Buck, S. M., Themanson, J. R., Pontifex, M. B., & Castelli, D. M. (2009). Aerobic fitness and cognitive development: Event-related brain potential and task performance indices of executive control in preadolescent children. *Developmental Psychology, 45*(1), 114–125; Hillman, C. H., Pontifex, M. B., Castelli, D. M., Khan, N. A., Raine, L. B., Scudder, M. R., . . . & Kamijo, K. (2014). Effects of

the FITKids randomized controlled trial on executive control and brain function. *Pediatrics, 134*(4):e1063-71.

70. See the comprehensive CDC research collection Health and Academics at: https://www.cdc.gov/healthyschools/health_and_academics/index.htm.

71. Howie, E. K., & Pate, R. R. (2012). Physical activity and academic achievement in children: A historical perspective. *Journal of Sport and Health Science, 1*(3), 160–169.

72. Centers for Disease Control and Prevention and SHAPE America—Society of Health and Physical Educators. (2017). *Strategies for recess in schools*. Atlanta, GA: Centers for Disease Control and Prevention, U.S. Department of Health and Human Services.

73. Ibid.

74. Curtin, M. (2017, December 29). The 10 top skills that will land you high-paying jobs by 2020, according to the World Economic Forum. *Inc.*

75. Author interview.

76. Hirsh-Pasek, K. (2018, January 29). Taking playtime seriously. *New York Times.*

77. Kathy Hirsh-Pasek, Senior Fellow, Global Economy and Development, Center for Universal Education Stanley; Debra Lefkowitz, Faculty Fellow, Department of Psychology, Temple University; Roberta Michnick Golinkoff, Unidel H. Rodney Sharp Professor of Education, University of Delaware. "Becoming brilliant: Reimagining education for our time." Brookings global education blog, May 20, 2016.

78. All-Party Parliamentary Group on a Fit and Healthy Childhood (2015). *Play: A report by the All-Party Parliamentary Group on a Fit and Healthy Childhood.*

79. Adapted from Ginsburg, K. R.; American Academy of Pediatrics Committee on Communications; American Academy of Pediatrics Committee on Psychosocial Aspects of Child and Family Health. (2007). The importance of play in promoting healthy development and maintaining strong parent–child bonds. *Pediatrics, 119*(1), 182–191; Milteer, R. M., Ginsburg, K. R.; Council on Communications and Media, & Committee on Psychosocial Aspects of Child and Family Health, American Academy of Pediatrics. (2012). The importance of play in promoting healthy child development and maintaining strong parent–child bonds: Focus on children in poverty. *Pediatrics, 129*, e204–e213; Murray, R., Ramstetter, C.; Council on School Health;

American Academy of Pediatrics. (2013). The crucial role of recess in schools. *Pediatrics, 131*(1), 183–188; and Yogman, M., Garner, A., Hutchinson, J., Hirsh-Pasek, K., & Golinkoff, R, M.; American Academy of Pediatrics Committee on Psychosocial Aspects of Child and Family Health, Council on Communications and Media. (2018). The power of play: A pediatric role in enhancing development in young children. *Pediatrics, 142*(3), e20182058. Also, AAP press release, "AAP considers recess a necessary break from the demands of school," December 31, 2012.

80. Yogman, M., Garner, A., Hutchinson, J., Hirsh-Pasek, K., & Golinkoff, R, M.; American Academy of Pediatrics Committee on Psychosocial Aspects of Child and Family Health, Council on Communications and Media. (2018). The power of play: A pediatric role in enhancing development in young children. *Pediatrics, 142*(3), e20182058.

81. Author interview.

82. Author interview.

83. Author interview.

84. See, for example, Siviy, S, & Panksepp, J. (2011). In search of the neurobiological substrates for social playfulness in mammalian brains. *Neuroscience and Biobehavioral Reviews, 35,* 1821–1830; Siviy, S. (2016). A brain motivated to play: Insights into the neurobiology of playfulness. *Behaviour, 153,* 819–844.

85. Author interview.

86. Author interview.

87. Author interview.

88. Author interview. In her article "Settling for Scores" in the December 27, 2017, issue of the *Atlantic,* Professor Diane Ravitch quoted the wise 1979 axioms of psychologist Donald Campbell: "The more any quantitative social indicator is used for social decision-making, the more subject it will be to corruption pressures and the more apt it will be to distort and corrupt the social processes it is intended to monitor"; and "Achievement tests may well be valuable indicators of general school achievement under conditions of normal teaching aimed at general competence. But when test scores become the goal of the teaching process, they both lose their value as indicators of educational status and distort the educational process in undesirable ways." Ravitch added: "For the last 16 years, American education has been trapped, stifled, strangled by standardized testing. Or, to be more precise, by federal and state

legislators' obsession with standardized testing. The pressure to raise test scores has produced predictable corruption: Test scores were inflated by test preparation focused on what was likely to be on the test. Some administrators gamed the system by excluding low-scoring students from the tested population; some teachers and administrators cheated; some so that more time could be devoted to the tested subjects. As a teaching tool, the tests are deeply flawed because they quash imagination, creativity, and divergent thinking. These are mental habits we should encourage, not punish." A 2018 report titled "How High the Bar?" published by the National Superintendents Roundtable and the Horace Mann League concluded that standardized tests are designed so that the vast majority of students in most countries cannot demonstrate "proficiency." The authors argued that the United States has set test score benchmarks so high that they are not useful, not credible, and designed so that most students will fail. The results are then used to criticize public schools, teachers, and teacher unions, and to drum up support for vouchers, charters, and school privatization. Dr. James Harvey, executive director of the National Superintendent's Roundtable, noted, "Many criticize public schools because only about one third of our students are deemed to be 'proficient' on NAEP [National Assessment of Educational Progress, a sample-based standardized testing regime] assessments. But even in Singapore—always highly successful on international assessments—just 39 percent of fourth-graders clear NAEP's proficiency benchmark."

89. See, for example, special issue of *Educational Management Administration & Leadership*, 36(2), 2008.

90. Strauss, V. (2014, May 1). Answer sheet: 6 reasons to reject Common Core K–3 standards—and 6 rules to guide policy *Washington Post*.

91. We believe that school systems should be "data informed" with a wide range of information, not "data driven" mainly by standardized test scores in a few subjects.

92. Sahlberg, P. (2006). Education reform for raising economic competitiveness. *Journal of Educational Change*, 7(4), 259–287.

93. See, for example, Adamson, F., Astrand, B., & Darling-Hammond, L. (2016). *Global Education Reform: How Privatization and Public Investment Influence Education Outcomes*. New York: Routledge.

94. See, for example, Abrams, S. (2016). *Education and the Commercial Mindset*. Cambridge, MA: Harvard University Press.

95. For a history of failed attempts at education reform during the Bush–Obama years and their impact on schools, see Ravitch, D. (2010). *The Death and Life of the Great American School System: How Testing and Choice are Undermining Education*. New York: Basic Books; Ravitch, D. (2013). *Reign of Error: The Hoax of the Privatization Movement and the Danger to Public Schools*. New York: Knopf; Merrow, J. (2017). *Addicted to Reform: A 12-Step Program to Rescue Public Education*. New York: The New Press. In Koretz, D. (2017). *The Testing Charade: Pretending to Make Schools Better,* Chicago: University of Chicago Press, Harvard education Professor Dan Koretz concluded that "The best estimate is that test-based accountability may have produced modest gains in elementary-school mathematics [author's note: which fade out before high school graduation] but no appreciable gains in either reading [author's note: in any grade] or high-school mathematics — even though reading and mathematics have been its primary focus." He added that "these meager positive effects must be balanced against the many widespread and serious negative effects," such as excessive testing and test preparation, displacing of actual instruction, "utterly absurd" teacher evaluation systems, the "corruption of the ideals of teaching," manipulation of tested populations (like finding ways to keep low achievers from being tested), outright cheating that has even led to criminal charges and imprisonment, score inflation, and the creation of "gratuitous and often enormous stress for educators, parents, and, most important, students." As for achievement gaps, Koretz concluded that "the trend data don't show consistent improvement" (6, 187, 190, 191).

96. Strauss, V., & Merrow, J. (2017, September 25). The "questionable questions" on today's standardized tests. *Washington Post*.

97. What's wrong with America's playgrounds and how to fix them: An interview with Joe L. Frost. *American Journal of Play, Fall,* 141–158, 2008.

98. Gordon, A. (2014, July 29). At this day camp, risks can be rewarding. *Toronto Star*.

99. Common Sense Media. (2015). *The Common Sense census: Media use by tweens and teens*. Also see Kaiser Foundation. (2010). *Generation M²: Media in the lives of 8- to 18-year-olds*; Pew Research Center. (2018). *Teens, social media and technology 2018*. Retrieved from http://www.pewinternet.org/2018/05/31/teens-social-media-technology-2018/

100. Miller, M., & Almon, J. (2009). *Crisis in the kindergarten: Why children need to play in school*. Alliance for Childhood.

101. Singer, D. G., Singer, J. L., D'Agostino, H., & DeLong, R. (2009). Children's pastimes and play in sixteen nations: Is free-play declining? *American Journal of Play* 1(3), 283–312.

102. Ikea Corporation. (2015). *The play report.*

103. Strauss, V., & Carlsson-Paige, N. (2015, November 24). How "twisted" early childhood education has become—from a child development expert. *Washington Post* online. Retrieved from https://www.washingtonpost.com/news/answer-sheet/wp/2015/11/24/how-twisted-early-childhood-education-has-become-from-a-child-development-expert/?utm_term=.d2cb0605515e

104. Abeles, V. (2016). *Beyond Measure: Rescuing an Overscheduled, Overtested, Underestimated Generation* (p. 107). New York: Simon & Schuster.

105. Jesse Hagopian, J. (2014). *More Than a Score: The New Uprising Against High-Stakes Testing* (p. 21). New York: Haymarket Books.

106. Parents Across America. (2013). *The power of play.* Retrieved from http://parentsacrossamerica.org/power-play/.

107. Merrow, J. (2017). *Addicted to Reform: A 12-step Program to Rescue Public Education* (p. 107). New York: The New Press.

108. Ibid.

109. Strauss, V. (2014, May 2). Answer Sheet: 6 reasons to reject Core K–3 standards—and 6 rules to guide policy. *Washington Post* online.

110. Yogman et al. (2018). The power of play.

111. Heim, J. (2016, September 6). Almost the entire D.C. school district is ignoring its PE requirements. *Washington Post.*

112. Ahmed-Ullah, N. (2011, October 25). Schools face new challenge: Return of recess. *Chicago Tribune.*

113. Roth, J., et al. (2003). What happens during the school day? Time diaries from a national sample of elementary school teachers. *Teachers College Record.*

114. Symons, M. (2016, January 21). Christie: Vetoed recess bill was "stupid." *Daily Record.*

115. *Neal Cavuto Show*, Fox News, January 20, 2016.

116. Gilson, K. (2013, April 18). CPS security chief bans dangerous bubbles from headquarters of America's third largest school system. *Substance News.*

117. Whitehouse, E., & Shafer, M. (2017, March 9). *State policies on physical activity in schools.* The Council of State Governments.

118. Ginsburg, K. R.; American Academy of Pediatrics Committee on Communications; American Academy of Pediatrics Committee on Psychosocial Aspects of Child and Family Health. (2007). The importance of play in promoting healthy child development and maintaining strong parent–child bonds. *Pediatrics, 119*(1), 182–191.

119. On costs and inaccuracies of standardized testing, see, for example, Shavelson, R., Linn, R., Baker, E., Ladd, H., Darling-Hammond, L., Shepard, L. A., . . . & Rothstein, R. (2010, August 27). *Briefing paper: Problems with the use of student test scores to evaluate teachers.* Economic Policy Institute; fairtest.org. (2007). *Fact sheet: The dangerous consequences of high-stakes standardized testing*; Nelson, H. (2013, July). *Testing more, teaching less: What America's obsession with student testing costs in money and lost instructional time.* American Federation of Teachers.

120. Hart, R., Casserly, M., Uzzell, R., Palacios, M., Corcoran, A., Spurgeon, L.; Council of the Great City Schools. (2015, October). *Student testing in America's great city schools: An inventory and preliminary analysis.*

121. Darling-Hammond, L. (2013, April 10). Editorial: Test and punish sabotages quality of children's education. *MSNBC.* Retrieved from http://www.msnbc.com/melissa-harris-perry/test-and-punish-sabotages-quality-childr

122. Ravitch, D. (2016, October 12). John King doubles down on importance of standardized tests; "reformers" cheer. dianeravitch.net

123. National Research Council. (2011). *Incentives and Test-Based Accountability in Education.* Washington, DC: National Academies Press.

124. Pellegrini, A. (2008). The recess debate: A disjuncture between educational policy and scientific research. *American Journal of Play, Fall,* 181–191.

125. Tienken, C. (2017, July 5). Students test scores tell us more about the community they live in than what they know. *The Conversation.*

126. Merrow, J. (2017, August 7). *The FreshEd Podcast.*

127. Solley, B. A. (2007, October 28). *On standardized testing: An ACEI position paper.* Retrieved from https://www.redorbit.com/news/education/1120085/on_standardized_testing_an_acei_position_paper/.

128. Russo, L. (2013). Play and creativity at the center of curriculum and assessment: A New York City school's journey to re-think curricular pedagogy. *Bordon, Journal of Education, 65*(1), 131–146.

129. Bartlett, T. (2011, February 20). The case for play: How a handful of researchers are trying to save childhood. *The Chronicle of Higher Education.*

130. Gates, B. (2016, April 3). A fairer way to evaluate teachers. *Washington Post.*

131. Chudacoff, H. (2008). *Children at Play: An American History* (p. 126). New York: NYU Press.

132. Burdette, H. L., & Whitaker, R. C. (2005). Resurrecting free play in young children: Looking beyond fitness and fatness to attention, affiliation, and affect. *Archives of Pediatrics and Adolescent Medicine, 159*(1), 46–50; citing Hofferth, S. L., & Sandberg, J. F. (2001). Changes in American children's use of time, 1981–1997. In T. Owens & S. L. Hofferth (Eds.), *Children at the Millennium: Where Have We Come From, Where Are We Going?* (pp. 193–229). Amsterdam: Elsevier Science Publishers.

133. Wisler, J. (n.d.) *Unstructured play is the parenting miracle we've all been waiting for (really).* Retrieved from http://www.scarymommy.com/unstructured-play-is-parenting-miracle/.

134. Elkind, D. (2007). *The Power of Play: How Spontaneous, Imaginative Activities Lead to Happier, Healthier Children* (p. 4). New York: Da Capo Press.

135. Christakis, E. (2016, January–February). The new preschool is crushing kids. *The Atlantic.*

136. Strauss, V. (May 1, 2014). Answer sheet: 6 reasons to reject Common Core K–3 standards. *Washington Post.* For an opposing argument that favors beginning formal reading instruction in kindergarten, see Hanson, R., & Farrell, D. (1992, January). Prescription for literacy: Providing critical educational experiences. *ERIC Digest.* Retrieved from https://www.ericdigests.org/1992-5/literacy.htm; and Hanson, R., & Farrell, D. (1995). The long-term effects on high school seniors of learning to read in kindergarten. *Reading Research Quarterly, 30*(4), 908. A key question is how best to support (and not penalize, overpressure, or discourage) children who are naturally disposed to formal reading and writing instruction at ages 6, 7, or 8 rather than 5.

137. Miller, E., & Almon, J. (2009). *Crisis in the kindergarten: Why children need to play in school.* Alliance for Childhood, National Society for the Study of Education.

138. For an opposing argument in favor of teaching advanced math in kindergarten, see Engel, M., Claessens, A., Watts, T., & Farkas, G. (2014, October 26). The misalignment of kindergarten mathematics content. Draft paper prepared for the Association for Public Policy Analysis and Management 2014 Fall Research Conference.

139. Wong, M. (2015, October 7). *Study finds improved self-regulation in kindergartners who wait a year to enroll.* Stanford News Center.

140. Suggate, S. (2009). School entry age and reading achievement in the 2006 Programme for International Student Assessment (PISA). *International Journal of Educational Research, 48*(3), 151–161.

141. Suggate, S. P., Schaughency, E. A., & Reese, E. (2013). Children learning to read later catch up to children reading earlier. *Early Childhood Research Quarterly, 28*(1), 33–48.

142. Ibid.

143. Morris, L. (2014, May 10). Political pressure takes the fun out of kindy, say academics. *Sydney Morning Herald.*

144. Schweinhart, L., & and Weikart, D. (1997). The High/Scope Preschool Curriculum Comparison Study through age 23. *Early Childhood Research Quarterly, 12*(2) 117–143. For a critique of the methodology and small sample size of the High/Scope study by "direct instruction" advocate Siegfried Engelmann, see Response to "The High/Scope Preschool Curriculum Comparison Study through age 23," (n.d.), at: http://darkwing.uoregon.edu/~adiep/zigrebut.htm

145. Marcon, R. A. (2002). Moving up the grades: Relationship between preschool model and later school success. *Early Childhood Research & Practice, 4*(1), n1. The study concluded, "Children's later school success appears to be enhanced by more active, child-initiated learning experiences. Their long-term progress may be slowed by overly academic preschool experiences that introduce formalized learning experiences too early for most children's developmental status. Pushing children too soon may actually backfire when children move into the later elementary school grades and are required to think more independently and take on greater responsibility for their own learning process." Also see Marcon, R. (1999). Differential impact of preschool models on development and early learning of inner-city children: A three-cohort study. *Developmental Psychology, 35*(2), 358–375.

146. Yogman, M., Garner, A., Hutchinson, J., Hirsh-Pasek, K., & Golinkoff, R, M.; American Academy of Pediatrics Committee on Psychosocial

Aspects of Child and Family Health, Council on Communications and Media. (2018). The power of play: A pediatric role in enhancing development in young children. *Pediatrics, 142*(3), e20182058.

147. David Berliner, John Popham, Diane Ravitch, and Daniel Koretz are among those scholars.

148. Evidence from large-scale case studies suggests that over-standardization does not benefit teachers and students. Perhaps the most interesting example is England, which launched a system-wide education reform in 1988 that for the first time brought tight external control to what and how teachers taught in the country's public schools. Based on an assumption that market-based choice for parents would work as it does in a marketplace, by raising efficiency and quality and lowering cost, the reform brought along the standardization of education services. Data from frequent standardized tests, the theory went, provided parents with information to help them choose "the best school" for their child. But, as mentioned earlier, research evidence shows that the reform didn't improve either the quality or equity of public school education in England. Similar research-informed conclusions have been made, for example, in the United States, Sweden, Australia, New Zealand, South Africa, and Chile.

149. Christakis, E. (2016, January–February). The new preschool is crushing kids. *The Atlantic*. Retrieved from https://www.theatlantic.com/magazine/archive/2016/01/the-new-preschool-is-crushing-kids/419139/.

150. Strauss, V., & Carlsson-Paige, N. (2015, November 24). Answer sheet: How "twisted" early childhood education has become—from a child development expert. *Washington Post* online.

151. Ibid.

152. Berdik, C. (2015, June 14). Is the Common Core killing kindergarten? *Boston Globe*.

153. Bassok, D., Latham, S., & Rorem, A. (2016, January 6). Is kindergarten the new first grade? *AERA Open*, https://doi.org/10.1177/2332858415616358

154. Walker, T. (2015, October 1). The joyful, illiterate kindergarteners of Finland. *The Atlantic*.

155. Ibid.

156. Ibid.

157. Kim, K. H. (2011). The creativity crisis: The decrease in creative thinking scores on the Torrance tests of creative thinking. *Creativity Research Journal, 23*(4), 285–295.

158. *Boston Globe,* June 14, 2015.

159. Ibid.

160. Nicholson, J., Bauer, A., & Wooly, R. (2016). Inserting child-initiated play into an American urban school district after a decade of scripted curricula complexities and progress. *American Journal of Play, 8*(2), 228–271.

161. Gray, P. (2011). The decline of play and the rise of psychopathology. *American Journal of Play, 3*(4), 443–463.

162. Gray, P. (2013, September 18). *The play deficit.* Retrieved from https://aeon.co/essays/children-today-are-suffering-a-severe-deficit-of-play.

163. Miller, E., & Almon, J. (2009). *Crisis in the kindergarten: Why children need to play in school.* Alliance for Childhood.

164. Ibid.

165. Haelle, T. (2018, May 16). Hospitals see growing numbers of kids and teens at risk for suicide. NPR; reporting on Plemmons, G., Hall, M., Doupnik, S., Gay, J., Brown, C., Browning, W., . . . Williams, D. (2018). Hospitalization for suicide ideation or attempt: 2008–2015. *Pediatrics, 141*(6), e20172426.

166. Abeles, V. (2016). *Beyond Measure: Rescuing an Overscheduled, Overtested, Underestimated Generation* (p. 15). New York: Simon & Schuster.

167. Association for Childhood Education International. (2017, May 9). *OECD's "Baby PISA" early learning assessment.* Retrieved from https://www.acei.org/acei-news/2017/5/9/oecds-baby-pisa-early-learning-assessment.

168. Merrow, J. (2016, September 5). The A.D.D. epidemic returns. *The Merrow Report* (online).

169. Schwarz, A. *ADHD Nation: Children, Doctors, Big Pharma, and the Making of an American Epidemic* (p. 3). New York: Simon & Schuster.

170. D'Agostino, R. (2014, April). The drugging of the American boy. *Esquire.*

171. Ibid.

172. Fulton, B., Scheffler, R., & Hinshaw, S. (2015). State variation in increased ADHD prevalence: Links to NCLB school accountability and state medication laws. *Psychiatric Services, 66,* 1074–1082.

173. D'Agostino, R. (2014, April). The drugging of the American boy. *Esquire*.

174. Evans, W., Morrill, M., & Parente, S. (2010). Measuring inappropriate medical diagnosis and treatment in survey data: The case of ADHD among school-age children. *Journal of Health Economics, 29*(5), 657–673.

175. Panksepp, J. (2008). Play, ADHD, and the construction of the social brain: Should the first class each day be recess? *American Journal of Play*, Summer, 55–79. In this paper, Panksepp predicted that future brain research will reveal that "(1) when properly evaluated, we will find that psychostimulants reduce the urge of human children to play; (2) a regular diet of physical play, each and every day during early childhood, will be able to alleviate ADHD-type symptoms in many children that would otherwise be on that 'clinical' track; (3) play will have long-term benefits for children's brains and minds that are not obtained with psychostimulants; (4) psychostimulants may sensitize young brains and intensify internally experienced urges that may, if socio-environmental opportunities are available, be manifested as elevated desires to seek drugs and other material rewards; and (5) if and when we finally get to human brain gene expression studies (methodologically almost impossible, since one needs brain tissue samples), we would anticipate that the profiles of gene-activation resulting from lots of play and lots of psychostimulants will be quite different in their brains." Researchers Anthony Pellegrini and Catherine Bohn have noted that "most children with attention-deficit hyperactivity disorder (ADHD) are boys, and they are especially vulnerable to the deleterious effects of prolonged periods of concentrated work without a break. Under less structured regimens, some of the same boys may not be diagnosed as ADHD." Regarding children in general, they added, "playful, not structured, breaks may be especially important in maximizing performance because unstructured breaks may reduce the cognitive interference associated with immediately preceding instruction." They suggested that "breaks during periods of sustained cognitive work should reduce cognitive interference and maximize learning and achievement gains," and "extending the American school day and school year, with more frequent recess periods, might positively affect children's cognitive performance and social competence, while

simultaneously providing parents with badly needed child care for more extended periods." Pellegrini, A. D., & Bohn, C. M. (2005). The role of recess in children's cognitive performance and school adjustment. *Educational Researcher, 34*(1), 13–19.

176. Ridgway, A., Northup, J., Pellegrini, A., & Hightshoe, A. (2003). Effects of recess on the classroom behavior of children with and without attention-deficit hyperactivity disorder. *School Psychology Quarterly, 18*, 253–268.

177. Cohen, P., Hochman, M., & Bedard, R. (2017, March 16). Is ADHD overdiagnosed and overtreated? *Harvard Health* blog.

178. Strauss, V., Miller, E., & Carlsson-Paige, N. (2013, January 29). Answer Sheet: A tough critique of Common Core on early education. *Washington Post* online. Retrieved from https://www.washingtonpost.com/news/answer-sheet/wp/2013/01/29/a-tough-critique-of-common-core-on-early-childhood-education/?utm_term=.2d3946eac0b8.

179. Ibid.

180. Ibid.

181. Ibid.

182. Kohn, D. (2015, May 16). Let the kids learn through play. *New York Times.*

183. Ibid.

184. Ibid.

185. Ibid.

186. Ibid.

187. Ibid.

188. Ibid.

189. Strauss, S., McLaughlin, G. B., Carlsson-Paige, N., & Levin, D. E. (2013, August 2) The disturbing shift underway in childhood classrooms. *Washington Post.*

190. Strauss, V., & Sluyter, S. (2014, March 23). Answer sheet: Kindergarten teacher: My job is now about tests and data—not children. I quit. *Washington Post.*

191. Teacher Blogs, Cody. A. (2012, September 26). Living in dialogue, guest post by Rog Lucido. How do high stakes tests affect our students? *EdWeek* blog. Retrieved from http://blogs.edweek.org/teachers/living-in-dialogue/2012/09/rog_lucido_how_do_high_stakes_.html.

192. Chasmar, J. (2013, November 25). Common Core testing makes children vomit, wet their pants: N.Y. principals. *Washington Times*.

193. Ohio Department of Education, Center for Curriculum and Assessment, Offices of Curriculum, Instruction and Assessment. (2007, October) *Ohio achievement tests: Grade 3, reading, directions for administration.*

194. Singer, S. (2017, August 2). Middle school suicides double as Common Core testing intensifies. *Huffington Post*. Retrieved from https://www.huffingtonpost.com/entry/middle-school-suicides-double-as-common-core-testing_us_59822d3de4b03d0624b0abb9.

195. McMahon, K. (2010, September 2). As a teacher, kindergarten is now not so exciting. *The Progressive*.

196. Strauss, V., McLaughlin, G. B., Carlsson-Paige, N., & Levin, D. (2013, August 2). Answer sheet: The disturbing shift underway in early childhood classrooms. *Washington Post* online. Retrieved from https://www.washingtonpost.com/news/answer-sheet/wp/2013/08/02/the-disturbing-shift-underway-in-early-childhood-classrooms/?utm_term=.4f0301e8c69a.

197. U.S. Department of Education Office for Civil Rights. (2014, March 21). *Civil rights data collection: Data snapshot (early childhood).*

198. Ibid.

199. Toppo, G. (2016, June 7). Black students nearly 4× as likely to be suspended. *USA Today*.

200. The impact of play deprivation on poor children is a special concern of Professor Rich Milner of the University of Pittsburgh, who studies sociology and urban education. He told us, "Play is of course an essential anchor to the development and learning of young children. And play is essential for all children—not just those from higher socio-economic backgrounds. My concern is that with an overemphasis on testing and test scores, some groups of students, especially those living below the poverty line, those whose first language is not English, those of color, and those with learning differences, may lose play time to focus on test prep—even in the early ages and grades. I worry though that 'play' opportunities are being streamlined with accountability systems in place that force some teachers to focus on traditional teaching methods and that do not allow students opportunities to explore, create, and develop skills through play." Echoing Milner's concerns,

Douglas Harris, Professor of Economics at Tulane University, points out the "potential irony that play might contribute positively to academic achievement, but more so in the long run than the short run, in which case reducing play is undermining the goal." Author interviews.

201. National Research Council, Division of Behavioral and Social Sciences and Education, Board on Testing and Assessment, Committee on Incentives and Test-Based Accountability in Public Education. (2018). *Incentives and Test-Based Accountability in Education* (pp. 4–26). Washington, DC: National Academies Press.

202. Cowan, L., & Mingo, C. (2012, May 2). A testing culture out of control. *New York Daily News*.

203. Domenech, D. (2013, May). Executive perspective. *School Administrator*.

204. Belknap, E., & Hazler, R. (2014). Empty playgrounds and anxious children. *Journal of Creativity in Mental Health, 9*(2), 210–231.

205. Toppo, G. (2016, May 17). GAO study: Segregation worsening in U.S. schools. *USA Today*.

206. Author interview.

207. Campanile, C. (2015, November 9). Principal says standardized testing is "modern day slavery." *New York Post*.

208. Cornerstone Academy for Social Action Middle School website, http://casaworldwide.org/principal-jamaal-bowman/.

209. Ibid.

210. Dewey, J. (1916). Democracy and Education. An introduction to the philosophy of education. New York: The Free Press, p. 194.

211. Nussbaum, D. (2006, December 10). Before children ask, "What's recess?" *New York Times*.

212. Deruy, E. (2016, September 13). Learning through play. *The Atlantic*.

213. Centers for Disease Control and Prevention and SHAPE America (Society of Health and Physical Educators). (2018). *Physical activity during school: Providing recess to all students*.

214. Johnson, D. (1998, April 9). Many schools putting an end to play. *New York Times*.

215. Ibid.

216. Ibid.

217. Blackwell, J. (2004, August). Recess: Forgotten, neglected, crossed off, or hidden. *Childhood Education*.

218. Patte, M. (2010). Is it still OK to play? *Journal of Student Wellbeing, 4*(1), 1–6.

219. Adams, C. (2011, March). Recess makes kids smarter. *Instructor,* Spring, 55–58.

220. Sohn, E. (2015, November 9). Recess: It's important. Does your child get enough of it? *Washington Post.*

221. Llopis-Jepsen, C. (2015, July 18). Elementaries not offering enough recess, advocates say. *Topeka Capital-Journal.*

222. French, R. (2014, August 31). School day recess and PE times diminish. *Atlanta Journal-Constitution.*

223. Anderson Cordell, S. (2013, October 23). Nixing recess: The silly, alarmingly popular way to punish kids. *The Atlantic.*

224. DiFulco, D. (2016, August 6). Parents push to boost recess in schools. *USA Today.*

225. Ibid.

226. Adams, C. (2011, March). Recess makes kids smarter, *Instructor,* Spring, 55–58.

227. Ibid.

228. De La Cruz, D. (2017, March 21). Why kids shouldn't sit still in class. *New York Times.*

229. Wurzburger, L. A. (2010). *Recess policy in Chicago Public Schools: 1855–2006* (Unpublished master's thesis). Paper 506. http://ecommons.luc.edu/luc_theses/506.

230. The Chronicle, Columbia College Chicago. (2012, January 27). *CPS students respond to new guidelines* [Video file]. YouTube. https://www.youtube.com/watch?v=DT3rGPlYZn0.

231. Sohn, E. (2015, November 9). Recess: It's important. Does your child get enough of it? *Washington Post.*

232. Chin, J., & Ludwig, D. (2013). Increasing children's physical activity during school recess periods. *American Journal of Public Health, 103*(7), 1229–1234.

233. Jarrett, O. (2013). *A Research-based case for recess.* US Play Coalition.

234. Robert Wood Johnson Foundation. (2009). *The state of play: Gallup survey of principals on school recess.*

235. Centers for Disease Control and Prevention. (1997). *Guidelines for school and community programs to promote lifelong physical activity among young people.* Atlanta, GA: Author.

236. Murray, R., Ramstetter, C.; Council on School Health; American Academy of Pediatrics. (2013). The crucial role of recess in school. *Pediatrics, 131*(1), 183–188.

237. The 2017 Wellness Policy of the New York City Department of Education states in no uncertain terms, "Physical activity during the school day (including but not limited to recess, physical activity breaks, or physical education) will not be withheld as punishment for any reason, nor will it be used as a punishment for any reason."

238. Christine Davis post on Arizonans for Recess and Wellness facebook page, September 12, 2018, accessed at https://www.facebook.com/photo.php?fbid=10216885009859073&set=gm.2091222257797693&type=3&theater&ifg=1.

239. Adams, C. (2011, March). Recess makes kids smarter. *Instructor*, Spring, 55–58.

240. Ibid.

241. Ferdman, R. (2015, January 16). The potentially significant flaw in how schools are serving lunch to kids. *Washington Post*.

242. Schulzke, E. (2014, August 10). Why has U.S. academic success dropped? The answer may be on the playground. *Deseret News*.

243. Fuller, L. (2017). *Recess before lunch*. National Education Association.

244. Just, J. P. D. (2015). Lunch, recess and nutrition: Responding to time incentives in the cafeteria. *Preventive Medicine*, 71(February), 27–30.

245. Overton, P. (2007, October 15). Playing first, eating later. *The Hartford Courant*.

246. Ramstetter, C., Murray, R., & Garner, A. (2010). The crucial role of recess in schools. *Journal of School Health, 80*(11), 517–526.

247. Reilly, K. (2017, October 23). Is recess important for kids or a waste of time? Here's what the research says. *Time*.

248. One structured/coached recess program, called Playworks, is popular among some school teachers and principals. The results of two recent studies of Playworks' impact on children's physical activity were mixed. One study of 29 schools, titled "The Impact of Playworks on Boys' and Girls' Physical Activity During Recess," by Martha Bleeker, Nicholas Beyler, Susanne James-Burdumy, and Jane Fortson, published in the January 21, 2015, *Journal of School Health*, concluded "Playworks had a significant impact on some measures of girls' physical activity, but no significant impact on measures of boys' physical activity."

Another study, by the same research team (plus Max Benjamin), titled "The Impact of Playworks on Students' Physical Activity During Recess: Findings from a Randomized Controlled Trial," published in the December 2014 issue of *Preventive Medicine,* stated, "Teachers in Playworks schools reported that students were more active during recess, but accelerometer and student survey measures showed either no impacts or marginally significant impacts." An interesting exercise would be to measure the impact of Playworks sessions on physical activity levels versus that of physical education classes, which can often involve a lot of standing and sitting around time, and also to measure its impact versus that of simple outdoor free-play recess periods overseen by trained school staff. Regardless of whether a program like Playworks is offered, children should be granted safely supervised daily blocks of free, unstructured outdoor play time, plus regular, and preferably daily, physical education.

249. Whitebread, D., Basilio, M., Juvalja, M., & Verma, M. (2012). *The importance of play: A report on the value of children's play with a series of policy recommendations.* Commissioned by Toy Industries of Europe.

250. Author interview.

251. Yan, A. (2016, December 27). Piano lessons, maths classes and hours of homework . . . a weekend in the life of China's stressed-out kids. *South China Morning Post.*

252. Students "drugged" in class ahead of *gaokao*. (2012, May 5). *China Daily.*

253. Larmer, B. (2014, December 31). Inside a Chinese test-prep factory. *New York Times.*

254. Yan, A. (2016, December 27). Piano lessons, maths classes and hours of homework . . . a weekend in the life of China's stressed-out kids. *South China Morning Post.*

255. Ibid.

256. Murray, J. (2014, November 18). Overtesting and China: A cautionary tale [radio broadcast]. WBUR.

257. Xueqin, J. (2010, December 8). The test Chinese schools still fail. *Wall Street Journal.*

258. Gray, P. (2013, September 18). *The play deficit.* Retrieved from https://aeon.co/essays/children-today-are-suffering-a-severe-deficit-of-play.

259. Private tutoring market in China—Drivers and forecasts from Technavio. *Business Wire,* April 21, 2017. Retrieved from https://

www.businesswire.com/news/home/20170421005379/en/
Private-Tutoring-Market-China.

260. Zhao, S. (2015, May 25). Tutoring centre's founder defends kindergarten interview ad campaign that went viral. *South China Morning Post.*

261. Blundy, R. (2017, April 22). All work and no play: Why more Hong Kong children are having mental health problems. *South China Morning Post.*

262. Author interview.

263. Choon, C. M. (2016, September 25). Seoul to cut homework for kids in P1 and P2. *Straits Times.*

264. Moon, L. (2018, June 9). Inside Asia's pressure-cooker exam system, which region has it the worst? *South China Morning Post.*

265. McDonald, M. (2011, May 22). Elite South Korean University rattled by suicides. *New York Times.*

266. Koo, S-W. (2014, August 1). An assault upon our children. *New York Times.*

267. Diamond, A. (2016, November 17). South Korea's testing fixation. *The Atlantic.*

268. Hesketh, T., Zhen, Y., Lu, L., Dong, Z. X., Jun, Y. X., & Xing, Z. W. (2010). Stress and psychosomatic symptoms in Chinese school children: Cross-sectional survey. *Archives of Disease in Childhood, 95*(2), 136–140.

269. Author interview. Similarly, in Poland, according to one expert, play is offered in kindergarten, but not in higher grades: "Children have the opportunity to play only during breaks between lessons. There is a conviction that during school lessons children are expected to learn in the traditional sense of the word. The Polish school does not recognize the developmental potential of children's play. It separates play from learning." Author interview with Ewa Lemańska-Lewandowska, Adjunct Professor, Department of Educational and Educational Studies and the Laboratory of Educational Change, Center for Research on Learning and Development at the Pedagogy Institute at the Faculty of Pedagogy and Psychology, at the University of Kazimierz Wielki in Bydgoszcz, Poland.

270. All-Party Parliamentary Group on a Fit and Healthy Childhood. (2015). *Play: A report by the All-Party Parliamentary Group on a Fit and Healthy Childhood.*

271. Ibid.
272. Ibid.
273. Moss, S. (2012). *Natural childhood*. Swindon, UK: National Trust.
274. Ibid.
275. Carrington, D. (2015, March 25). Three-quarters of UK children spend less time outdoors than prison inmates—survey. *The Guardian*.
276. Institute of Education, University of London. (2013). *The social value of breaktimes and lunchtimes in schools*. Research Briefing No 59. London: Author.
277. Gill, E. (2016, May 3). Parents explain why their children are "on strike" over tests for six-year-olds. *Manchester Evening News*.
278. Ibid.
279. Richardson, H. (2017, April 16). Teachers back moves towards primary SATS boycott. *BBC News*. Retrieved from https://www.bbc.com/news/education-39592777
280. Ibid.
281. Evans, M. (2011, February 8). Analysis: What does "ready for school" mean? *Nursery World*.
282. Whitebread, D. (2014, July 11). Hard evidence: At what age are children ready for school? *The Conversation*.
283. Gaunt, C. (2018, February 27). Campaigners publish case against the baseline. *Nursery World*, reporting on *Baseline testing: Why it doesn't add up*, Association for Professional Development in Early Years.
284. Abeles, V. (2016). *Beyond Measure: Rescuing an Overscheduled, Overtested, Underestimated Generation* (p. 160). New York: Simon & Schuster.
285. Brown, F., & Patte, M. (2012). *Rethinking Children's Play* (p. 145). London: A&C Black.
286. Kwon, Y-I. (2002). Changing curriculum for early childhood education in England. *Early Childhood Research and Practice, 4*(2).
287. University of Cambridge. (2009). *Introducing the Cambridge Primary Review: Children, their world, their education*. Cambridge, UK: Author.
288. Robinson, N. (2018, March 7). Calls for NAPLAN review after report reveals no change in decade of results. *ABC News Australia*.
289. Topsfield, J. (2012, November 26). NAPLAN tests take heavy toll. *Sydney Morning Herald*.
290. Ibid.

291. Seith, E. (2018, August 2). *Call to abolish tests that leave P1s "shaking."* Retrieved from https://www.tes.com/news/call-abolish-tests-leave-p1s-shaking.

292. Scottish National Standardised Assessments [website]. https://standardisedassessment.gov.scot.

293. Author interview.

294. Author interview.

295. Author interview.

296. Author interview.

297. Meredith, J., & Doyle, W. (2012). *A Mission from God: A Memoir and Challenge for America* (p. 264). New York: Doubleday.

298. Latest edition: Sahlberg, P. (2015). *Finnish Lessons 2.0.: What Can the World Learn from Educational Change in Finland?* New York: Teachers College Press.

299. Jung, C. G. (2014). *Collected Works of C.G. Jung, Volume 6: Psychological Types* (p. 123). Princeton, NJ: Princeton University Press.

300. Author interview.

301. Author interview.

302. Author interview.

303. Author interview.

304. On the Finnish childhood education system, see Abrams, S. (2011, January 28). The children must play. *The New Republic*; Hancock, L. (2011, September). Why are Finland's schools successful? *Smithsonian Magazine*; Partanen, A. (2011, December 29). What Americans keep ignoring about Finland's school success. *The Atlantic.* On the history of Finland and class size: see Sam Abrams in http://parentsacrossamerica.org/what-finland-and-asia-tell-us-about-real-education-reform/: "These reductions in class size were won by Finland's teachers' union (Opestusalan Ammattijarjesto, or OAJ) as a concession from the government when education authorities nullified tracking. In 1972, authorities postponed tracking from fifth grade to seventh. In 1985, authorities postponed tracking from seventh grade to tenth. The response from the OAJ was acceptance of the termination of tracking as wise but only if class sizes were reduced, as it would be too difficult for teachers to teach heterogeneous groups if classes remained large. In addition to science classes, all classes that involve any machinery or lab equipment are capped at 16. This includes cooking (which all seventh-graders are required to take), textiles (or sewing),

carpentry, and metal shop." On ideal class sizes, Leonie Haimson, Executive Director of Class Size Matters, told us in an email communication: "There is very little research on this but what there is shows the smaller the better—though there is no particular threshold that needs to be met for benefits to accrue to the kids in the class. Several elite prep schools like Exeter cap class sizes at 12; no more than can fit around their 'Harkness table.' What I"ve found through experience and anecdotal evidence is that the ideal class size for any school, public or private, is 15 or less. Whether or not that is achievable is another question. Class sizes in grades K-3 really should be capped at 18 or less, at about 23 students in middle school and no more than 25 in high school."

305. Another problem is indoor air quality: Fully 9 percent of Finnish pupils began the 2018/2019 school year in temporary buildings because their schools were infected with mold and had to be renovated, a chronic problem in the often damp nation of Finland. See Mould problems drive thousands of Finnish school children into temporary barracks, *YLE News*, September 13, 2018.

306. Sahlberg, P. (2012, September 6). How gender equality could help school reform. *Washington Post.*

307. UNICEF. (2017). *Innocenti Report Card 14: Building the future: Children and the sustainable development goals in rich countries.* Retrieved from https://www.unicef-irc.org/publications/pdf/RC14_eng.pdf.

308. World Economic Forum. (2018). *The global gender gap report.* Retrieved from http://www3.weforum.org/docs/WEF_GGGR_2018.pdf.

309. Ibid.

310. James Heckman, quoted in Kristoff, N. (2011, October 20). Occupy the classroom. *New York Times.*

311. Watson, J. (2012). Starting well: Benchmarking early education across the world. Economist Intelligence Unit, *The Economist.*

312. Christakis, E. (2016, January–February). The new preschool is crushing kids. *The Atlantic.*

313. For families where both parents choose to work, Finnish law guarantees the right to a municipal kindergarten spot to children younger than 7. About 40 percent of 1- and 2-year-olds take advantage of this right while the rest of the children stay home with mother, father, or another adult. Three out of four 3- to 5-year-olds take part in daily early

childhood education and care in either public, private, or home-based day care. Early childhood education is heavily subsidized in all of these arrangements, with the maximum monthly fee determined by parents' wealth per child in Helsinki being about $300. All 6-year-olds must attend publicly funded half-day preschool either in their kindergarten or neighborhood primary school prior to starting primary school at the age of 7.

314. Author interview.

315. Finnish Schools on the Move website: https://liikkuvakoulu.fi/english.

316. Association for Childhood Education International. (2009). *Childhood obesity & testing: What teachers can do.* Retrieved from http://www.teachhub.com/childhood-obesity-testing-what-teachers-can-do.

317. Bangsbo, J., Krustrup, P., Duda, J., Hillman, C., Andersen, A. B., Weiss, M., . . . & Elbe, A-M. (2016). The Copenhagen Consensus Conference 2016: Children, youth, and physical activity in schools and during leisure time. *British Journal of Sports Medicine, 50*(19). doi:10.1136/bjsports-2016-096325.

318. Rhea, D., Rivchun, A., & Pennings, J. (2013). The LiiNk Project: Implementation of a recess and character development pilot study with grades K & 1 children. *Texas Association for Health, Physical Education, Recreation & Dance Journal (TAHPERD),* Summer, 14–35.

319. Background on Debbie Rhea's thinking are from interviews with Professor Rhea; details and quotes on the LiiNK program in this chapter are from author interviews with and information provided by Deborah Rhea, Amber Beene, Doug Seiver, Debbie Clark, and Bryan McLain; Texas Christian University LiiNK Project, End of Year Report (2015–16); Rhea, D. (2016). Recess: The forgotten classroom. *Instructional Leader, 29*(1), 1–4; Rhea, D., Rivchun, A., & Pennings, J. (2016). The LiiNk Project: Implementation of a recess and character development pilot study with grades K & 1 children. *Texas Association for Health, Physical Education, Recreation & Dance Journal (TAHPERD),* Summer, 14–35; Rhea D., & Nigaglioni, I. (2016, February). Outdoor playing = Outdoor learning. *Educational Facility Planner Journal.*

320. Increasing recess can help school grades? NewsOn6.com (Chattanooga, OK), May 17, 2017. Retrieved from http://www.newson6.com/story/35457235/increasing-recess-can-help-school-grades.

321. McLogan, J. (2017, October 27). *Patchogue schools experiment with expanded recess, less homework.* CBS New York. Retrieved from https://newyork.cbslocal.com/2017/10/27/patchogue-medford-homework/.

322. *Pat-Med debuts before school play program.* Patch.com, January 25, 2018. Retrieved from https://patch.com/new-york/patchogue/pat-med-debuts-school-play-program.

323. Except where indicated, Dr. Hynes's thoughts, quotes, and details on his school district's play initiatives are from author interviews.

324. Chang Jing, C. (2016, October 26). How did "Anji Play" go global? (J. Coffino, Trans.). *China Education Daily.*

325. Author interview.

326. Jing, C. (2016, October 26). How did "Anji Play" go global? (J. Coffino, Trans.). *China Education Daily.*

327. Coffino, J. (2016, March 21). *This 21st century Maria Montessori is changing China, and we should all be paying attention.* Medium.com. In an interview with the authors, Coffino elaborated on the deeply Chinese roots of Anji Play: "Confucian culture stresses a human-centered world view and respect for the essence of human nature, and that because the freedom of play is essential to the nature of childhood, a pedagogy that derives from a human-centered view would therefore advocate for self-determined play in childhood. Traditional Chinese culture advocates for the value of the natural world, and the oneness of man and nature. Moreover, both Daoism and Confucian thought emphasize the unique knowledge and learning of the child, that education should follow natural development, accord with the individual characteristics of each learner, and that self-direction and independent thought are critical qualities of learning. Laozi emphasized the need for adults to return to the qualities of childhood as a means of learning deeply and naturally. Ming dynasty Confucian scholar Wang Yangming believed that the education of the child should center around the joy that the child derives from play guided by their own interests, and that to limit that trajectory is to limit the natural growth of the child. While the Ming dynasty scholar Li Zhi emphasized that adults should maintain the spirit of the child in themselves, that essential spirit of the child should be venerated and protected in the process of education."

328. Author interview, translated by Jesse Coffino.

329. *China Education Daily*, May 7, 2017.

330. Boesveld, S. (2015, January 25). When one New Zealand school tossed its playground rules and let students risk injury, the results were surprising. *National Post* (Canada).
331. SBS Dateline, Journeyman Pictures. *The school with a radical "no rules" policy* YouTube video posted November 24, 2014. Retrieved from https://www.youtube.com/watch?v=qG2MhjBOSLQ.
332. Bruce McLachlan at TEDxBondUniversity. *Play at Swanson School.* YouTube video posted October 2, 2014. Retrieved from https://www.youtube.com/watch?v=uADHiCuq1SI.
333. McLachlan, B. (2015, Winter). The no rules playground. *Leadership in Focus.*
334. Farmer, V. L., Williams, S. M., Mann, J. I., Schofield, G., McPhee, J. C., & Taylor, R. W. (2017). Change of school playground environment on bullying: A randomized controlled trial. *Pediatrics, 139*(5), e20163072.
335. Research and information for this section were provided to the authors by Inspiring Scotland.
336. Zaharia, M., & Ungku, F. (2017, January 8). In the hunt for new ideas, Singapore eases obsession with grades. *Reuters.*
337. Vasagar, J., & Kang, B. (2016, September 29). Singapore's strict schools start to relax. *Financial Times.*
338. Author interview.
339. July 25, 2018, Keynote Address by Minister for Education Ye Kung Ong, at the Economic Society of Singapore Dinner.
340. July 11, 2018, Singapore Government News.
341. Teng, A. (2016, April 17). Going beyond grades: Evolving the Singapore education system. *Straits Times.*
342. Ibid.
343. Rubin, C. M. (2017, August 14). The global search for education: Will Singapore continue to lead in 2030? *Huffington Post.*
344. Teng, A. (2018, September 28). Learning is not a competition: No more 1st, 2nd or last in class for primary and secondary students. *South China Morning Post.*
345. Mokhtar, F. (2018, September 28). Changes made, now the next challenge. *TODAY* (Singapore).
346. Yng, N. J. (2014, January 24). In Japan's pre-schools, children must play. *TODAY* (Singapore); Yng, N. J., & Chia, A. (2014, February 19). Lessons for Singapore from Asia's pre-schools. *TODAY* (Singapore).

347. Clavel, T. (2014, March 2). Thinking outside the usual white box. *The Japan Times.*

348. Moriyama RAIC International Prize award document, 2017.

349. Ibid.

350. Ha, T-H. (2015, April 23). *Inside the world's best kindergarten.* Ideas. Ted.com. Retrieved from https://ideas.ted.com/inside-the-worlds-best-kindergarten/.

351. Block, I. (2017, October 2). *Tokyo kindergarten by Tezuka Architects lets children run free on the roof.* Retrieved from https://www.dezeen.com/2017/10/02/fuji-kindergarten-tokyo-tezuka-architects-oval-roof-deck-playground/.

352. Ibid.

353. Moriyama Prize award document, 2017.

354. Bozikovic, A. (2017, September 19). Fuji kindergarten awarded $100,000 global architecture prize. *Globe and Mail.*

355. Block, I. (2017, October 2). *Tokyo kindergarten by Tezuka Architects lets children run free on the roof.*

356. Zann, L. (2015, January 30). Croatia: Journey to my ancestral home. *The Chronicle Herald* (Halifax).

357. Jenkin, M. (2016, June 2). Wild things: How ditching the classroom boosts children's mental health. *The Guardian.*

358. Branson, R. (2014, November 10). *The importance of play.* Retrieved from https://www.virgin.com/richard-branson/importance-play.

359. See Sir Ken Robinson's website: http://sirkenrobinson.com.

360. de Braganza, A. (2013, August 12). To love somebody: Remembering Janusz Korczak. *Times of Israel* (blog).

361. Kuper, L. (2013, September 3). 10 commandments for new teachers. Retrieved from https://www.theguardian.com/teacher-network/teacher-blog/2013/sep/03/nqt-10-commandments-new-teachers; Goldstein, D. (2014). *The Teacher Wars: A History of America's Most Embattled Profession.* New York: Knopf Doubleday Publishing Group. Note: some versions of this quote have it as "elastic joy" rather than "ecstatic joy."

362. McEwan, E. (1998). *The Principal's Guide to Raising Reading Achievement* (p. 3). Newbury Park, CA: Corwin Press.

363. Lutkehaus, N. (2008). *Margaret Mead: The Making of an American Icon* (p. 261). Princeton, NJ: Princeton University Press. Interestingly,

although this quote is widely, and probably reliably, attributed to Margaret Mead, the original primary source has yet to be found.

364. Hughes, C., Daly, I., White, N., et al. (2015). Measuring the foundations of school readiness: Introducing a new questionnaire for teachers—the Brief Early Skills and Support Index. *British Journal of Educational Psychology, 85*(3), 332–356.

365. Center on Media and Child Health. *#MorePlayToday*. Retrieved from http://cmch.tv/moreplaytoday/.

366. See the provocative, cliché-busting article, Kirschner, P. A., & van Merriënboer, J. G. J. (2013, June). Do learners really know best? Urban legends in education. *Educational Psychologist*.

367. Kardaras, N. (2016, December 17). Kids turn violent as parents battle "digital heroin" addiction. *New York Post*.

368. Yogman, M., Garner, A., Hutchinson, J., Hirsh-Pasek, K., & Golinkoff, R, M.; American Academy of Pediatrics Committee on Psychosocial Aspects of Child and Family Health, Council on Communications and Media. (2018). The power of play: A pediatric role in enhancing development in young children. *Pediatrics, 142*(3), e20182058.

369. Kardaras, N. (2016, August 31). Screens in schools are a $60 billion hoax. *Time*.

370. Retter, E. (2017, April 21). Billionaire tech mogul Bill Gates reveals he banned his children from mobile phones until they turned 14. *The Mirror*.

371. Bilton, N. (2014, September 10). Steve Jobs was a low-tech parent. *New York Times*.

372. Carmody, T. (2012, January 17). What's wrong with education cannot be fixed with technology: The other Steve Jobs. *Wired*.

373. Richtel, M. (2011, October 11). A Silicon Valley school that doesn't compute. *New York Times*.

374. *The View*, ABC Network, May 15, 2012.

375. Interview with Mary Harris, *The Leonard Lopate Show*, WNYC radio, December 7, 2017.

376. Bowles, N. (2018, October 26). A dark consensus about screens and kids begins to emerge in Silicon Valley; Silicon Valley nannies are phone police for kids: The digital gap between rich and poor kids is not what we expected. *New York Times* online. Retrieved from https://www.nytimes.com/2018/10/26/style/phones-children-silicon-valley.html.

377. Ferdman, R. A. (2015, September 15). The problem with one of the biggest changes in education around the world. *Washington Post* online. Retrieved from https://www.washingtonpost.com/news/wonk/wp/2015/09/15/how-much-computers-at-school-are-hurting-kids-reading/?utm_term=.d272d4c94d57.

378. For a contrary view, see Zheng, B., Warschauer, M., & Chin-Hsi Lin, C-H. (2016). Learning in one-to-one laptop environments: A meta-analysis and research synthesis. *Review of Educational Research, 86*(4). The article reviewed 65 journal articles and 31 doctoral dissertations published from January 2001 to May 2015 to examine the effect of one-to-one laptop programs on teaching and learning in K–12 schools. From the article's abstract: "A meta-analysis of 10 studies examines the impact of laptop programs on students' academic achievement, finding significantly positive average effect sizes in English, writing, mathematics, and science. In addition, the article summarizes the impact of laptop programs on more general teaching and learning processes and perceptions as reported in these studies, again noting generally positive findings."

379. Milteer, R. M., Ginsburg, K. R.; Council on Communications and Media, & Committee on Psychosocial Aspects of Child and Family Health, American Academy of Pediatrics. (2012). Clinical report: The importance of play in promoting healthy child development and maintaining strong parent–child bonds: Focus on children in poverty. *Pediatrics, 129*, e204–e213.

380. Growing Up Digital (GUD) Alberta. Website: https://www.teachers.ab.ca/Public%20Education/EducationResearch/Pages/GrowingUpDigital(GUD)Alberta.aspx.

381. Kardaras, N. (2017). *Glow Kids: How Screen Addiction Is Hijacking Our Kids—and How to Break the Trance.* New York: St. Martin's Griffin.

382. Kardaras, N. (2016, 17). Kids turn violent as parents battle "digital heroin" addiction, *New York Post.*

383. Kardaras, N. (2016, August 31). Screens in schools are a $60 billion hoax. *Time.*

384. Kardaras, N. (2016, 17). Kids turn violent as parents battle "digital heroin" addiction, *New York Post.*

385. Riley, N. S. (2018, February 11). America's real digital divide. *New York Times.*

386. Beland, L-P., & Richard Murphy, R. (2015, May). Ill communication: Technology, distraction & student performance. CEP Discussion Paper No. 1350. Centre for Economic Performance.

387. Higgins, S., Xiao, Z., & Katsipataki, M. (2012). *The impact of digital technology on learning: A summary for the Education Endowment Foundation*. Durham, UK: Durham University.

388. Mangen, A., Walgermo, B., & Brønnick, K. (2013). Reading linear texts on paper versus computer screen: Effects on reading comprehension. *International Journal of Educational Research, 58*, 61–68.

389. Boesveld, S. (2011, September 8). Students give e-learning a grade of incomplete. *National Post* (Canada).

390. Rieger, S. (2015, December 3). Screen time is bad for kids' development: University of Alberta researchers. *Huffington Post Canada*.

391. Kardaras, N. (2016, August 27). It's "digital heroin": How screens turn kids into psychotic junkies. *New York Post*.

392. For problems and limitations of screens in schools, see Parents Across America. (2016). *Our children @ risk: PAA reports detail dangers of EdTech*; and Cimarusti, D. (2018). *Online learning: What every parent should know*. Network for Public Education.

393. Passage adapted with permission from Brown, F., & Patte, M. (2013). *Rethinking Children's Play*. New York: Bloomsbury.

394. Rule 23, United Nations Standard Minimum Rules for the Treatment of Prisoners (Nelson Mandela Rules, adopted 2015), United Nations Office on Drugs and Crime, retrieved from: http://www.unodc.org/documents/justice-and-prison-reform/GA-RESOLUTION/E_ebook.pdf.

395. Institute of Medicine [now called National Academy of Medicine]. (2013). Educating the student body: Taking physical activity and physical education to school, 6, 7. Retrieved from http://www.nationalacademies.org/hmd/Reports/2013/Educating-the-Student-Body-Taking-Physical-Activity-and-Physical-Education-to-School.aspx.

SELECT BIBLIOGRAPHY

This book is based on author interviews with a panel of over 70 international academic experts and educators; our personal observations and conversations with teachers, parents, and students during field visits to schools and kindergartens in the United States, Finland, Canada, Singapore, Australia, New Zealand, Japan, China, Iceland, Norway, Sweden, England, Scotland, Croatia, and around the world; and our critical review of a wide range of research literature on childhood education and play.

We are grateful to these experts for generously agreeing to share their ideas, opinions, and research discoveries with us. They are as follows:

Sophie Alcock, Senior Lecturer, School of Education, Victoria University of Wellington, New Zealand

Joshua Aronson, Associate Professor of Applied Psychology, Steinhardt School of Culture, Education, and Human Development, New York University, New York City

Amber Beene, Principal, Saginaw Elementary School, Fort Worth, Texas

Jo Boaler, Professor, Mathematics Education, Stanford Graduate School of Education, Palo Alto, California

Robert Boruch, University Trustee Chair Professor of Education and Statistics, Co-Director, Center for Research and Evaluation in Social Policy (CRESP), Human Development and Quantitative Methods Division, Graduate School of Education, University of Pennsylvania, Philadelphia

Jamaal Bowman, Founding Principal of Cornerstone Academy for Social Action Middle School, South Bronx, New York

Milda Bredikyte, Associate Professor, Lithuanian University of Educational Sciences, Vilnius

Stig Brostrom, Professor Emeritus, Danish School of Education, Aarhus University, Aarhus, Denmark

Fraser Brown, Professor of Playwork, Core Member of the Institute for Health and Wellbeing, Leeds Beckett University; Co-Editor, *International Journal of Play*

Judith Butler, President of World Organization for Early Childhood—Ireland, Course Coordinator, Early Years Education, Department of Sport, Leisure & Childhood Studies, Cork Institute of Technology, Cork, Ireland

Nancy Carlsson-Paige, Professor Emerita, Child Development, Lesley University, Cambridge, Massachusetts; co-founder, Defending the Early Years

Christine Chen, Asia Pacific Early Education Development Federation, Founder, President of the Association for Child Care Educators (ACCE) and Founder and current President, Association for Early Childhood Educators (AECES), Singapore

Debbie Clark, Principal, Oak Point Elementary School, Oak Point, Texas

Eric Contreras, Principal, Stuyvesant High School, New York City

Barbara Darrigo, Retired Principal, P.S. 149—the Sojourner Truth School, Harlem, New York

Bruce Fuller, Professor of Education and Public Policy, University of California, Berkeley

Gene Glass, Senior Researcher, National Education Policy Center, University of Colorado Boulder; Regents' Professor Emeritus, Arizona State University, Phoenix

Jeanne Goldhaber, Associate Professor Emeritus, College of Education and Social Services, University of Vermont

Ian Goldin, Oxford University Professor of Globalisation and Development, Director of the Oxford Martin Programme on Technological and Economic Change, Senior Fellow at the Oxford Martin School, Professorial Fellow at the University's Balliol College

Pentti Hakkarainen, Professor, Lithuanian University of Educational Sciences, Vilnius

Heikki Happonen, Professor of Education, University of Eastern Finland, Head of the Finnish Association of University Teacher Training Schools

Douglas Harris, Professor of Economics, Schleider Foundation Chair in Public Education, Director, Education Research Alliance for New Orleans, Tulane University; Non-Resident Senior Fellow, Brookings Institution

Stephen P. Hinshaw, Professor, Department of Psychology, University of California, Berkeley; Professor in Residence and Vice-Chair for Child and Adolescent Psychology, Department of Psychiatry, UCSF Weill Institute for Neurosciences, University of California, San Francisco

Kathy Hirsh-Pasek, Senior Fellow, Global Economy and Development, Center for Universal Education, Stanley and Debra Lefkowitz Faculty Fellow, Department of Psychology, Temple University, Philadelphia

Michael Hynes, Superintendent of Schools, Patchogue-Medford School District, Long Island, New York

Sekiichi Kato, Principal, Fuji Kindergarten, Tokyo

Lori Korner, Principal, Patchogue-Medford School District, Long Island, New York

Gloria Ladson-Billings, President, National Academy of Education; Professor, Department of Curriculum & Instruction, Kellner Family Distinguished Professor in Urban Education, University of Wisconsin–Madison

Ewa Lemańska-Lewandowska, Adjunct Professor, Department of Educational and Educational Studies and the Laboratory of Educational Change, Center for Research on Learning and Development, Pedagogy Institute at the Faculty of Pedagogy and Psychology, University of Kazimierz Wielki, Bydgoszcz, Poland

Henry Levin, William H. Kilpatrick Professor of Economics and Education, Teachers College, Columbia University, New York City

Susan Linn, Lecturer on Psychiatry, Harvard Medical School; Research Associate, Boston Children's Hospital

Ulina Mapp, President, World Organization for Early Childhood Education–Panama; Professor, Director of Research and Postgraduate Studies, ISAE University, Panama City

Erum Mariam, Director of Institutional Development, BRAC University, Bangladesh

Smita Mathur, Associate Professor, College of Education, Department of Early, Elementary, & Reading Education, James Madison University, Harrisonburg, Virginia

Chika Matsudaira, Associate Professor, Social Welfare, University of Shizuoka, Japan

Helen May, Emeritus Professor of Education, University of Otago, New Zealand

Bryan McLain, Principal, Eagle Mountain Elementary School, Fort Worth, Texas

Deborah Meier, Senior Scholar, New York University Steinhardt School of Education; Founding Principal, Central Park East Elementary Schools, New York City; author, *These Schools Belong to You and Me*

Rich Milner, Professor of Education, Helen Faison Professor of Urban Education, Professor of Sociology, Social Work, and Africana Studies, Director, Center for Urban Education, University of Pittsburgh

Stellakis Nektarios, Assistant Professor, Department of Educational Science and Early Childhood Education, University of Patras, Greece; Regional Vice-President for Europe, World Organization for Early Childhood Education

Chee Mg Ng, former Minister for Education, Republic of Singapore

Pak Tee Ng, Associate Professor, National Institute of Education, Singapore

Julie Nicholson, Associate Professor of Practice, School of Education, Mills College; Deputy Program Director, WestEd Center for Child and Family Studies, Sausalito, California

Nel Noddings, Lee L. Jacks Professor of Education, Emerita, Stanford University; past President of the National Academy of Education, the Philosophy of Education Society, and the John Dewey Society

Pedro Noguera, Distinguished Professor of Education, Graduate School of Education and Information Studies, University of California, Los Angeles

Kolbrún Pálsdóttir, Associate Professor, Program Director for the Leisure and Youth Programme, School of Education, University of Iceland, Reykjavik

Anthony Pellegrini, Professor Emeritus, Department of Educational Psychology, College of Education, University of Minnesota

Sergio Pellis, Professor and Board of Governors Research Chair, Department of Neuroscience, University of Lethbridge, Alberta, Canada

Jonathan Plucker, Julian C. Stanley Professor of Talent Development, School of Education, Johns Hopkins University, Baltimore, Maryland

Catherine L. Ramstetter, PhD, Health Educator; Co-author of American Academy of Pediatrics 2013 Policy Statement "The Crucial Role of Recess in Schools"

Diane Ravitch, Research Professor of Education, Steinhardt School of Culture, Education, and Human Development, New York University; Founder and President of the Network for Public Education (NPE)

Rob Reich, Professor of Political Science, Stanford University, Palo Alto, California

Deborah Rhea, Associate Dean of Research and Health Sciences, Harris College of Nursing and Health Sciences, Professor, Department of Kinesiology, Texas Christian University, Fort Worth

Eszter Salamon, President, European Parents Association

Ellen Beate Hansen Sandseter, Professor, Queen Maud University College of Early Childhood Education, Norway

Barbara Schneider, John A. Hannah University Distinguished Professor in the College of Education and the Department of Sociology, Michigan State University, East Lansing

Doug Seiver, Principal, Chavez Elementary School, Little Elm, Texas

Serap Sevimli-Celik, Assistant Professor, Elementary and Early Childhood Education, College of Education, Middle East Technical University (METU), Ankara, Turkey

Selma Simonstein, President, Chilean National Committee of the World Organization for Early Childhood Education; Professor, Metropolitan University of Education Sciences, Santiago, Chile

Stephen Siviy, Professor of Psychology, Gettysburg College, Gettysburg, Pennsylvania

Erin Skahill, Principal, Patchogue-Medford School District, Long Island, New York

Reesa Sorin, Associate Professor, Coordinator, Early Childhood Education, College of Arts, Society and Education, Division of Tropical Environments and Societies, James Cook University, Queensland, Australia

Deborah Stipek, Judy Koch Professor of Education and former Dean of the Graduate School of Education, Stanford University, Director of Heising-Simons Development and Research in Early Math Education Network

Marcelo Suárez-Orozco, Wasserman Dean and Distinguished Professor of Education, Graduate School of Education & Information Studies, University of California, Los Angeles

William G. Tierney, Wilbur Kieffer Professor of Higher Education, University Professor & Co-director, Pullias Center for Higher Education, University of Southern California, Los Angeles

Charles Ungerleider, Professor Emeritus, Educational Studies, University of British Columbia

Tony Wagner, Expert in Residence, Innovation Lab, Harvard University; Senior Research Fellow, Learning Policy Institute

Cheng Xueqin, Founder, Anji Play, China

Hirokazu Yoshikawa, Courtney Sale Ross University Professor of Globalization and Education, Steinhardt School of Culture, Education, and Human Development, New York University, New York City

Yong Zhao, Foundation Distinguished Professor in the School of Education, University of Kansas; Professorial Fellow at the Mitchell Institute for Health and Education Policy, Victoria University, Australia; Global Chair at the University of Bath, UK

Jonathan Zimmerman, Professor of Education and History, University of Pennsylvania, Philadelphia

The expert titles and affiliations are as of the writing of this book and for identification only, and the author's opinions, interpretations, conclusions, and any errors are, of course, exclusively our own.

RESEARCH SOURCES

There is a vast research literature on the childhood benefits of various forms of play. Much of it is limited by the ethical difficulties of doing valid long-term interventional research on children, by small sample sizes, short research periods or less-than-ideal research designs, and by the fact that much of the research has been focused on Western and younger populations. These are important caveats to keep in mind.

Key research sources on play include the academic journals the *American Journal of Play* and the *International Journal of Play*, as well as the research papers, books, and presentations listed here.

Abrams, S. E. (2011, January 17). The children must play. *The New Republic*. Retrieved from https://newrepublic.com/article/82329/education-reform-finland-us.

Barros, R. M., Silver, E. J., & Stein, R. E. K. (2009). School recess and group classroom behavior. *Pediatrics, 123*(2), 431–436.

Bassok, D., Claessens, A., & Engel, M. (2014, June 4). The case for the new kindergarten: Challenging and playful. *Education Week*. Retrieved from http://www.edweek.org/ew/articles/2014/06/04/33bassok_ep.h33. html.

Baumer, S., Ferholt, B., & Lecusay, R. (2005). Promoting narrative competence through adult–child joint pretense: Lessons from the Scandinavian educational practice of playworld. *Cognitive Development, 20,* 576–590.

Becker, D. R., McClelland, M. M., Loprinzi, P., & Trost, S. G. (2014). Physical activity, self-regulation, and early academic achievement in preschool children. *Early Education & Development, 25*(1), 56–70.

Bickham, D., Kavanaugh, J., Alden, S., & Rich, M. (2015). *The state of play: How play affects developmental outcomes.* Center on Media and Child Health, Boston Children's Hospital.

Bodrova, E., Germeroth, C., & Leong, D. J. (2013). Play and self-regulation: Lessons from Vygotsky. *American Journal of Play, 6*(1), 111.

Bodrova, E., & Leong, D. J. (2015). Vygotskian and post-Vygotskian views on children's play. *American Journal of Play, 7,* 371–388.

Bonawitz, E., Shafto, P., Gweon, H., Goodman, N. D., Spelke, E., & Schulz, L. (2011). The double-edged sword of pedagogy: Instruction limits spontaneous exploration and discovery. *Cognition, 120*(3), 322–330.

Brown, S., with Vaughan, C. (2009). *Play: How It Shapes the Brain, Opens the Imagination, and Invigorates the Soul.* New York: Avery.

Brussoni, M., Gibbons, R., Gray, C., Ishikawa, T., Sandseter, E. B. H., Bienenstock, A., . . . & Pickett, W. (2015). What is the relationship between risky outdoor play and health in children? A systematic review. *International Journal of Environmental Research and Public Health, 12*(6), 6423–6454.

Brussoni, M., Olsen, L., Pike, I., & Sleet, D. (2012). Risky play and children's safety: Balancing priorities for optimal development. *International Journal of Environmental Research and Public Health, 9,* 3134–3148.

Burdette, H. L., & Whitaker, R. C. (2005). Resurrecting free play in young children: Looking beyond fitness and fatness to attention, affiliation, and affect. *Archives of Pediatrics & Adolescent Medicine, 159*(1), 46–50.

Burghardt, G. (2005). *The Genesis of Animal Play: Testing the Limits.* Cambridge, MA: MIT Press.

Center on the Developing Child at Harvard University. (2014). *Enhancing and practicing executive function skills with children from infancy to adolescence.* Retrieved from http://developingchild. harvard.edu/wp-content/uploads/2015/05/Enhancing-and-Practicing-Executive-Function-Skills-with-Children-from-Infancy-to-Adolescence-1.pdf.

Center on the Developing Child at Harvard University. (2016). *From best practices to breakthrough impacts: A science-based approach to building a more promising future for young children and families.* Retrieved from https://developingchild.harvard.edu/resources/from-best-practices-to-breakthrough-impacts/.

Centers for Disease Control and Prevention. (2010). *The association between school-based physical activity, including physical education, and academic performance.* Atlanta, GA; Centers for Disease Control and Prevention, U.S. Department of Health and Human Services. Retrieved from https://www.cdc.gov/healthyyouth/health_and_academics/pdf/pa-pe_paper.pdf.

Cheng Pui-Wah, D., Reunamo, J., Cooper, P., Liu, K., & Vong, K. P. (2015). Children's agentive orientations in play-based and academically focused preschools in Hong Kong. *Early Child Development and Care, 185*(11–12), 1828–1844.

Christakis, D. A. (2016). Rethinking attention-deficit/hyperactivity disorder. *JAMA Pediatrics, 170*(2), 109–110.

Christakis, D. A., Zimmerman, F. J., & Garrison, M. M. (2007). Effect of block play on language acquisition and attention in toddlers: A pilot randomized controlled trial. *Archives of Pediatrics and Adolescent Medicine, 161*(10), 967–971.

Christakis, E. (2016). *The Importance of Being Little.* New York: Viking Press.

Conklin, H. (2015, March 3). Playtime isn't just for preschoolers—Teenagers need it, too. *Time.* Retrieved from http://time.com/3726098/learning-through-play-teenagers-education/.

Council on Physical Education for Children. (2001). *Recess in elementary schools.* A position paper from the National Association for Sport and Physical Education.

Diamond, A. (2012). Activities and programs that improve children's executive functions. *Current Directions in Psychological Science, 21,* 335–341.

Diamond, A. (2014). Want to optimize executive functions and academic outcomes? Simple, just nourish the human spirit. *Minnesota Symposium on Child Psychology, 37,* 205–232.

Diamond, A, & Lee, K. (2011). Interventions shown to aid executive function development in children 4 to 12 years old. *Science, 333*(6045), 959–964.

Elkind, D. (2007). *The Power of Play: How Spontaneous, Imaginative Activities Lead to Happier, Healthier Children.* New York: Da Capo Press.

Elkind, D. (2008). The power of play: Learning what comes naturally. *American Journal of Play,* Summer, 1–6.

Fein, G. G. (1981). Pretend play in childhood: An integrative review. *Child Development, 52*(4), 1095–1118.

Fisher, K. R., Hirsh-Pasek, K., Newcombe, N., & Golinko, R. M. (2013). Taking shape: Supporting preschoolers' acquisition of geometric knowledge through guided play. *Child Development, 84,* 1872–1878.

Fletcher, R., St George, J., & Freeman, E. (2012). Rough and tumble play quality: Theoretical foundations for a new measure of father-child interaction. *Early Child Development and Care, 183*(6), 746–759.

Fortson, J., James-Burdumy, S., Bleeker, M., et al. (2013). *Impact and implementation findings from an experimental evaluation of Playworks: Effects on school climate, academic learning, student social skills and behavior.* Princeton, NJ: Robert Wood Johnson Foundation.

Fuller, B., Bein, E., Bridges, M., Kim, Y., & Rabe-Hesketh, S. (2017). Do academic preschools yield stronger benefits? Cognitive emphasis, dosage, and early learning. *Journal of Applied Developmental Psychology, 52,* 1–11.

Gertler, P., Heckman, J., Pinto, R., Zanolini, A., Vermeerch, C., Walker, S., & Grantham-McGregor, S. (2014). Labor market returns to an early childhood stimulation intervention in Jamaica. *Science, 344*(6187), 998–1001.

Ginsburg, K. R.; American Academy of Pediatrics Committee on Communications; American Academy of Pediatrics Committee on Psychosocial Aspects of Child and Family Health. (2007). The importance of play in promoting healthy child development and maintaining strong parent–child bonds. *Pediatrics, 119*(1), 182–191.

Goldstein, J. (2012). *Play in children's development, health and well-being. Toy industries of Europe.* Retrieved from https://www.toyindustries.eu/resource/play-childrens-development/.

Graham, G., Holt-Hale, S., & Parker, M. (2005). *Children Moving: A Reflective Approach to Teaching Physical Education* (7th ed.). New York: McGraw-Hill.

Gray, A. (2017, Jan. 27). *What does the future of jobs look like? This is what experts think.* World Economic Forum. Retrieved from https://www. weforum.org/agenda/2017/01/future-of-jobs-davos-2017.

Gray, P. (2009). Play as a foundation for hunter-gatherer social existence. *American Journal of Play, 1*(4), 476–522.

Gray, P., (2013). *Free to Learn: Why Unleashing the Instinct to Play Will Make Our Children Happier, More Self-Reliant, and Better Students for Life.* New York: Basic Books.

Haapala, E. A., Väistö, J., Lintu, N., Westgate, K., Ekelund, U., Poikkeus, A. M., Brage, S., . . . & Lakka, T. A. (2017). Physical activity and sedentary time in relation to academic achievement in children. *Journal of Science and Medicine in Sport, 20*(6), 583–589.

Hassinger-Das, B., Hirsh-Pasek, K., & Michnick Golinkoff, R. (2017). The case of brain science and guided play: A developing story, young children. *National Association for the Education of Young Children (NAEYC), 72*(2). Retrieved from https://www.naeyc.org/resources/pubs/yc/may2017/case-brain-science-guided-play.

Heckman J. (2015). Keynote address. In R. Winthrop (Ed.), *Soft Skills for Workforce Success: From Research to Action.* Washington, DC: Brookings Institution. Retrieved from https://www.brookings.edu/events/soft-skills-for-workforce-success-from-research-to-action/.

Hillman, C. (2014). An introduction to the relation of physical activity to cognitive and brain health, and scholastic achievement. *Monographs of the Society for Research in Child Development, 79*, 1–6.

Hillman, C. H., Pontifex, M. B., Castelli, D. M., Khan, N. A., Raine, L. B., Scudder, M. R., . . . & Kamijo, K. (2014). Effects of the FITkids randomized controlled trial on executive control and brain function. *Pediatrics, 134*(4). Retrieved from http://pediatrics.aappublications. org/content/134/4/e1063.

Hirsh-Pasek, K., & Golinkoff, R. M. (2003). *Einstein Never Used Flash Cards: How Our Children Really Learn—And Why They Need to Play More and Memorise Less.* Emmaus, PA: Rodale.

Hirsh-Pasek, K., Golinkoff, R. M., Berk, L., & Singer, D. G. (2009). *A Mandate for Playful Learning in Preschool: Presenting the Evidence.* New York: Oxford University Press.

Howard, J., & McInnes, K. (2013). The impact of children's perception of an activity as play rather than not play on emotional well-being. *Child: Care, Health and Development, 39*(5), 737–742.

Huizinga, J. (1950). *Homo Ludens: A Study of the Play Element in Culture.* New York: Roy Publishers.

Hurwitz, S. (2003). To be successful—let them play! *Child Education, 79*(2), 101–102.

Isenberg, J., & Quisenberry, N. (2002). A position paper of the Association for Childhood Education International, PLAY: Essential for all children. *Journal of Childhood Education, 79*(1), 33–39.

Jarrett, O. S. (2002). Recess in elementary school: What does the research say? *ERIC Digest*, Retrieved from https://eric.ed.gov/?id=ED466331.

Jarrett, O. (2014). *A research-based case for recess.* Position paper for the US Play Coalition.

Jarrett, O. S., Maxwell, D. M., Dickerson, C., Hoge, P., Davies, G., & Yetley, A. (1998). Impact of recess on classroom behavior: Group effects and individual differences. *Journal of Educational Research, 92*(2), 121–126.

Jenkins, J. M., Duncan, G. J., Auger, A., Bitler, M., Domina, T., & Burchinal, M. (2018). Boosting school readiness: Should preschool teachers target skills or the whole child? *Economics of Education Review, 65*, 107–125.

Kinoshita, I. (2008, January). Children's use of space of the fourth generation (today) with reviewing the three generation's play maps (1982). Presented at the IPA 17th triennial conference "Play in a Changing World." Hong Kong.

Koretz, D. (2017). *The Testing Charade: Pretending to Make Schools Better.* Chicago: University of Chicago Press.

LaFreniere, P. (2011). Evolutionary functions of social play: Life histories, sex differences, and emotion regulation. *American Journal of Play 3*, 464–488.

Layton, T. J., Barnett, M. L., Hicks, T. R., & Jena, A. B. (2018). Attention deficit–hyperactivity disorder and month of school enrollment. *New England Journal of Medicine, 379*, 2122–2130.

Lester, S., & Russell, W. (2008). *Play for a Change: Play, Policy and Practice: A Review of Contemporary Perspectives.* London: Play England.

Lester, S., & Russell, W. (2010). *Children's Right to Play: An Examination of the Importance of Play in the Lives of Children Worldwide.* The Hague: Bernard van Leer Foundation.

Lillard, A. S., Lerner, M. D., Hopkins, E. J., Dore, R. A., Smith, E. D., & Palmquist, C. M. (2013). The impact of pretend play on children's development: A review of the evidence. *Psychological Bulletin, 139*, 1–34.

Lim, S. S., Updike, R. L., Kaldjian, A. S., Barber, R. M., Cowling, K., York, H., . . . & Murray, C. J. L. (2018). Measuring human capital: A systematic analysis of 195 countries and territories, 1990–2016. *Lancet, 392*(10154), P1217–P1234.

Liu, C., Solis, S. L., Jensen, H., Hopkins, E. J., Neale, D., Zosh, J. M., Hirsh-Pasek, K., & Whitebread, D. (2017). *Neuroscience and learning through play: A review of the evidence (research summary)*. Billund, Denmark: The Lego Foundation. Retrieved from https://www.legofoundation.com/media/1064/neuroscience-review_web.pdf.

Mahar, M. T. (2011). Impact of short bouts of physical activity on attention-to-task in elementary school children. *Preventive Medicine, 52*(Suppl. 0), S60–S64.

Mahar, M. T., Murphy, S. K., Rowe, D. A., Golden, J., Shields, A. T., & Raedeke, T. D. (2006). Effects of a classroom-based program on physical activity and on-task behavior. *Medicine and Science in Sports and Exercise, 38*(12), 2086–2094.

Marcon, R. A. (2002). Moving up the grades: Relationship between preschool model and later school success. *Early Childhood Research & Practice, 4*(1), n1.

McElwain, N., & Volling, B. (2005). Preschool children's interactions with friends and older siblings: Relationship special city and joint contributions to problem behavior. *Journal of Family Psychology, 19*(4), 486–496.

Miller, E., & Almon, J. (2009). *Crisis in the kindergarten: Why children need to play in school*. Alliance for Childhood, National Society for the Study of Education.

Milteer, R. M., Ginsburg, K. R.; Council on Communications and Media, & Committee on Psychosocial Aspects of Child and Family Health, American Academy of Pediatrics. (2012). Clinical report: The importance of play in promoting healthy child development and maintaining strong parent–child bonds: Focus on children in poverty. *Pediatrics, 129*, e204–e213.

Murray, R., Ramstetter, C.; Council on School Health; American Academy of Pediatrics. (2013). The crucial role of recess in school. *Pediatrics, 131*(1), 183–188.

National Association for Sport and Physical Education. (2002). *Active start: A statement of physical activity guidelines for children from birth to age 5* (2nd ed.). Retrieved from http://www.aahperd. org/naspe/ standards/nationalGuidelines/ActiveStart.cfm.

National Association of Early Childhood Specialists in State Departments of Education. (2002). *Recess and the importance of play: A position statement on young children and recess.* Washington, DC: National Association of Early Childhood Specialists in State Departments of Education.

Nicholson, J., Bauer, A., & Wooly, R. (2016). Inserting child-initiated play into an American urban school district after a decade of scripted curricula complexities and progress. *American Journal of Play, 8*(2), 228–271.

Nicolopoulou, A., Cortina, K. S., Ilgaz, H., Cates, C. B., & de Sá, A. B. (2015). Using a narrative- and play-based activity to promote low-income preschoolers' oral language, emergent literacy, and social competence. *Early Childhood Research Quarterly, 31*, 147–162.

OECD. (2015). *Students, computers and learning: Making the connection.* Paris: OECD.

OECD (2016). *PISA 2015 Results (Volume I). Excellence and equity in education.* Paris: OECD.

Panksepp, J., Burgdorf, J., Turner, C., & N. Gordon. (2003). Modeling ADHD type arousal with unilateral frontal cortex damage in rats and beneficial effects of play therapy. *Brain and Cognition, 52*, 97–105.

Pellegrini, A. D. (1980). The relationship between kindergartners' play and achievement in prereading, language, and writing. *Psychology in the Schools, 17*(4), 530–535.

Pellegrini, A. D. (2009). *The Role of Play in Human Development.* Oxford: Oxford University Press.

Pellegrini, A. D., & Bohn, C. M. (2005). The role of recess in children's cognitive performance and school adjustment. *Educational Researcher, 34*(1), 13–19.

Pellegrini, A. D., & Davis, P. D. (1993). Relations between children's playground and classroom behavior. *British Journal of Educational Psychology, 63*, 88–95.

Pellegrini, A. D., Dupuis, D., & Smith, P. K. (2007). Play in evolution and development. *Developmental Review, 27*(2), 261–276.

Pellegrini, A. D., & Gustafson, K. (2005). Boys' and girls' uses of objects for exploration, play, and tools in early childhood. In A. D. Pellegrini & P. K. Smith (Eds.), *The Nature of Play: Great Apes and Humans* (pp. 113–135). New York: Guilford Press.

Pellegrini, A. D., & Holmes, R. M. (2006). The role of recess in primary school. In D. Singer, R. Golinkoff, & K. Hirsh-Pasek (Eds.), *Play = Learning: How Play Motivates and Enhances Children's Cognitive and Socio-Emotional Growth.* Oxford: Oxford University Press.

Pellegrini, A. D., Huberty, P. D., & Jones, I. (1995). The effects of recess timing on children's classroom and playground behavior. *American Educational Research Journal, 32,* 845–864.

Pellegrini, A. D., & Smith, P. K. (1993). School recess: Implications for education and development. *Review of Educational Research, 63*(1), 51–67.

Pellegrini, A. D., & Smith, P. K. (1998). Physical activity play: The nature and function of a neglected aspect of play. *Child Development, 69,* 577–598.

Pellis, S. M., & Pellis, V. (2007). Rough and tumble play and the development of the social brain. *Current Directions in Psychological Science 16*(2), 95–98.

Pellis, S., & Pellis, V. (2009). *The Playful Brain.* Oxford: Oneworld Publications.

Pellis, S., & Pellis, V. (2011). Rough and tumble play: Training and using the social brain. In P. Nathan & A. D. Pellegrini (Eds.), *The Oxford Handbook of the Development of Play* (pp. 245–259). New York: Oxford University Press.

Pellis, S. M., Pellis, V. C., & Bell, H. C. (2010). The function of play in the development of the social brain. *American Journal of Play, 2,* 278–296.

Pellis, S. M., Pellis, V. C., & Himmler, B. T. (2014). How play makes for a more adaptable brain: A comparative and neural perspective. *American Journal of Play, 7*(1), 73–98.

Piaget, J. (1962). *Play, Dreams, and Imitation in Childhood.* New York: W.W. Norton.

Plomin, R., & Asbury, K. (2005). Nature and nurture: Genetic and environmental influences on behavior. *Annals of the American Academy of Political and Social Science, 600,* 86–98.

Pyle, A., & Danniels, E. (2017). A continuum of play-based learning: The role of the teacher in play-based pedagogy and the fear of hijacking play. *Early Education and Development, 28*(3), 274–289.

Ramstetter, C. L., Murray, R., & Garner, A. S. (2010). The crucial role of recess in schools. *Journal of School Health, 80*(11), 517–526.

Ramstetter, C., & Murray, R. (2013). American Academy of Pediatrics policy statement: The crucial role of recess in schools. *Pediatrics, 131*(1).

Retrieved from http://pediatrics.aappublications.org/content/131/1/183.

Ravitch, D. (2013). *Reign of Error: The Hoax of the Privatization Movement and the Danger to America's Public Schools*. New York: Alfred A. Knopf.

Rubin, K. H., Fein, C. G., & Vandenberg, B. (1983). Play. In E. M. Hetherington (Ed.), *Handbook of Child Psychology (Vol. 4), Socialization, Personality, and Social Development* (pp. 693–774). New York: Wiley.

Saggar, M., Quintin, E. M., Kienitz, E., Bott, N. T., Sun, Z., Hong, W. C., . . . & Hawthorne, G. (2015). Pictionary-based fMRI paradigm to study the neural correlates of spontaneous improvisation and inaugural creativity. *Scientific Reports, 5.*

Sahlberg, P. (2006). Education reform for raising economic competitiveness. *Journal of Educational Change, 7*(4), 259–287.

Sahlberg, P. (2012, September 6). How gender equality could help school reform? *Washington Post.*

Sahlberg, P. (2015). *Finnish Lessons 2.0. What Can the World Learn from Educational Change in Finland?* New York: Teachers College Press.

Sahlberg, P. (2016). Global educational reform movement and its impact on teaching. In K. Mundy, A. Green, R. Lingard, & A. Verger (Eds.), *The Handbook of Global Policy and Policymaking in Education* (pp. 128–144). New York: Wiley-Blackwell.

Sahlberg, P. (2018). *FinnishED Leadership: Four Big, Inexpensive Ideas to Transform Education*. Thousand Oaks, CA: Corwin Press.

Sandseter, E. (2011). Children's risky play from an evolutionary perspective. *Evolutionary Psychology, 9*, 257–284.

Schulz, L. E., & Bonawitz, E. B. (2007). Serious fun: Preschoolers engage in more exploratory play when evidence is confounded. *Developmental Psychology, 43*(4), 1045–1050.

Schwab, K., & Samans, R. (2016). *The future of jobs. Employment, skills and workforce strategy for the fourth Industrial Revolution*. The World Economic Forum. Retrieved from http://www3.weforum.org/docs/WEF_Future_of_Jobs.pdf.

SHAPE America. (2016). *Guide for recess policy*. Reston, VA.

Shields, A., & Ciccetti, D. (1998). Reactive aggression among maltreated children: The contributions of attention and emotion dysregulation. *Journal of Clinical Child Psychology, 24*, 381–395.

Shonko, J., & Phillips, D. (2000). *From Neurons to Neighborhoods: The Science of Early Childhood Development. Institute of Medicine, Committee on*

Integrating the Science of Early Childhood Development, Board on Children, Youth and Families. Washington, DC: National Academies Press.

Singer, D., Golinko, R., & Hirsh-Pasek, K. (2006). *Play = Learning: How Play Motivates and Enhances Children's Cognitive and Social-Emotional Growth.* Oxford: Oxford University Press.

Siviy, S. M. (2016). A brain motivated to play: Insights into the neurobiology of playfulness. *Behaviour, 153,* 819–844.

Siviy, S. M., & Panksepp, J. (2011). In search of the neurobiological substrates for social playfulness in mammalian brains. *Neuroscience and Biobehavioral Reviews, 35,* 1821–1830.

Spinke, M., Newberry, R., & Bekoff, M. (2001). Mammalian play: Training for the unexpected. *Quarterly Review of Biology, 76,* 141–168.

Stroud, J. E. (1995). Block play: Building a foundation for literacy. *Early Childhood Education Journal, 23*(1), 9–13.

Sutton-Smith, B. (1997). *The Ambiguity of Play.* Cambridge, MA: Harvard University Press.

Thompson, R. A. (2001). Development in the first years of life. *The Future of Children, 11*(1), 20–33.

Trawick-Smith, J., Swaminathan, S., Baton, B., Danieluk, C., Marsh, S., & Szarwacki, M. (2017). Block play and mathematics learning in preschool: The effects of building complexity, peer and teacher interactions in the block area, and replica play materials. *Journal of Early Childhood Research, 15,* 433–448.

UN Committee on the Rights of the Child (CRC). (2013). *General comment No. 17 (2013) on the right of the child to rest, leisure, play, recreational activities, cultural life and the arts (art. 31), 17 April 2013,* CRC/C/GC/17. Retrieved from http://www.refworld.org/docid/51ef9bcc4.html.

Urban, M. (2019). The *Shape of Things to Come* and what to do about Tom and Mia: Interrogating the OECD's International Early Learning and Child Well-Being Study from an anti-colonialist perspective. *Policy Futures in Education.* Retrieved from https://doi.org/10.1177/1478210318819177.

Vygotsky, L. S. (1967). Play and its role in the mental development of the child. *Soviet Psychology, 5,* 6–18.

Vygotsky, L. (1978). *Mind in Society—The Development of Higher Psychological Processes.* Cambridge, MA: Harvard University Press.

Vygotsky, L. S. (1978). The role of play in development. In *Mind in Society* (pp. 92–104). Cambridge, MA: Harvard University Press.

Wallace, C. E., & Russ, S. W. (2015). Pretend play, divergent thinking, and math achievement in girls: A longitudinal study. *Psychology of Aesthetics, Creativity, and the Arts, 9*(3), 296–305.

Weisberg, D. D. S., Hirsh-Pasek, K., & Golinko, R. M. (2013). Guided play: Where curricular goals meet a playful pedagogy. *Mind, Brain, and Education, 7*(2), 104–112.

Weisberg, D. S., Hirsh-Pasek, K., Golinkoff, R. M., Kittredge, A. K., & Klahr, D. (2016). Guided play: Principles and practices. *Current Directions in Psychological Science, 25*(3), 177–182.

White, R. (2013). *The power of play: A research summary on play and learning*. Minneapolis: Minnesota Children's Museum.

White, R. E., & Carlson, S. M. (2016). What would Batman do? Self-distancing improves executive function in young children. *Developmental Science, 19*(3), 419–426.

Whitebread, D., Neale, D., Jensen, H., Liu, C., Solis, S. L., Hopkins, E., Hirsh-Pasek, K., & Zosh, J. M. (2017). *The role of play in children's development: A review of the evidence (research summary)*. Billund, Denmark: The Lego Foundation. Retrieved from https://www.legofoundation.com/media/1065/play-types-_-development-review_web.pdf.

Wolfgang, C. H., Stannard, L. L., & Jones, I. (2001). Block play performance among preschoolers as a predictor of later school achievement in mathematics. *Journal of Research in Childhood Education, 15*(2), 173–180.

Yogman, M., Garner, A., Hutchinson, J., Hirsh-Pasek, K., & Golinkoff, R, M.; American Academy of Pediatrics Committee on Psychosocial Aspects of Child and Family Health, Council on Communications and Media. (2018). The power of play: A pediatric role in enhancing development in young children. *Pediatrics, 142*(3), e20182058.

Zachariou, A., & Whitebread, D. (2015). Musical play and self-regulation: Does musical play allow for the emergence of self-regulatory behaviours? *International Journal of Play, 4*(2), 116–135.

Zelazo, P. D., Blair, C. B., & Willoughby, M. T. (2017). *Executive Function: Implications for Education* (NCER 2017-2000). Washington, DC: National Center for Education Research, Institute of Education Sciences.

Zhao, Y. (2014). *Who's Afraid of the Big Bad Dragon? Why China Has the Best (and the Worst) Education System in the World*. San Francisco: Jossey-Bass.

Zosh, J. M., Hassinger-Das, B., Toub, T. S., Hirsh-Pasek, K., & Golinkoff, R. (2016). Playing with mathematics: How play supports learning and

428 ■ Select Bibliography

the Common Core state standards. *Journal of Mathematics Education at Teachers College, 7*, 45–49.

Zosh, J. M, Hirsh-Pasek, K., Golinkoff, R. M., & Dore, R. A. (2017). Where learning meets creativity: The promise of guided play. In R. Beghetto & B. Sriraman (Eds.), *Creative Contradictions in Education: Cross Disciplinary Paradoxes and Perspectives* (pp. 165–180). New York: Springer International Publishing.

Zosh, J. M., Hirsh-Pasek, K., Hopkins, E. J., Jensen, H., Liu, C., Neale, D., . . . & Whitebread, D. (2018) Accessing the inaccessible: Redefining play as a spectrum. *Frontiers in Psychology, 9*, 1124.

Zosh, J. M., Hopkins, E. J., Jensen, H., Liu, C., Neale, D., Hirsh-Pasek, K., . . . & Whitebread, D. (2017). *Learning through play: A review of the evidence (white paper)*. Billund, Denmark: Lego Foundation. Retrieved from https://www.legofoundation.com/media/1063/learning-through-play_web.pdf.

ABOUT THE AUTHORS

Pasi Sahlberg is a globally renowned educator, author, speaker, and scholar, and one of the world's most respected authorities on educational improvement.

Pasi has served as schoolteacher and as Director General of Finland's Ministry of Education and Culture in Helsinki, as Senior Education Specialist in the World Bank in Washington, DC, and as a visiting professor at Harvard University.

In 2016 he was awarded the Lego Prize in recognition of his work for children's education, creativity, and the right to play. He is currently a professor of education policy at the Gonski Institute for Education of the University of New South Wales, Sydney, Australia.

Pasi's areas of interest and expertise include teaching and learning, school improvement, international education issues, and educational leadership. He has published numerous articles, chapters, and books on education and given over 500 keynote presentations around the world. He has advised several governments and leaders about educational reforms, including those in Finland, Sweden, Scotland, Australia, Canada, and Iceland. His book *Finnish Lessons 2.0: What Can the World Learn from Educational Change in Finland* won the prestigious Grawemeyer Award in 2013 and he was awarded the 2014 Robert Owen Award in Scotland for being an inspirational educator and champion of equity in education.

Pasi is the father of three boys. Learn more on his website: pasisahlberg.com and on Twitter: @pasi_sahlberg.

William Doyle is a *New York Times* bestselling author and TV producer.

Since 2015 he has served as a Fulbright Scholar, a Scholar in Residence and lecturer on media and education at the University of Eastern Finland, and as advisor to the Ministry of Education and Culture of Finland, which is ranked the world's #1 childhood education system by UNICEF, the Organization for Economic Cooperation and Development (OECD), and the World Economic Forum.

William is executive producer of the 2017 History Channel documentary *Transition of Power: The Presidency*; co-producer of the 2014 PBS documentary film special *Navy Seals: Their Untold Story* and co-author of the companion book; author of *An American Insurrection: James Meredith and the Battle of Oxford, Mississippi, 1962*; co-author of civil rights giant James Meredith's *A Mission from God*; and author of the acclaimed 2015 book *PT 109: An American Epic of War, Survival and the Destiny of John F. Kennedy*.

Previously, he won the Writers Guild of America Award for Best TV Documentary for his A&E White House history special and served as Director of Original Programming for HBO. He is winner of the American Bar Association Silver Gavel Award and the American Library Association Alex Award and is a Robert F. Kennedy Book Award Finalist. His articles on education have appeared in the *Washington Post, Los Angeles Times, USA Today, New York Daily News,* and the *Sydney Morning Herald.* Twitter: @williamdoylenyc

William lives in New York City with his wife and 11-year-old son, who attends public school in New York City and part of the year attends a university teacher training "lab" school in Finland.

In 2017 the authors were appointed as Rockefeller Foundation Bellagio Center Resident Fellows to work on this book.

INDEX